$1.00

THE BOOMERS RETIRE

A GUIDE FOR FINANCIAL ADVISORS AND THEIR CLIENTS

4th Edition

Lynn Biscott,
CFP, FELLOW OF FPSC™

CARSWELL®

A Cataloging record for this publication is available from Library and Archives Canada

ISBN 978-0-7798-6363-1 (2014 edition)

Composition: Computer Composition of Canada

Printed in Canada by Thomson Reuters

 **THOMSON REUTERS**

CARSWELL, A DIVISION OF THOMSON REUTERS CANADA LIMITED

One Corporate Plaza
2075 Kennedy Road
Toronto, Ontario
M1T 3V4

Customer Relations:
Toronto 1-416-609-3800
Elsewhere in Canada/U.S. 1-800-387-5164
Fax 1-416-298-5094
www.carswell.com
carswell.orders@thomsonreuters.com

This book is dedicated to Lillian Gilpin, who was the best role model for a successful retirement that anyone could hope to meet.

Table of Contents

Table of Contents

Table of Contents

Acknowledgements

Writing a book like this one and updating it through several editions cannot be done without the help and support of many other people. I would particularly like to thank the following friends and colleagues for their help and suggestions in reviewing materials:

Michel Brisebois, Pl. Fin., Oka, Quebec

Kathleen Clough, CFP, RFP, TEP, PWL Capital Inc., Toronto

Barbara L. Garbens, CFP, RFP, BL Garbens and Associates Inc., Toronto

William Jack, CFP, FCIA, CPCA, William D. Jack and Associates Ltd., Toronto

Fernanda Leitao, FLMI, CEBS, FTL Consulting, Richmond Hill, Ontario

Patrick Longhurst, CFP, FCIA, Patrick Longhurst Advisory Services Inc., Toronto

Mary Prime, CFP, Toronto

Stephen Smith, CFP, RFP, PRP, Yorkminster Insurance Brokers Limited, Port Hope, Ontario

Susan Stefura, CFP, RFP, FCSI, TEP, FELLOW OF FPSC™, Bespoke Financial Consulting Inc., Toronto

Susan Viger, PFP, CFP, Toronto

I would also like to thank the following organizations for graciously providing examples and illustrations to support the text:

Canada Mortgage and Housing Corporation

Canada Revenue Agency

Phillips, Hager & North Investment Management Ltd.

Salvation Army Canada

Finally, I would like to thank my husband, Peter Eberhardt, for his encouragement and support during the time I spent writing and researching updates.

Chapter 1: Retirement — What Does it Mean Today?

Since this book was first published in 2008, we have seen many changes that impact on the financial wellbeing of our retired and about-to-be retired clients. Both the Canada and Quebec Pension Plan retirement benefits are now available at age 60, regardless of whether the recipient is working or not. The age of eligibility for Old Age Security is being raised, and clients now have the opportunity to decide when they would like the benefit to start. We continue to see the decline of defined benefit pension plans in favour of more flexible but less predictable plans such as defined contribution plans or the new Pooled Registered Retirement Plans.

Clients who are seeking guaranteed income in retirement have been disappointed by recent changes to Guaranteed Minimum Withdrawal Benefit products, but have expressed renewed interest in traditional annuity products. And concern about rising health care costs in retirement has sparked interest in long term care insurance.

There is more emphasis on training advisors on how to help their clients make the most tax-effective use of the various sources of income that will support them throughout their retirement years. It is hoped that this book will play a role in these efforts.

The second way in which this book may be useful is that there is growing recognition of the importance of attending to both quantitative and qualitative issues when

1

dealing with a mature group of clients. In the early days of financial planning, much more emphasis was placed on the quantitative side. But retirement isn't just about the money. Quality of life becomes more important as we age, and issues such as where to live or how best to leave a legacy, which have both a qualitative and quantitative component, come to the fore. While advisors "of a certain age" may intuitively understand the nuances of these issues, younger advisors may need some direction. For that reason, this book brings together the life planning and financial planning issues that go hand-in-hand for the mature client.

The Demographic Background

There is no doubt that the Canadian population is aging. Human Resources and Social Development Canada reported that the median age of the population in 1971 was 26.2 years, while in 2011 it reached 41 years[1].

Canadians age 65 and older are the fastest growing age group in the country. The chart on the next page illustrates the actual and projected growth of this age group from 1971 up to 2051.

---

[1] The median is the point where half the population is younger and half is older.

Percentage of Canadian Population Age 65 and Older, 1971 - 2051

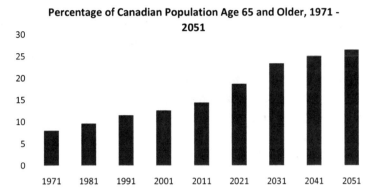

Percentage of Canadian Population Age 65 and Older, 1971 - 2051

Source: Statistics Canada. Estimates of Population, Canada, the Provinces and Territories (Persons).

The chart shows a gradual increase in the percentage of Canadians age 65 and older from 1971 up to 2011. But the rate of increase will accelerate dramatically between 2005 and 2036, with the number of seniors in Canada more than doubling during that period[2]. Population aging will continue past 2036, but at a slower rate of growth.

There are several reasons for this trend, including decreased fertility rates, increased life expectancy, and the effects of the baby boom[3], which have been well documented by David Foot and others. But the implications for the financial planning community are significant. While there will always be a need to help clients in the accumulation stage with decisions about saving for retirement, paying down debt, and educating children, much more attention is now being paid to developing strategies appropriate for

---

[2] In 2011, seniors represented 14.8 percent of the total population of Canada. In 2041, Statistics Canada predicts that seniors will represent 24 percent of the total population.

[3] Baby boomers represent a larger proportion of the population in Canada than in any other country.

those in the withdrawal stage. As the financial planning profession has evolved, more emphasis is being placed on
managing wealth in the retirement years.

Increasing life expectancy is the demographic component that will likely have the greatest impact on retirees
themselves. Many clients are not aware of current statistics,
particularly those relating to remaining life expectancy at
age 65. In any given year, life expectancy (in terms of age)
at 65 is typically higher than life expectancy at birth. This
is because of "survivorship bias": those who die young are
removed from the database.

When considering the impact on retirement, life expectancy from age 65 is the more important statistic. This is
because increases in life expectancy at birth do not necessarily imply an equivalent increase in the number of years
that people might spend in retirement. For example, life
expectancy at birth increased by 20 years between 1926
and 1996, but life expectancy at 65 only increased by four
years over that same time frame[4]. Most of the gains in life
expectancy over that period were due to an increase in the
numbers of people living up to age 65, not beyond that age.

But over the past decade, according to a report[5] released
in April 2014 by the Office of the Superintendent of Financial
Institutions (OSFI), life expectancy at age 65 has climbed
by two years. A decrease in deaths as a result of heart
disease in the 65+ age group has been largely responsible
for this trend.

The table on the next page shows a comparison of life
expectancy statistics at age 65 for 1921, 1991 and 2012,
showing the expected age for 65-year-old males and fe-
males.

---

[4] Health Canada. Aging: Financial Impacts on the Health Care System.

[5] OSFI. Mortality Projections for Social Security Programs in Canada.

Life Expectancy at Age 65

Year	Males Only	Females Only
1921	78.3	78.9
1991	80.6	84.7
2012	84.2	87.0

Sources: Statistics Canada, OSFI.

What these numbers mean is that a 65-year-old man today has a 50 percent chance of living to age 84.2. It follows then that 50 percent of that age cohort will live to be older than 84.2. In fact, according to research done by Sun Life Global Investments, for a 65-year-old couple, there is at least a 25 percent chance that one of the two will live to be age 93.

While these numbers may be useful to review with clients, they should also realize that they have a good chance of living even longer than these statistics suggest. Statistics are based on the entire population, including lower income people, who tend to have shorter lifespans, as well as those with serious medical conditions. It's quite likely that most of a financial advisor's clients would still be alive beyond the stated ages.

The combination of increasing life expectancy and younger retirement ages means that retirees today can expect to spend perhaps 20 to 25 years of their lives in retirement. And, of course, many of our clients will be retired for much longer than that. While 25 years of leisure may sound quite appealing on a typical workday, it raises the very serious concern of how to go about supporting oneself for that length of time without working. Throughout the accumulation years, our major concern is setting aside enough money for retirement and ensuring that it grows to produce the level of income clients and advisors hope for. In the distribution phase, the focus shifts to protecting what's already built up, and looking at how to access the different sources of income available in order to produce the best after-tax result. Retired clients today are worried about outliving their money, and advisors need to help them choose the products and strategies that will minimize that likelihood.

Another concern sparked by increased longevity is the issue of health care as we get older. Study after study has shown that health care is a major concern of retirees. As we age, the possibility of becoming physically or mentally disabled, or suffering from a life-threatening illness, increases. What impact will this have on our quality of life, and our ability to pay for the care we may need? Because of the advances in medicine and health care that have taken place and are continuing to evolve, people are now surviving illnesses that would have been a death sentence years ago. While this is definitely a positive development, it means that many retirees will have to be prepared to fund medical expenses and long-term care arrangements as they age.

What's Different about Retirement Today?

To answer that question, let's compare retirement today to retirement back in the 1950s. At that time, the average retirement age was 67, while average life expectancy was 69. CPP had not yet been introduced, and although RRSPs were introduced in 1957, they were not widely available until the early 1970s.

No More Early Retirement?

We have seen how life expectancy has increased dramatically over the past several decades, but how about retirement age? Here's where things get interesting. When this book was first published in 2008, we reported that the average age of retirement in Canada was on the decline. However, over the past five years, we have seen a reversal of this trend across all categories of workers, as illustrated in the table below.

Average Age of Retirement across Canada

	1976	2006	2013
Men	65.3	62.1	63.7
Women	63.9	60.7	62.3
Self-employed	66.4	64.7	66.8
Private sector employees	65.0	61.8	63.7
Public sector employees	63.5	59.5	61.1

Source: Statistics Canada CANSIM table 282-0051.

There are a number of factors contributing to this recent trend towards later retirement, including financial need, increased flexibility in the workplace, and changing attitudes towards retirement.

Financial Need

For various reasons, Canadians have not been highly successful in planning and saving for retirement. By and large, we choose to spend money today instead of setting it aside for our future. As a result, many of us reach our late fifties with insufficient resources and, in some cases, large debt loads. This trend has been exacerbated by the market turmoil of recent years, so that even those who had a reasonable level of retirement savings may have seen a dramatic decline in the value of their nest egg.

A second factor that contributes to financial need is a general lack of financial literacy on behalf of the Canadian public. Many people don't understand some of the most basic concepts related to money management, such as the power of compound returns over time, or how a seemingly small management fee can eat away at portfolio returns year after year. As a result, they make decisions that are not necessarily in their best interest if their goal is retirement security.

Thirdly, many boomers are members of the sandwich generation, spending money taking care of the needs of their elderly parents as well as those of their young adult children, who are still living at home while they attempt to launch themselves into the world. These conflicting demands make it even more difficult to focus on setting aside money for retirement, which may seem like a mirage off in the distance.

And finally, in the past, higher percentages of employees belonged to employer pension plans. In 1979, 48 percent of the workforce age 15 and over was covered by an employer plan.[6] Statistics Canada reported that, at the end of 2011, about 38 percent of employees were members of registered pension plans, down from 40 percent in 2001. Not only do fewer Canadians belong to pension plans, the plans themselves are changing. At one time, the defined benefit (DB) plan was the only game in town. Now, defined contribution (DC) plans are becoming more prevalent, particularly in the private sector. In fact, the distribution of DB and DC plans is such that the majority of DB plan members are employed in the public sector, whereas the majority of DC plan members are employed in the private sector. The increasing popularity of DC plans as well as other retirement savings vehicles such as group RRSPs means that retirees have limited sources of guaranteed lifetime income to rely on in retirement, adding to their concern about running out of money.

---

[6] Statistics Canada. Pension Plans in Canada: Overview of Pension Plans in Canada as of January 1, 2003. Ottawa. Statistics Canada. 2004.

Increased Flexibility in the Workplace

Fortunately for the boomers, the workplace has become increasingly flexible and welcoming to those who wish to continue to work, either on a full-time or part-time basis. Effective December 2012, Canada has repealed the legislative provisions that allowed for mandatory retirement for employees governed by federal employment and human rights legislation. All other jurisdictions in Canada have already dealt with this issue. Therefore, as of December 2012, mandatory retirement is considered discriminatory under human rights legislation for virtually all employees in Canada, except for situations where age is deemed to be a *bona fide* and reasonable requirement for a specific employment or occupation. This exception usually applies to public safety occupations such as firefighters.

While the demise of mandatory retirement means that Canadians will be able to work past the age of 65, it doesn't mean that we have to, and many of us will choose not to. This has created a labour crisis for many employers, who are now faced with the bulk of their workforce heading into their retirement years, and not enough younger workers to fill the gap. While the baby boom in Canada was the largest in the world, the decline in birth rates following the boom was also the most dramatic in Canada. To cope with the labour shortage, and encourage older employees to stay on the job, employers have become more flexible in offering work arrangements that appeal to older workers, such as part-time work, job sharing, seasonal employment, and contract work.

Making a gradual transition into retirement is a win-win situation for employers and employees. For employers, gradual retirement provides the means to retain valuable employee knowledge and experience, and encourage the transfer of knowledge and skills to more junior staff through extended opportunities for mentoring and training. For employees, it means that retirement doesn't have to be an all

9

or nothing affair. They could choose to move into retirement at an earlier age by gradually reducing their commitment to the paid workforce while supplementing their employment earnings with pension income. Or they could be enticed to stay on the job for a few years longer by the prospect of a part-time schedule.

Over the past several years, some employers have offered incentives for employees to transition gradually to retirement. For example, some defined benefit pension plans allow employees to reduce the number of hours worked in the two years prior to retirement, while still contributing to the pension plan on the basis of a full-time salary. These two years are then considered to be full-time years when calculating the employee's eventual pension entitlement.

However, regulations under the federal *Income Tax Act* acted as a disincentive to phased retirement. Employees were prohibited from accruing benefits under a defined benefit pension plan if they were already receiving an income from that plan, or from a different defined benefit plan offered by the same or a related employer. This regulation meant that employees could not transition to retirement by working part-time and continuing to accrue pensionable service, while receiving a partial pension to supplement their earnings.

Amendments to the *Income Tax Regulations*, the federal *Pension Benefits Standards Act* and the federal *Pension Benefits Standards Regulations* came into force in 2009 in order to allow employees to receive a pension while continuing to accrue future service, under certain conditions. In addition, the *ITA* previously had a restriction that bridge benefits could only be paid at the same time as a retiree was receiving a lifetime basic pension benefit. This restriction has been removed. Employees will accrue pension benefits based on their actual earnings while in the phased retirement period.

In addition to the federal jurisdiction, provisions for phased retirement are now in effect in Alberta, British Columbia, Manitoba, Nova Scotia, Ontario and Quebec. In the remaining provinces (New Brunswick, Newfoundland and Labrador, Prince Edward Island and Saskatchewan), phased retirement is not specifically addressed under pension legislation; therefore, its status is somewhat unclear.

Remember that the legislation doesn't require employers to provide phased retirement - it just says they can do it if they want to. Each employer must decide if they want to pass an amendment to their plan to put phased retirement in place. Clients need to understand that this is entirely voluntary on the part of employers, and many employers, particularly those in the private sector, may choose not to offer such a program. There's no law that says they have to.

Advisors should also note that plans set up for individuals who are connected with their employer continue to be subject to the old rules. This would include, for example, Individual Pension Plans (IPPs) set up for employees who do not deal at arm's length with the employer, or who own 10 percent or more of the shares of the employer.

In addition to changes affecting defined benefit pension plan members, both Canada Pension Plan and Quebec Pension Plan now allow members to start collecting a retirement pension beginning at age 60, even if they are still working full-time. Additional changes to CPP and QPP are described in Chapter 2, Sources of Retirement Income: Government Benefits.

Changing Attitudes towards Retirement

The boomer generation is one with very high expectations. We want to continue to have it all during retirement – we don't want to have to pare down our lifestyle, we want to travel and enjoy ourselves, keep in shape, maybe continue some work if the mood strikes us. In the past, many people fully expected to live a more modest lifestyle when they retired. Today, many retirees will want to maintain at least the same standard of living they enjoyed while they were working, if not improve on it.

Inflation

Given the length of time that many people will be spending in retirement, inflation becomes even more of a concern. In March 2014, the Bank of Canada reported that the total Consumer Price Index (CPI) showed a 1.5 percent increase over the previous year. Since the Bank started tracking the CPI in 1914, prices have increased on average by 3.08 percent per year. If we assume that inflation will continue at this level in future, what would be the impact on the income your clients would need to buy the same goods and services as they move through retirement? Let's assume that they want to be able to spend $50,000 per year. The chart below shows how their income requirements would change throughout potentially 30 years of retirement, based on a 3.08 percentage increase annually. Table 1 at the end of this chapter shows the impact of different inflation rates on income requirements.

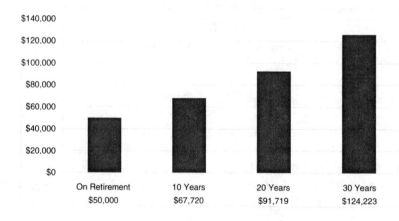

While, in the past, retirees have tended to spend less as they got older, it's dangerous to assume that this trend will hold true in future, given the rising costs of health care and assisted living. Advisors need to work with their clients on strategies that will help to maintain their purchasing power throughout the retirement years.

Diversified Sources of Income

The old linear model, where Canadians moved through three distinct life stages (school, work, and leisure) is being replaced by a cyclical model that mixes these three components together in varying amounts throughout a lifetime. Think about the high school students who take a year or so off to travel and perhaps work before starting university. Think about the mid-career professionals who take time off for an advanced degree, or to train for a different line of work. Many people today will retire from their primary career, perhaps take a break for a couple of years to relax and travel, and then pursue further work interests at a later date, either in the same or a different field.

One of the benefits of this cyclical model is that it allows retirees to add employment income to other sources such as CPP, OAS, employer pensions, and personal savings. Under the traditional retirement concept, most people earned full-time salaries until the day they retired, and then lived on their pensions or retirement savings. Today's retiree, on the other hand, will likely have a blend of income streams from many different sources. For some clients, this causes concern, because they tend to look at each individual source in isolation and see it as being rather small and insignificant. A reduced pension taken at an early age can look somewhat paltry compared to a full-time salary. But your client needs to be reminded that the employer pension is only one of many potential sources of income to be considered. Government benefits, in particular, often make a greater contribution than clients expect.

In fact, receiving income from a variety of sources can be seen as a form of diversification. We all know that we can reduce investment risk by holding various asset classes in the portfolio. Similarly, we can reduce "income risk" by having a number of different sources of income. Modest levels of income from pensions and government benefits can supplement earnings from part-time, contract, or consulting work as well as regular withdrawals from an investment portfolio.

The challenge for the new retiree is in blending together income from the government, former employers, and personal resources in the most effective way possible.

Let's take a look at how these sources of income work, what they provide, and how clients can optimize the returns from each one.

TABLE 1

AMOUNTS NEEDED AFTER RETIREMENT TO HAVE THE SAME PURCHASING POWER AS $100 AT RETIREMENT

Years From Retirement Date	Annual Inflation Rates						
	2%	3%	4%	5%	6%	8%	10%
0 (retirement)	100	100	100	100	100	100	100
1	102	103	104	105	106	108	110
5	110	116	122	128	134	147	161
10	122	134	148	163	179	216	259
11	124	138	154	171	190	233	285
12	127	143	160	180	201	252	314
13	129	147	167	189	213	272	345
14	132	151	173	198	226	294	380
15	135	156	180	208	240	317	418
16	137	160	187	218	254	343	459
17	140	165	195	229	269	370	505
18	143	170	203	241	285	400	556
19	146	175	211	253	303	432	612
20	149	181	219	265	321	466	673
21	152	186	228	279	340	503	740
22	155	192	237	293	360	544	814
23	158	197	246	307	382	587	895
24	161	203	256	323	405	634	985
25	164	209	267	339	429	685	1,083
28	174	229	300	392	511	863	1,442
30	181	243	324	432	574	1,006	1,745

Chapter 2: Sources of Retirement Income — Government Benefits

Many clients (and advisors too) ignore the significant contributions that CPP/QPP and OAS make towards retirement income. While few of us expect to live on government benefits alone, they do provide a base to build on. At today's benefit rates, a 65-year-old couple with maximum entitlement could expect to receive over $38,000 per year from these plans. It's worthwhile understanding about how the plans work and how to make the most of them.

It's also important to keep up to date with changes to government benefits as they occur. Since the first edition of this book was published in 2008, significant changes have taken place both to CPP and OAS. As our population ages, we may continue to see some fine-tuning applied to all types of government retirement benefits. The good news is that most changes have been introduced with enough lead time so that retirees can plan for the impact on retirement income.

Canada Pension Plan/Québec Pension Plan (CPP/QPP)

The Canada Pension Plan was introduced in 1966 to provide a retirement benefit to working Canadians. The Quebec Pension Plan broadly mirrors the CPP in most respects. The retirement benefits provided under the two plans are virtually identical, although the contribution rate for QPP will increase slightly each year from 2012 to 2017 in order to improve the funding of the plan. Any differences in the administration of the two plans will be highlighted throughout the chapter. Anyone between the ages of 18 and 65 who works in Canada on more than a casual basis (outside of Quebec) must contribute to CPP. Between ages 65 and 70, additional contributions are optional for those who continue to have employment income. Contributions beyond age 70 are not permitted. In Quebec, QPP contributions are required for anyone over the age of 18 who has employment income.

Employers make matching contributions on behalf of their employees. The self-employed contribute at a double rate, which covers both the employee and employer share.

The operation of the two plans is co-ordinated through a series of agreements between the federal and Quebec governments. Benefits from either plan are based on pension credits accumulated under both. Dual contributors who live outside of Quebec when they make their application receive their benefits from CPP; dual contributors who live in Quebec at the time of application receive their benefits from QPP.

The maximum retirement pension at age 65 is currently $1,038.33 per month (as of January 2014). However, not everyone receives the maximum amount. Benefits are calculated based on the number of years the applicant contributed, and the level of earnings on which contributions were made. For CPP, an individual statement of contributions can be requested on-line at www.servicecanada.gc.ca, as well as an estimate of the benefit that the client can expect to receive at age 65. For QPP, contributors may view their statements on-line or request a printed statement at www.rrq.gouv.qc.ca.

Benefits are indexed to inflation, and the amount of the benefit is adjusted in January of each year to match increases in the Consumer Price Index.

Recipients are entitled to the full amount of their CPP benefit, even if they leave Canada in retirement. The taxation of the benefit, however, will depend on whether or not the recipient is considered to be a non-resident for tax purposes, and, if so, the tax treaty in effect between Canada and the recipient's country of residence. The standard rate of withholding tax that applies to CPP benefits paid to non-residents is 25 percent, although lower rates may apply depending on the tax treaty in effect. See Table 3 at the end of this chapter for a list of current withholding tax rates.

Getting the Maximum Benefit Entitlement

Current studies show that not all Canadians get the full benefits they are entitled to. This can happen because people don't always know that they have to apply to receive government benefits, or they don't complete the paperwork properly. While the government doesn't take the initiative to ensure that we all get our full entitlement, this is a role that financial advisors can play for their clients. One area that is frequently missed is the Child Rearing Provision.

Retirement benefits are calculated based on the number of years of contributions, as well as the level of contributions made each year. If an applicant was out of the workforce for a period of time, or had low earnings, their retirement benefit would normally be less than the maximum amount. However, there is an exception if those periods of lower earnings were related to caring for children.

Where a child was born after December 31, 1958, the parent can apply for the Child Rearing Provision at the same time as they apply for the CPP/QPP retirement benefit. This provision acts to exclude any period where the child was under the age of seven from the contributory period, increasing the applicant's average lifetime earnings, thereby increasing the retirement benefit. Under CPP, either parent is entitled to use the Child Rearing Provision, but they cannot both use it for the same period of time.

For example, Margaret was employed outside the home until her daughter, Cynthia, was born in 1985. Margaret then stayed at home until Cynthia started school in 1991. When Margaret eventually applies for her retirement benefit, the period from the month following Cynthia's birth up until Margaret returns to work full-time can be excluded. With this Child Rearing Provision, Margaret's retirement benefit will be $735 per month. If the Child Rearing Provision were not applied, Margaret's retirement benefit would have been $650 per month.

However, suppose that Margaret stayed at home from the time Cynthia was born until the end of 1987, when she returned to work. At the beginning of 1988, Margaret's husband Bob lost his job and spent the remainder of the year at home with Cynthia while he completed his Master's degree. When it comes time to apply for their CPP retirement benefits, Margaret could apply for the time between Cynthia's birth and the end of 1987, while Bob could apply for 1988.

Under QPP, the parent who received family allowance benefits is the only one who is entitled to apply for the Child Rearing Provision.

When Should Clients Apply?

CPP retirement benefits can start anytime between age 60 and 70, regardless of whether the applicant still has employment income. With QPP, the applicant's expected earnings from employment in the coming year must be less than 25 percent of the yearly maximum pensionable earnings, or $13,125 in 2014. Note that QPP has provisions for phased retirement, where individuals between the ages of 55 and 69 can reduce their work hours and continue to contribute to QPP at their original rate, under certain circumstances. See the section "Quebec Pension Plan – opportunities for phased retirement" for a more detailed explanation of this arrangement.

Early retirement can result in lower CPP/QPP benefits for two reasons. First, if the applicant decides to take CPP/QPP early, the amount of the benefit is reduced by a certain percent per month for each month that the applicant is under age 65.[1] This is a permanent reduction – the payment does not increase once the recipient reaches age 65. Second, CPP/QPP calculates the full retirement pension based on contributions over a working life from 18 to 70 years of age, or until the applicant begins to collect the retirement benefit, if that is prior to age 70. Although there are special provisions for those who started work before CPP/QPP was introduced in 1966, as well as for those who have periods of low or no contributions for various reasons, leaving the workforce in one's fifties, or even reducing employment earnings below the yearly maximum pensionable earnings (YMPE), can result in the contributor not being entitled to receive the maximum amount at age 65. Note that the current YMPE level as of 2014 is $52,500.

CPP applicants who wait until past age 65 will receive an increase of a certain percent per month for each month that they are over age 65. At age 70, an amount equal to 142 percent of the amount payable at age 65 would be paid out. Under QPP, applicants at age 70 are eligible to receive 130 percent of the amount payable at age 65. Further increases beyond age 70 are not provided.

Clients who are considering early retirement, at least on a transitional basis, may wonder whether they are better

---

[1] The monthly reduction under CPP is .56% for 2014, .58% for 2015, and .60% for 2016. Under QPP, the monthly reduction is 0.50%.

off to wait until age 65 to collect their full CPP benefit, or to take the reduced benefit at age 60. The following factors should be considered as part of the decision process:

- Anticipated life expectancy. This comes into play when evaluating the break-even point between the two options.

- Current cash flow. If the client receives the retirement benefit at an early age, does that reduce or eliminate the need to draw on investments to cover expenses? Or will the benefit be invested for future growth?

- Tax bracket. If the client continues to work, the benefits could be subject to tax at a fairly high rate.

- The bird in the hand approach. If we knew exactly how long we were going to live, we could calculate mathematically the exact age that we should start to receive CPP/QPP in order to get the most out of the plan. Lacking that information, many people believe that it's best to take the benefit as soon as possible so as not to miss out should they die prematurely. This approach has some merit, particularly for couples where each spouse is entitled to CPP/QPP in his or her own right. Bear in mind that survivor benefits are only paid to the extent that the surviving spouse needs them to top up their own CPP/QPP benefit to the maximum allowed.

- Exposure to the OAS clawback. Taking benefits early reduces the amount that is received each year. For some clients, this could mean reducing exposure to the OAS clawback.

Be aware of how the retirement benefit is calculated if the client stops working at 60, but waits until 65 to apply for CPP. The retirement benefit will be calculated based on contributions from age 18 up until the benefit starts. If Liz stops working at 60, but her "contributory period" continues to age 65, her record will show five years of zero contributions. This will be counted against her when the retirement benefit is calculated.

Post Retirement Benefit (PRB)

As stated above, clients aged 60 to 65 who are already collecting a retirement benefit but continue to work must continue to contribute to CPP. For clients aged 65 to 70, additional contributions are voluntary. The contributions go towards the Post Retirement Benefit, which is an amount that increases retirement income the following year, even where the client is already receiving the maximum amount.

The contribution rates are the same as for the basic CPP program. However, they do not count towards eligibility or increase the amount of any other benefits payable. They are also not subject to credit splitting or income sharing.

Service Canada has a calculator that can be used to estimate the annual amount of PRB that could be received: https://srv111.services.gc.ca/PRB_01.aspx.

Quebec Pension Plan – Opportunities for Phased Retirement

The Quebec Pension Plan has been innovative in creating opportunities that support the concept of a gradual transition to retirement. Employees in Quebec can choose from two options if they wish to pursue phased retirement. First, those who are between the ages of 55 and 69 can reduce their working hours, but continue to contribute to QPP as if their earnings had not been reduced. This means that lower- and middle-income employees can cut back their hours, perhaps to part-time status, without jeopardizing the eventual amount of their QPP benefit. Higher income employees, in effect, have always had this opportunity, since a reduction in their hours and earned income could still leave them above the threshold for maximum QPP contributions. This option is available to employees whose employers are willing to agree to the reduction in hours worked. It is not available to self-employed workers, unless they have incorporated their businesses and are drawing salaries as employees.

The second option is for employees aged 60 to 65. If their hours and wages have been reduced by at least 20 percent under a phased retirement agreement, or their estimated employment earnings for the coming year are less than $13,125 (in 2014), they can apply for early QPP benefits while they are still working.

With QPP, anyone whose employment earnings exceed the $3,500 basic exemption must contribute to the plan, regardless of age. Under Bill 68, which was passed on June 18, 2008, a retirement pension supplement is paid to those who are already receiving a QPP retirement benefit, but continue to work. The retirement pension supplement came into effect on January 1, 2009. Calculated as 0.5 percent of the earnings on which the retiree contributed during the previous year, the supplement is added to the regular monthly benefits in addition to annual indexation. Even those who are already receiving the maximum retirement benefit are entitled to this additional supplement.

The Régie des rentes du Québec, which governs private pension plans registered in Québec as well as QPP, has also extended this concept to private pension plans. If an employee is less than ten years away from normal retirement age, and his or her work hours are reduced, the employee can apply to receive benefits from the private pension to offset the loss of employment income. Employees must reach an agreement with their employer in order to take advantage of these provisions. See Chapter 3, Sources of Retirement Income – Employer Plans for a more detailed discussion of this scheme.

Sharing the Pension

Both CPP and QPP allow couples (married, common law, or same sex partners) to share their pension payments, as long as both are at least 60 years old. This method of income splitting can result in a lower tax bill for the couple. Spouses may apply to receive an equal share of the pensions they both earned during the years they were together.

To take a traditional example, let's look at Steve and Paula. They've been married since age 18 when Steve started working. Paula has never worked outside of the home. At age 65, Steve's CPP benefit has been calculated to be $800 per month. If he and Paula apply to split the benefit, CPP will pay $400 to Steve each month, and $400 to Paula. Assuming that Steve is in a higher tax bracket than Paula, this will produce ongoing tax savings throughout their retirement years.

In this example, Steve and Paula were married for the 47 years that Steve contributed to CPP. If they had been married for 20 years, only the portion of the benefit that Steve earned during that 20-year period would be eligible for sharing with Paula.

If both spouses are entitled to receive a retirement benefit, the amount of the pensions is pooled together and divided according to the credits earned during the time they were together. This could still be to their advantage, if there is a substantial difference between the pensions.

Pension sharing ends on divorce, death, 12 months after separation, or if the recipient and spouse decide to end the arrangement, which they can do at any time if it no longer meets their needs.

Pensions earned under the QPP may also be split, although the conditions of eligibility are somewhat different.

Additional information on CPP/QPP pension splitting is covered in Chapter 6, Tax Planning Tips and Strategies.

Survivor Benefits

The Canada Pension Plan provides for the payment of survivor benefits to the surviving spouse and dependent children of those who have made CPP contributions for a minimum qualifying period. There are three types of benefits available:

- lump-sum death benefit
- surviving spouse's benefit
- children's benefit

For those contributors who worked in Quebec and contributed to the Quebec Pension Plan, the rules are very similar. Instances where the benefits or calculations differ are noted.

In all cases, the surviving spouse must apply for the benefits - they don't come automatically. Failure to apply can mean the loss of benefits the client was entitled to receive.

In order for the survivors to be eligible to receive any benefits, the deceased must have made contributions to the CPP for at least three years. If the deceased's total contributory period was longer than nine years, they must have contributed in at least one-third of the calendar years in their contributory period. For example, suppose the contributor died at 48. Their total contributory period, from age 18 to 48, was 30 years. They would have had to contribute to CPP for at least ten years in order for their survivors to qualify for benefits. If the contributory period was more than 30 years, at least ten years' worth of contributions are required.

As with all CPP benefits, reciprocal social security agreements between Canada and other countries provide for the co-ordination of benefits between countries. If the deceased contributed to another country's social security program, their years of contribution to that program may be added to their periods of contribution to the CPP in order to meet the qualifying requirements. Check with Service Canada for information about the reciprocal agreement with the specific country involved.

Lump-sum Death Benefit

The CPP death benefit is a one-time lump-sum payment made to the estate of the deceased. The amount of the benefit depends on how much, and for how long, the deceased paid into CPP. In order to calculate the payment, CPP works out the amount that the deceased's retirement pension would have been if they had been age 65 when they died. The death benefit is equal to six months' worth of this calculated amount, up to a set maximum for the year of death. As of January 1, 1998, the maximum CPP death benefit has been limited to $2,500.

The QPP death benefit is a one-time lump-sum payment of $2,500 made to the estate of the deceased.

The executor or administrator of the deceased's estate should apply for the death benefit as soon as possible and certainly within 12 months after the death. CPP cannot make retroactive payments after this point. The benefit is usually paid within six to twelve weeks of application.

Understanding the tax treatment of the death benefit is important. Like all CPP benefits, it is fully taxable. It can be declared either on the trust return filed for the estate, or included as part of the income of the surviving spouse. It is not to be filed as part of the final tax return for the deceased. The advisor will want to choose the return that is subject to the lowest tax rate for the reporting of the death benefit.

Surviving Spouse's Benefit

The surviving spouse's benefit is a monthly pension paid to the surviving spouse of the deceased contributor. It applies to both legally married and common-law spouses of the same or opposite sex[2]. CPP defines a common-law spouse as a person with whom the deceased was living in a conjugal relationship for at least one year. Under QPP, common-law (de facto) spouses must have lived together for at least three years, unless they have a child together, in which case only one year is required. If the spouses were separated at the time of death, and there is no cohabiting common-law spouse, the separated surviving spouse may qualify for the benefit.

The amount of the monthly pension depends on four factors:

- the deceased's history of contributions to CPP (how much and for how long)
- the age of the surviving spouse
- whether the surviving spouse is supporting dependent children
- whether the surviving spouse is already receiving a CPP disability or retirement pension

CPP first calculates how much the deceased's retirement pension would have been if he or she had been age 65 at death. A surviving spouse who is 65 or older would be eligible to receive 60 percent of this amount. As of January 2014, the maximum monthly pension is $623.00. Spouses aged 45 to 64, as well as those who are under 45 and either disabled or raising a dependent child, receive a flat-rate portion, plus 37.5 percent of the calculated amount, to a maximum of $567.91 per month under CPP as of January 2014.

The calculation of the maximum amounts payable under QPP is slightly different. A spouse under age 45, who is

---

[2] Quebec refers to "civil union" as the equivalent to marriage for same-sex couples.

not disabled and not raising a dependent child, is eligible for the flat-rate portion, plus 37.5 percent of the calculated amount, minus 1/120 for each month he or she is under age 45 at the time the deceased passed away. Spouses who are under age 35, not disabled, and not raising a dependent child, do not receive a pension until they either reach age 65 or become disabled. There is an exception to this rule if the deceased contributed to both CPP and QPP, and the surviving spouse lives in Quebec. In that case, the surviving spouse is eligible for a survivor pension under the age of 35.

If the surviving spouse is already receiving a CPP retirement or disability pension, it can be combined with the survivor pension, and received as one monthly payment. However, there is a maximum allowable payment, so that spouses do not necessarily receive the total of both amounts. The ceiling is based on the maximum disability or retirement pension payable, as applicable.

The survivor benefit continues even if the widow or widower remarries. If he or she is widowed a second time, only one survivor benefit will be paid. It will, however, be the larger of the two.

Survivor benefits are paid monthly, beginning with the month after the contributor's death. Payments can be made by direct deposit, which most people find to be the most convenient method. Payments are taxable in the hands of the surviving spouse. Benefits are indexed every January 1 to keep them in line with increases in inflation.

For more information on CPP, contact www.service canada.gc.ca. For more information on QPP, contact www.rrq.gouv.qc.ca.

Will CPP and QPP be There for Us?

Many retired Canadians are concerned that CPP will run out of money in the near future. Underfunding of the plan was a legitimate concern in the 1990s, when studies predicted that CPP would run out of money by 2015. However, a number of changes were implemented at that time to keep the system sustainable. The changes took effect in 1998 and have been very successful in turning the situation around.

One major change is that contribution rates were increased from the original rate of 3.6 percent of earnings (for employees and employers combined) up to the current combined level of 9.9 percent. Accelerated contribution rates mean that CPP is building up a surplus as an investment fund. In fact, the long-range goal is that current contributions will cover 70 percent of benefits paid, while investment income will cover 30 percent.

The investment strategy of the CPP has been improved as well. Previously, CPP funds were loaned out to the provinces at a relatively low rate of return. Now, the CPP Investment Board manages current contributions, where they are invested in a diversified portfolio of equities, fixed income investments, and alternative investments such as infrastructure.

As well, other changes were made in order to protect the retirement benefits that are paid out by CPP. The lump sum death benefit was frozen at $2,500 and the yearly basic exemption (YBE) was frozen at $3,500. The requirements for receiving a disability pension were also tightened up.

In December 2009, Bill C-51, which dealt with the most recent changes to CPP, received Royal Assent. The first changes appeared in 2011, and full implementation of the changes will take place gradually over several years. The major changes are summarized below:

- As of 2012, individuals are able to take the CPP retirement benefit as early as age 60 without any work interruption or reduction in hours worked or earnings. However, those who continue to work are required to contribute to CPP. Contributions are mandatory for workers under age 65 and voluntary for workers age 65 and older. These contributions will result in increased retirement benefits.

- Previously, CPP dropped out 15 percent of low-income or no-income years in an individual's contribution history when calculating the retirement benefit. The drop-out provision was increased to 16 percent in 2012 and to 17 percent in 2014. This change improves the basic retirement pension for virtually all CPP contributors.

- The early pension reduction, originally 0.5 percent for each month that the pension is taken before age 65, will gradually increase to 0.6 percent, over a period of five years beginning in 2012.

- The late pension augmentation, originally 0.5 percent for each month that the pension is taken after age 65 and up to age 70, was increased to 0.7 percent as of 2014.

With the exception of the low income dropout years, these changes are designed to level the playing field between those who take CPP early and those who wait until 65 or later. Because of increasing life expectancy, the original system resulted in an actuarial advantage to taking the benefit early. When fully implemented, the changes will eliminate that advantage.

The most recent Actuarial Report on the CPP that was tabled in Parliament in December 2013 showed that "the legislated contribution rate of 9.9% is sufficient to financially sustain the Plan over the long term".

Similarly with QPP, the latest actuarial report as of December 31, 2012 showed that "the Plan is financially healthy and that the measures implemented by the government in 2011 to improve the financial situation [increases to the contribution rate] have been effective".

Old Age Security (OAS)

Old Age Security (OAS) benefits are financed through federal government general tax revenues, and are available as early as age 65, as long as applicants meet specific OAS residence requirements. An applicant's employment history is not a factor in determining eligibility, nor does the applicant need to be retired.

A minimum of ten years' residence in Canada after the age of 18 is required in order to receive the OAS benefit while in Canada. However, the amount of the benefit is determined by how long the applicant has lived in Canada, according to the following rules:

- an applicant who has lived in Canada for at least 40 years after the age of 18 qualifies for the full amount of the OAS benefit

- an applicant who does not meet the above test may still receive the full amount of the OAS benefit if he or she was 25 or older on July 1, 1977, lived in Canada for ten years immediately prior to applying for OAS, and:

  - lived in Canada on July 1, 1977, or

  - had lived in Canada before July 1, 1977, after reaching age 18, or

  - possessed a valid immigration visa on July 1, 1977.

Certain exceptions are allowed for absences outside Canada where the applicant was working for a Canadian employer, or was married to someone working abroad for an international organization.

An applicant who does not meet the requirements for a full OAS benefit may qualify for a partial pension. Note that if the applicant elects a partial pension at age 65, the amount will not increase to the full pension at some future date when he or she meets the residence requirements.

Clients should apply for OAS six months prior to the date they want the benefits to begin. Late applicants can receive retroactive payments, but only back to their 65th birthday, or up to one year prior to the application for benefit, whichever is less.

OAS benefits are indexed quarterly. The maximum monthly benefit as of June 2014 was $551.54.

Once an OAS benefit has been approved, it may be paid indefinitely to a recipient living outside Canada, as long as the recipient lived in Canada for at least 20 years after the age of 18. Otherwise, payment is continued only for six months after the recipient leaves Canada. The benefit can be reinstated if the recipient subsequently returns to live in Canada.

The taxation of the benefit when the recipient lives outside of Canada will depend on whether or not the recipient is considered to be a non-resident for tax purposes, and, if so, the tax treaty in effect between Canada and the recipient's country of residence. The normal rate of withholding tax for non-residents is 25 percent; however, this is reduced where there is a specific tax treaty in effect. See Table 3 at the end of this chapter for a listing of withholding tax rates applicable to non-residents.

Many retirees are concerned that they will not benefit from OAS because of the "clawback" of the benefit applied to higher income earners. However, to put this into perspective, be aware that only about five percent of OAS recipients are affected by the clawback at all, while only two percent have incomes so high that they receive nothing from OAS.

The clawback was instituted in 1989 to reduce the amount of the benefit payable to those whose net income exceeds an annual threshold. For 2014, the threshold amount is $71,592. The annual benefit is reduced by 15 percent of the amount that net income exceeds the threshold amount, up to the maximum of the total annual OAS benefit. For 2014, the full amount of the OAS benefit is clawed back for those whose net income is higher than $115,716. The chart below can be used to estimate the effect of the OAS clawback.

OAS Benefit Reduction

Estimated annual net income	$_____
Minus	$71,592
	$_____
	X0.15
Equals annual reduction	$_____
Annual OAS benefit	$ 6,619
Minus annual reduction	$_____
Equals reduced annual benefit	$_____

OAS payments are reduced at source based on the retiree's previous year's income tax return. When the retiree files a tax return for the current year, the benefit amount is adjusted based on actual net income for the year.

Reducing the Impact of the Clawback

To ensure that clients get the maximum benefit from the OAS program, advisors need to look for ways to keep net income below the threshold level. Here are some strategies that clients can use to help reduce the effect of the clawback:

- Apply to receive CPP/QPP as soon as eligible, in order to minimize the annual income received from these plans.

- Where appropriate, apply to share CPP/QPP payments between spouses, in order to reduce the benefit received by the spouse with the higher income.

• Consider reporting a portion of the higher income earner's employer pension income in the name of the lower income spouse.

• Defer claiming some RRSP deductions until after OAS benefits have commenced, in order to reduce net income. Although contributions to one's own RRSP must be made before age 71, unused deductions can be carried forward indefinitely.

• Plan RRSP withdrawals carefully. Some individuals choose not to withdraw funds at all prior to age 71, in order to minimize the effects of the clawback for that period. For others, it may make sense to start to withdraw funds before OAS benefits have begun in order to reduce income later on.

• Consider the timing of conversion of RRSP funds to a RRIF or annuity. It may be best to wait until age 71 if minimum withdrawals or regular monthly payments will trigger the clawback.

• When opening a RRIF, base the withdrawal schedule on the age of the younger spouse, in order to minimize the income that must be drawn each year.

• Consider reporting a portion of the higher income earner's RRIF or annuity income in the name of the lower income spouse. This can be done where the original recipient is age 65 or older.

• Consider triggering gains on investments and stock options before receiving OAS or spread the income inclusion out over a number of years. If the investments would likely have to be realized in the early years of receiving OAS, it may be better to pay the taxes before OAS begins and avoid the clawback.

• Make use of the Tax-Free Savings Account (TFSA)

to hold fixed income investments such as bonds and GICs that are otherwise fully taxable. Consider transferring existing bonds and GICs from non-registered accounts into a TFSA each year up to the allowable limit.

- Hold tax-favoured investment vehicles such as prescribed annuities and T-series investment funds in non-registered accounts, in order to reduce taxable income. While dividends from Canadian companies are usually considered to be tax-favoured, be aware that they act to increase rather than reduce net income, due to the gross-up and tax credit system.

Benefits for Lower Income Retirees

The OAS program also provides two benefits for lower income individuals: the Guaranteed Income Supplement (GIS) and the Allowance.

The GIS is a monthly benefit paid to residents of Canada who receive the basic OAS pension, but who have little or no other income. Initially, clients must apply in writing to receive the GIS. However, eligibility in subsequent years is calculated automatically for those who file an annual income tax return. Unlike the basic OAS benefit, the GIS is not subject to tax. It is reported as part of total income, but then is subject to an offsetting deduction. The amount of the benefit depends on marital status and income. If the applicant is married or living in a common-law relationship, the combined income of the applicant and spouse will be taken into consideration in determining eligibility and calculating the benefit.

The maximum monthly GIS benefit for a recipient who is single or married to a non-pensioner is $747.86 per month (as of June 2014). The maximum amount for a recipient who is married to a pensioner or to an Allowance recipient is $495.89 per month (as of June 2014).

The income cut-off levels (as of June 2014) are as follows:

- single applicant: $16,728

- married to a non-pensioner or an Allowance recipient: $40,080 (combined income)

- married to a pensioner: $22,080 (combined income)

The GIS benefit will continue to be paid outside of Canada only for six months following the recipient's departure.

The Allowance is a monthly benefit paid to the spouse, widow, or widower of an OAS recipient. Applicants must be Canadian residents between the ages of 60 and 64, and must have lived in Canada for at least 10 years after turning 18. The combined annual income of the applicant and the pensioner spouse, or the annual income of the surviving spouse, must be below certain limits.

The Allowance ceases once the recipient becomes eligible for a basic OAS benefit at age 65, if the recipient leaves Canada for more than six months, or if a widow or widower remarries.

The maximum Allowance benefit for a spouse of an OAS recipient is $1,047.43 per month. The maximum for a widow or widower is $1,172.65 per month.

The current income cut-off levels are: $30,912 (combined) for a married recipient and $22,512 for a widowed recipient. All benefit amounts are current as of June 2014.

Recent Changes to OAS

Unlike CPP, OAS is funded through general tax revenues, and it is one of the most costly federal programs to run. Currently, there are nearly five million Canadians over the age of 65. Given current population trends, it's predicted that by 2030, there will be 9.3 million of us over 65. The cost of the OAS program is projected to increase from $36 billion per year (2010 numbers) to $106 billion per year in 2030. By that time, we will have twice as many retirees supported by half as many working Canadians. Without changes the OAS program would certainly be in jeopardy by that time.

Bill C-38, which was passed by the legislature in June 2012, addresses this issue by making the following changes to the OAS program:

- The age of eligibility for OAS and GIS benefits will gradually increase from 65 to 67 during the period 2023 to 2029. Those born prior to April 1, 1958 will not be affected by the changes. Those born in 1963 or later will not be eligible for OAS until they reach age 67. In between those two dates, there is a sliding scale that determines age of eligibility, which will fall somewhere between ages 65 and 67.

This increase to the age of eligibility brings our program into line with virtually every other country in the 34-member Organization for Economic Co-operation and Development (OECD).

In spite of the outcry from various seniors' lobby groups, increasing the age of eligibility for OAS is an entirely rea-sonable approach, given the increase in life expectancy that has taken place since OAS was created. The program was introduced in 1952, with an eligibility age of 70, at a time when average life expectancy was less than that. Today, the eligibility age is 65, with an average life expectancy of approximately 82, meaning that, on average, retirees collect the benefit for 17 years.

- Effective July 2013, OAS applicants have the option to defer receipt of their benefits for up to five years past their age of eligibility in exchange for an actu-arially increased pension. For each month of deferral, the monthly pension will be increased by 0.6%.

The government has also begun a proactive enrolment process that removes the need for seniors to apply for the OAS benefit. Proactive enrolment is being phased in between 2013 and 2016. At the time of writing, it appears that seniors are required to complete application forms if they choose to defer their benefits.

For more information on OAS, contact www.servicecanada.gc.ca.

Employment Insurance

Employment Insurance (EI) has been designed as a financial safety net to protect Canadians from hardship when they lose their jobs through no fault of their own, and are actively looking for other employment. There are some situations where clients transitioning into retirement could be entitled to apply for EI.

Most often, this is seen where a corporation or public sector organization is planning a restructuring that will result in the loss of jobs, and offers voluntary early retirement packages to employees. Arrangements can be made between the employer and EI officials to ensure that employees who take advantage of a voluntary separation package will not lose their entitlement to benefits under EI. As long as the layoff is considered permanent, and the employee's departure protects the job of another whose employment would otherwise be terminated, the employee who voluntarily accepts the package will qualify for EI benefits.

Another situation where at least one of a retiring couple might qualify for EI is where one spouse relocates for business reasons, and the other voluntarily leaves his or her job in order to accompany the relocating spouse.

However, advisors should be aware that payments such as retiring allowances and regular pension income may be taken into consideration when determining the waiting period for collecting benefits or the amount of benefit that can be received. See the discussion below for further details.

EI benefits are calculated based on 55 percent of insurable earnings. Maximum insurable earnings in 2014 are $48,600 per year; therefore, the maximum EI benefit is $514.04 per week. Benefits are normally payable for up to 45 weeks, although the exact payment period will vary according to the employee's contribution and claim history, as well as the unemployment rate in the region at the time the employee makes the claim. A local EI office should be contacted in order to determine the exact maximum payment period for the client.

Employees who decide to accept a voluntary early retirement package and are considering the advantages of claiming EI benefits should be aware of the following:

- A claimant must be in Canada and must be actively seeking work in order to continue to receive benefits. Regular reports must be submitted to EI every two weeks for monitoring.

- There is a standard waiting period of two weeks prior to receiving EI benefits. However, any separation payments the retiree receives from the employer, whether paid in cash or transferred to an RRSP, will extend the waiting period. This applies to vacation pay, payment of unused sick days, retiring allowances, and severance pay. EI calculates the number of weeks of regular employment income represented by the separation payments and adds this figure to the standard two-week period.

- Any work done during the waiting period or while on claim must be reported to EI and can potentially reduce the benefits paid out. Claimants are allowed to earn up to 25 percent of their weekly benefit, or $50, whichever is greater, without any reductions being made. However, any earnings over this level will reduce the EI benefit dollar for dollar. Note that, for EI purposes, earned income includes employer pension income, as well as CPP/QPP retirement benefits. Payments from personal RRSPs, survivor pensions, or disability pensions do not affect the calculation of EI benefits.

• When it comes time to file a tax return for the year that EI benefits were received, the claimant may have to pay back some of the benefit, depending on the level of his or her net income, even if the source of the net income is from investments or RRSP withdrawals. For the year 2014, a portion will have to be repaid if net income is $60,750 or more. Note that there is an exemption on this clawback for those who are claiming regular benefits for the first time in the past ten years.

If a client genuinely intends to seek other employment, it may make sense to consider applying for EI when she signs off on an early retirement offer. However, applying for employer pensions and CPP/QPP to start at the same time may be counterproductive. These payments may have the effect of reducing the EI benefit received, and they also could increase net income to the level where some of the benefit would have to be repaid at tax time. The advisor may want to consider the benefit of having employer pensions and CPP/QPP start after the EI entitlement period ends.

For example, Marilyn, age 60, takes an early retirement offer from her employer in December 2014. She intends to look for other employment, but is concerned about her prospects. She could take a reduced pension effective immediately, or she could wait until January 2016 to receive her full pension. Marilyn estimates that she would be entitled to receive EI benefits until October 2015, unless she finds employment first. It may be best for Marilyn to wait until

January 2016 to receive her full pension, and to delay receipt of her CPP benefits to November 2015. Marilyn's advisor will need to prepare a detailed analysis in order to determine the best outcome for her situation.

For more information on EI, contact www.service canada.gc.ca.

TABLE 1

CANADA PENSION PLAN BENEFIT RATES 2014

Type of Benefit	Maximum Monthly Amount
Retirement pension at age 65	$1,038.33
Survivors benefit under age 65	$ 567.91
Survivors benefit at age 65 and over	$ 623.00
Children's benefit[3]	$ 230.72
Disability benefit	$1,236.35
Combined survivors and retirement benefit at age 65	$1,038.33
Combined survivors and disability benefit	$1,236.35
Lump sum death benefit	$2,500.00

Source: www.servicecanada.gc.ca.

---

[3] The children's benefit is payable to the child of a deceased or disabled CPP contributor. The child must be under 18, or under 25 and in school full-time in order to be eligible.

TABLE 2

QUEBEC PENSION PLAN BENEFIT RATES 2014

Type of Benefit	Maximum Monthly Amount
Retirement pension at age 65	$1,038.33
Survivors benefit age 45 to 64[4]	$ 846.94
Survivors benefit at age 65 and over	$ 623.00
Orphan's benefit – child of deceased contributor[5]	$ 230.72
Children's benefit – child of disabled contributor[6]	$ 73.25
Disability benefit	$1,236.32
Combined survivors and retirement benefit at age 65	$1,038.33
Combined survivors and disability benefit	$1,236.32
Lump sum death benefit	$2,500.00

Source: www.rrq.gouv.qc.ca.

---

[4] Benefit under age 45 depends on health and family situation.

[5] The child must be under 18 in order to be eligible.

[6] The child must be under 18 in order to be eligible.

TABLE 3

NON-RESIDENT WITHHOLDING TAX ON GOVERNMENT BENEFITS

The normal rate of non-resident withholding tax is 25 percent. The countries listed below have a tax treaty with Canada that lowers this rate as shown.

Country of residence	OAS benefits	CPP or QPP pension	CPP or QPP death benefit
Argentina	15%	15%	25%
Australia	15%	15%	15%
Bangladesh	15%	15%	25%
Barbados	15%	15%	25%
Brazil[1]	25% or 0%	25% or 0%	25% or 0%
Bulgaria	15%	15%	25%
Cyprus[2]	15%	15%	25%
Dominican Republic	18%	18%	25%
Ecuador[3]	15%	15%	25%
Finland	20%	20%	25%
Germany	15%	15%	25%
Hungary	15%	15%	25%
Israel	15%	15%	25%
Ireland[4]	15%	15% or 0%	15%

[1] If you are both a resident and a national of Brazil, you are entitled to the lower rate. To get this exemption, you must file the NR5 form and provide evidence of your nationality.

[2] You are exempt from tax on the first CAN $10,000 (or its equivalent in Cyprus pounds whichever is higher) of the total of your pensions from Canada. To get this exemption, you must file the NR5 form.

[3] No tax is payable if your pension payments from Canada are not above CAN $12,000 (or the equivalent in Ecuadorian currency). To get this exemption, you must file the NR5 form.

[4] The 15% rate is for any portion of your CPP or QPP benefit payments related to self-employed earnings. The 0% rate applies to CPP or QPP benefits related to other employment earnings.

The Boomers Retire

Country of residence	OAS benefits	CPP or QPP pension	CPP or QPP death benefit
Italy[5]	15%	15%	25%
Ivory Coast	15%	15%	25%
Kenya	15%	15%	25%
Malaysia	15%	15%	25%
Malta	15%	15%	25%
Mexico	15%	15%	25%
Netherlands	25%	15%	25%
New Zealand[6]	15%	15%	15%
Norway	15%	15%	25%
Papua-New Guinea	15%	15%	25%
Peru	15%	15%	25%
Philippines[7]	25%	25%	25%
Poland	15%	15%	25%
Portugal[8]	15%	15%	25%
Romania[9]	25% or 15%	25% or 15%	25%
Senegal[10]	15%	15%	25%
Spain	15%	15%	25%

[5] You are exempt from tax on the first CAN $10,000 (or the equivalent of 6197.48 euros, if that is higher) of your Canadian pensions. To get this exemption, you must file the NR5 form.

[6] You are exempt from tax if your Canadian pensions are not above CAN $10,000. To get this exemption, you must file the NR5 form.

[7] No tax is payable if your pension payments from Canada are not above CAN $5,000 (or the equivalent in Philippine pesos). To get this exemption, you must file the NR5 form.

[8] No tax is payable if your pension payments from Canada are not above CAN $12,000 (or the equivalent in euros). To get this exemption, you must file the NR5 form.

[9] OAS and CPP/QPP benefits are taxed at 15% if they are also taxable in Romania. To get this reduced tax rate, you must file the NR5 form and provide evidence that the benefits you receive are also taxable in Romania.

[10] You are exempt from tax on the first CAN $12,000 (or its equivalent in Senegalese currency) of the total of your periodic pensions from Canada. To get this exemption, you must file the NR5 form.

Sources of Retirement Income — Government Benefits

Country of residence	OAS benefits	CPP or QPP pension	CPP or QPP death benefit
Sri Lanka	15%	15%	25%
Tanzania	15%	15%	25%
Trinidad & Tobago	15%	15%	25%
United Kingdom of Great Britain and Northern Ireland	0%	0%	25%
United States	0%	0%	0%
Zambia	15%	15%	25%
Zimbabwe	15%	15%	25%

Source: www.servicecanada.gc.ca.

TABLE 4

ADJUSTMENT FACTORS FOR EARLY RECEIPT OF CPP RETIREMENT BENEFITS

Year Benefit Begins	Amount Benefit Reduced from Age 65 Entitlement[7]
2014	.56%
2015	.58%
2016 and later	.60%

---

[7] Retirement benefit is reduced by stated percentage for each month prior to age 65 when benefit is taken early.

Chapter 3: Sources of Retirement Income — Employer Plans

This chapter addresses the various sources of income that originate from employer plans. While employer attitudes towards funding retirement programs for employees are changing, many clients will have some portion of their retirement income paid out from these sources. According to Statistics Canada, 38 percent of employees were members of registered pension plans (RPPs) by the end of 2011, down from 40 percent in 2001. Of that 38 percent, 73 percent were in traditional defined benefit (DB) plans, compared with 83 percent a decade earlier. Typically, these plans are not well understood by clients, and the advisor can play an important role in helping to clarify some of the issues that must be addressed.

Registered Pension Plans

One of the challenges that advisors face in counselling clients about pension plans is that pension legislation is not uniform across Canada. The individual provinces each have their own legislation in place, which governs the pension plans of companies registered in their respective jurisdictions. In addition, the federal *Pension Benefits Standards Act (PBSA)* governs private sector pension plans in the following industries: banks, railways, airlines, shipping, broadcasting, and telecommunications. Federal legislation also applies to plans for federal employees, including those working for federal Crown corporations, and public and private sector plan members in Yukon, the Northwest Territories, and Nunavut. In order to take advantage of tax benefits, pension plans must also meet certain requirements under the *Income Tax Act.*

Registered pension plans sponsored by employers include defined benefit and defined contribution or money purchase varieties, as well as plans that combine some of the features of both. Most defined benefit plan members work in the public sector. Increasingly, private sector employers are moving away from the expense, risk and red tape associated with operating a defined benefit plan, and are introducing defined contribution plans or other forms of retirement savings such as group RRSPs.

Defined Benefit (DB) Plans

A defined benefit plan specifies the amount of the pension benefit payable at retirement by way of a formula based on years of service and level of earnings. The level of earnings included in the calculation could be based on earnings over the employee's entire period of service with the employer, or the calculation could reflect only the last (or the best) three to five years of earnings. Employees may or may not be required to contribute to the plan. Even if the employee does not contribute, the fact that he is a member of the plan will give rise to a pension adjustment (PA), which will reduce his ability to contribute to an RRSP.

There is a standard formula for determining the PA related to a specific year's participation in the plan for all types of defined benefit pensions. For 1997 and later years, the formula is as follows:

$$PA = (9 \times \text{benefit entitlement}) - \$600$$

For years prior to 1997, the offset amount was $1,000 instead of $600. The benefit entitlement is calculated by multiplying the employee's current pensionable earnings by the unit percentage used by the pension plan. For example, if the plan was based on two percent of earnings, and the employee was earning $80,000, the calculation would be:

$$PA = (9 \times (2\% \times 80{,}000)) - \$600 = \$13{,}800$$

Although employees sometimes bemoan the lack of RRSP room they have, the reality is that the more generous the pension plan, the larger the PA, and thus, the smaller the amount of RRSP room the employee earns each year.

Retirement income projections from a defined benefit plan can be calculated based on the plan formula and assumptions about salary growth rates and future years of service. The annual pension statements that employers provide do not usually project future increases in salary.

Some of the features of defined benefit plans that should be considered in preparing retirement income projections include:

- Are future retirement benefits fully or partially indexed to inflation?

- Are retirement benefits integrated with CPP retirement benefits?

- What is the definition of earned income used by the plan?

- What provisions are there for early retirement benefits?

- What optional forms of income are available on retirement?

Maximum DB Pension Benefit

The *Income Tax Act* sets limits on the maximum annual pension that can be paid out from a defined benefit pension plan. The maximum amount is determined by multiplying a dollar limit by the number of years of pensionable service the plan member has to his or her credit.

For 2014, the dollar limit is $2,770.00. This limit is indexed annually to the increase in the average industrial wage as reported by Statistics Canada.

Highly paid individuals will be caught by these limits. In many cases, their employers operate Supplementary Employee Retirement Plans (SERPs) or Retirement Compensation Arrangements (RCAs) that serve to ensure that highly compensated employees remain whole from a pension perspective. For example, a retired teacher with 20 years of service might be entitled to an annual pension of $60,000 according to the terms of his pension plan. However, the maximum that can be paid out of a DB plan for 20 years of service is $55,400. In that case, although the teacher only receives one cheque each month, he will report $55,400 on line 115 of his tax return (pension income) and $4,600 on line 130 (other income). The difference is significant because only the pension income is eligible for income splitting with a spouse or partner. These unregistered plans will be discussed later in this chapter.

Defined Contribution (DC) Plans

A defined contribution plan specifies the contribution to be made each year by the employer and the employee, usually as a percentage of earnings. Employees have the ability to invest their contributions as they see fit, at least within the range of options offered by the plan. Future retirement income is unknown until the point of retirement, since it is partially dependant on the investment return earned by the plan.

Projecting retirement income from a defined contribution plan can be done in the same way that projecting income from an RRSP is done. Advisors will need to make assumptions about future level of contributions, years of service, and return on investment.

At retirement, the employee has the option of using the pension funds to purchase an immediate or deferred annuity, or to transfer the funds into a Locked-in Retirement Account (LIRA).

Hybrid Plans

Many employers today offer pension plans that are hybrids of defined benefit and defined contribution plans. Most hybrid designs are geared to provide larger values through the DC component for younger, more mobile workers, and more predictable values from the DB component for those closer to retirement. While hybrid plans may appear to offer the best of both worlds, the communication challenges should not be underestimated. Most planners are aware of how difficult it is for many clients to understand the basic DB plan, without introducing any further complications. Some common hybrid plan designs are outlined below.

Combination Plans

These plans feature a core DB pension that is supplemented by an additional DC component. Typically, the DB pension is funded solely by the employer, while members can choose to contribute to the DC plan if they wish. The DB formula needs to be low enough to allow room for DC contributions.

Flexible Plans

These plans are similar to the combination plans, but the DC component is designed so as to avoid inclusion in the pension adjustment calculation. On termination, the balance in the DC account is used to purchase ancillary benefits on the DB pension, such as bridge benefits to age 65, inflation protection, improved survivor benefits, or smaller early retirement reductions. It is up to the plan member to decide how much to contribute to the DC account and, at retirement, to determine which benefits to buy. With this arrangement, planners should ensure that their clients do not over-contribute to the DC account – funds that exceed the value of benefits a member can purchase are usually forfeited.

"Greater Of" Plans

With this arrangement, terminating members receive the greater of the pension that can be purchased with their DC account or the stated DB benefit. In this case, the DB benefit acts as a guaranteed income. With these plans, there is typically a much narrower selection of investments available for the DC component to prevent employees from taking on excessive investment risk.

Decisions to be Made at Retirement

Immediate Versus Deferred Pension

Clients who are retiring from a defined benefit plan before normal retirement age sometimes have the option of taking an immediate pension at a reduced amount, versus leaving their entitlement in the plan and taking an unreduced pension in a few years' time. This decision will depend, in part, on the client's plans for the intervening years. If the client plans on having some other sources of income, such as part-time employment or consulting work, there may be no need to draw the pension income right away. If the other sources of income are substantial, the pension income could be exposed to tax at a relatively high level.

On the other hand, it's important to consider the rate of reduction that is used to calculate the immediate retirement benefit. In some situations, the reduction will be so small that the gain in annual income achieved by waiting to receive the unreduced amount is far outweighed by receiving one or two years of pension income under the immediate pension benefit. Advisors can use spreadsheets to show clients the difference in total cash received up to specific ages under both scenarios.

Commuted Value versus Monthly Pension

Another option that is sometimes presented to members of defined benefit plans is to take the commuted value of the plan on termination and transfer it into a Locked-in Retirement Account (LIRA). This option is appealing to clients who feel that they will be able to achieve better investment performance than the professional money managers responsible for investing the pension funds. However, there are many factors that must be considered before such a decision is made.

Advisors should calculate the annual rate of return that would need to be achieved by investing the commuted value and producing an income equivalent to the monthly pension. In most cases, it's unlikely that a sufficient rate of return could be produced by guaranteed investments. Since a pension plan is essentially a guaranteed investment, this is the appropriate comparison to use. Growth-oriented investments may produce a higher rate of return, but these returns are not guaranteed. The portfolio required to produce the desired level of income must be evaluated with the client's risk tolerance in mind.

Another significant factor is that the *Income Tax Act* places a cap on the amount that can be transferred from a defined benefit pension plan to a LIRA. Excess funds will be taxable, unless the client has RRSP contribution room available. This means that there is a possibility that only part of the pension funds will be working in a tax-sheltered environment, making it even more of a challenge to reach the required rates of return.

Some pension plans provide additional features that may not be reflected in the commuted value. For example, some employers provide medical, life insurance, and other retiree benefits only if the retiree takes the monthly pension option. The value of these benefits can be significant, and should be included in the comparison. Also, some pensions, particularly public sector plans, are fully indexed to inflation. Many private sector plans provide ad hoc increases that would not be reflected in the commuted value.

One of the advantages to choosing the commuted value option is in the area of estate protection. If a client dies while holding the commuted value in a LIRA, LIF, or LRIF, the full amount can be transferred to a spouse or common law partner's registered plan on a tax-deferred basis. If there is no spouse or common law partner, the after-tax value of the plan can be paid to the client's estate. Although pension plans provide for a certain portion of the retirement benefit to continue to a surviving spouse, or to be paid to the estate of a retiree under certain circumstances, the protection is generally much more limited than the commuted value would provide. This suggests that the client's current state of health and family history can have a bearing on the decision to take the commuted value. For a client who is terminally ill, for example, greater estate protection may be a more significant factor.

Advisors should not ignore the state of health of the employer and the pension plan itself. If there is a risk that the employer could declare bankruptcy, or the plan is in a serious deficit situation, taking the commuted value may be the safest course of action. On the other hand, a healthy company with a large surplus in the plan might distribute a portion of that surplus to members if the plan is wound up.

Survivor Benefits

While all jurisdictions provide for the continuation of at least 60 percent of the retiree's monthly pension benefit to a surviving spouse, spouses or common law partners can waive their rights to the survivor pension, as long as they apply to do so within the applicable timeframe. Many pension plans also offer an opportunity to increase the benefit provided to the surviving spouse, at the cost of a lower pension benefit for the retiree.

Advisors need to weigh these options carefully, taking the spouse's needs for income into consideration. Another alternative that should be explored is the use of life insurance to provide a benefit for the surviving spouse. Sometimes, the monthly insurance premiums are less than the drop in after-tax income that the survivor benefit option would entail.

Phased Retirement

As discussed in Chapter 1, phased retirement will gradually become more common across Canada as more employers offer the opportunity for employees to work and collect a pension at the same time as they continue to accrue pensionable service. Advisors will need to be aware of this trend, and work with their clients to identify possible opportunities that may suit their clients' lifestyles and financial objectives.

Pooled Registered Pension Plans (PRPPs)

Bill C-25, a federal *Act Relating to Pooled Registered Pension Plans*, came into force in December 2012. This Act is designed to create a new type of pension plan that will be available to employees of organizations that come under federal jurisdiction (banks, transportation, broadcasting, telecommunications), as well as employees and the self-employed in Yukon, Northwest Territories and Nunavut.

The basic structure of the federal PRPP is intended to be similar to a defined contribution pension plan. It is up to each individual employer to decide whether or not to offer a PRPP, and if one is offered, the employer can choose whether or not to contribute. Both employer and employee contributions are subject to the overall limits for retirement savings that apply to RRSPs and other registered pension plans. Locking-in and portability provisions are similar to the rules currently governing federally-regulated pension plans.

PRPPs are not administered by individual employers. The "pooled" aspect indicates that they are maintained and offered by a variety of financial institutions, and employers are able to shop around and select a plan to offer their employees. Similarly, the self-employed are able to choose from the available providers.

Where employers offer a PRPP, employees are automatically enrolled, but will retain the right to opt out of the plan within 60 days of enrollment. Employers may set a default contribution rate for employees, but employees can move this rate up or down, as long as their contributions to all forms of retirement savings remain within the established limits.

Because the structure is similar to a defined contribution plan, employees who participate will need to make investment choices. The regulations specify that plan members are to be given a maximum of six investment options, including a default option. The default option must be represented either by a balanced fund or a portfolio of investments designed to take the member's age into account, e.g. a lifecycle fund. Members have 60 days to select an option before the default option automatically applies. As with a DC plan, these choices should be examined with regard to the client's overall investment strategy and holdings.

In order for those who work for provincially-regulated companies to participate, each province must pass similar enabling legislation. Quebec introduced Bill 80, *An Act Respecting Voluntary Retirement Savings Plans (VRSPs)* in June 2012. The following September, the Bill died as a result of the provincial election. In May 2013, the new provincial government introduced Bill 39, which is substantially similar to Bill 80. The structure of the VRSP is very similar to the PRPP, with the following exceptions: employers with at least five employees who do not already offer a pension plan must offer a VRSP by January 1, 2014; the default contribution rate for employees will be set by regulation rather than by the plan sponsor.

In May 2013, both Alberta and Saskatchewan passed legislation introducing PRPPs in their respective jurisdictions. The legislation, which is broadly similar to the federal plan, will come into effect once the regulations have been drafted and approved.

In February 2014, the British Columbia government reintroduced Bill 9, which would allow for the creation of PRPPs for small and medium-sized businesses, as well as the self-employed in that province. As with Alberta and Saskatchewan, the legislation closely mirrors that introduced by the federal government in 2012.

Locked-in Retirement Accounts

Locked-in RRSPs (LIRAs)

If a vested employee decides to take the commuted value of his or her pension, the funds must be transferred to a Locked-in Retirement Account (LIRA), also known as a locked-in RRSP. Some jurisdictions favour one term over the other, but they are essentially synonymous. Note that the term "locked-in retirement account" is also used more generally to describe any structure that holds locked-in funds.

As mentioned earlier, the *Income Tax Act* places a limit on the amount that can be transferred to a LIRA. Excess amounts are paid out in cash and will be included in the recipient's taxable income. However, if the recipient has RRSP room available, the excess amount can be paid directly to the RRSP on a tax-deferred basis.

While pension plans are governed by the jurisdiction where the pension plan is registered, locked-in funds are usually governed by the province where the locked-in plan was opened. The only exception to this applies to funds originating from a federally regulated pension plan. As discussed earlier, the federal *Pension Benefits Standards Act (PBSA)* governs private sector pension plans in the following industries: banks, transportation (railways, airlines, shipping), broadcasting, and telecommunications. Federal legislation also applies to plans for federal employees, including those working for federal Crown corporations, and public and private sector plan members in Yukon, the Northwest Territories, and Nunavut. Funds transferred out of a federally regulated pension plan are subject to federal rules regarding locked-in funds, regardless of where the locked-in plan is opened.

From the investment point of view, these plans are identical to RRSPs. However, because they are set up to receive funds transferred from a pension plan, they are subject to different rules regarding access to the money. As a general rule, a cash withdrawal cannot be made from an ongoing LIRA.

A LIRA may be converted to a Life Income Fund (LIF), Locked-in Retirement Income Fund (LRIF), Prescribed Retirement Income Fund (PRIF), or used to purchase a life annuity. Note that the availability of these options and the rules surrounding conversion differ from jurisdiction to jurisdiction. Table 2 at the end of this chapter summarizes the rules that were in effect as of May 2014. As this is an area of ongoing change, planners may wish to consult the pension regulator for the jurisdiction in question. Contact information for pension regulators is shown under Table 1 at the end of this chapter.

In general, clients can access the funds as early as age 55 or the earliest retirement date specified by the pension plan from which the funds were transferred (usually ten years prior to normal retirement age). Special rules allow individuals who work in public safety occupations to retire with an unreduced pension five years earlier than other pension plan members. These occupations include firefighters, police officers, corrections officers, commercial airline pilots, and air traffic controllers. Just as with a regular RRSP, the funds must be transferred to a retirement income vehicle by the end of the year the plan holder turns 71.

On death of the plan holder, the value of the LIRA can be transferred to the surviving spouse on a tax-deferred basis, and, at that point, the lock-in may or may not be removed, depending on the jurisdiction in question. See Table 2 at the end of this chapter.

Clients who may have received pension funds from more than one employer do not need to set up multiple LIRAs. However, they should be aware that, if the plans are consolidated, the more onerous lock-in rules will apply to the whole plan.

Under certain circumstances, funds in a LIRA can be unlocked. While the specific requirements will differ from jurisdiction to jurisdiction, in general, one of the following four situations must apply:

- Serious financial hardship
- Shortened life expectancy
- The assets in the LIRA are below a certain dollar amount (ranging from 10 percent to 50 percent of the YMPE, or $5,250 to $26,250 in 2014)

- Non-residency

Assets held in a LIRA are protected from creditors under pension legislation.

Life Income Funds (LIFs)

Both the LIF and the LRIF are retirement income funds that are used to hold monies that have been transferred from a LIRA. Like the LIRA, these plans are subject to regulation under the *Income Tax Act* as well as pension legislation. *Income Tax Act* regulations provide for the same minimum annual withdrawal schedule that applies to RRIFs.

A LIF is basically a variation of a RRIF that is set up to receive funds from a locked-in retirement account (LIRA), and provides for a lifetime retirement income by restricting both the minimum and maximum withdrawals from the plan. The investment rules and minimum withdrawal rules are the same as those that apply to RRIFs. However, pension standards legislation provides for additional limitations on the amounts that may be withdrawn, in order to ensure that the plan assets will remain sufficient to provide a lifetime retirement income.

There is a specific formula that is used to calculate the amount of the maximum withdrawal, based on what the plan holder would receive if the LIF funds were used to purchase a term certain annuity to age 90, using current interest rates. The maximum amount, therefore, is not a set percentage, but varies according to prevailing interest rates. The higher the interest rate, the higher the maximum withdrawal allowed.

While the minimum withdrawal is set by the *Income Tax Act*, and is the same in all jurisdictions, the maximum withdrawal is determined differently, but is generally calculated based on the age of the plan holder and long term interest rates. The federal *Pension Benefits Standards Act* uses the CANSIM rate (the interest rate on a long term Government of Canada bond) of the previous November, i.e. the rate for November 2014 is used to determine the withdrawal schedule for 2015. All the provinces use a minimum CANSIM rate of six percent; however, because their calculations are different, the maximum LIF withdrawal percentages will not be the same. See Table 3 at the end of this chapter for the maximum LIF withdrawal percentages for 2014.

At the time of writing, Newfoundland is the only remaining jurisdiction that requires the plan holder to use the funds to purchase a life annuity by the end of the calendar year he or she reaches age 80. For plan holders with a spouse or partner, the life annuity must be a joint and survivor annuity, unless the spouse waives his or her right to this income. In all other jurisdictions, there is no longer any requirement to annuitize at any age.

LIFs are available in all jurisdictions across Canada, except for Saskatchewan, which stopped issuing new LIFs as of April 1, 2002. Ontario legislation has provided for a product called a "new LIF" since January 1, 2008. Here, the maximum withdrawals are based on the greater of the existing LIF table and the investment earnings in the previous year.

The minimum age at which a LIF can be established is set by the relevant pension standards legislation governing the plan from which the funds originated. This differs from jurisdiction to jurisdiction, but generally 55 is the minimum age. In Ontario, it is defined as within ten years of normal retirement date under the terms of the pension plan. British Columbia sets a minimum of age 55, unless the pension plan allowed for the payment of a retirement pension at an earlier age. The Alberta government allows for the establishment of a LIF as early as age 50. In Manitoba, New Brunswick and Quebec, a LIF can be opened at any age.

If the LIF holder dies prior to converting the plan to a life annuity, and there is a surviving spouse, the funds must normally be transferred to the surviving spouse. In most jurisdictions, the funds can be paid out directly to the spouse, which would have immediate tax implications, or they could be transferred to another retirement vehicle in the spouse's name. Normally, the locked-in aspect disappears on the death of the original LIF holder; however, this does not apply to plans set up under federal jurisdiction. Here, the surviving spouse continues to be subject to the lock-in. In the absence of a surviving spouse or other designated beneficiary, the funds in the LIF will be paid to the estate of the plan holder.

Locked-in Retirement Income Funds (LRIFs)

The LRIF was created in Alberta and introduced in 1993. One of the major advantages of the LRIF at that time was that it was structured so that it never had to be turned into an annuity. However, since that time, most jurisdictions have removed the requirement for LIFs to be annuitized, so there is no longer a difference between LIFs and LRIFs with regard to that aspect.

However, there is a difference in the calculation of the maximum withdrawal amount.

The minimum withdrawal schedule for an LRIF is the same as for a LIF or a RRIF, but the maximum withdrawal is calculated based on the investment earnings of the plan, rather than the age of the annuitant.

If the maximum is not withdrawn in any given year, the balance may be carried forward and withdrawn in future years.

An LRIF does not guarantee a survivor benefit payable to the plan holder's spouse or partner. Therefore, the written consent of the spouse or partner is required to establish the plan. In addition, the spouse or partner must be named as designated beneficiary of the LRIF.

Where available, the LRIF provides more flexibility in cash flow for the plan holder than does the LIF. At the time of writing, only Newfoundland continues to offer LRIFs.

Prescribed RRIFs (PRIFs)

A newer innovation in the world of retirement income is the prescribed RRIF. Offered only in Manitoba and Saskatchewan at the time of writing, the PRIF provides the greatest level of flexibility for dealing with funds from a pension plan, as there is no cap on the withdrawals that can be made each year. The only difference between a PRIF and a RRIF is that, because the PRIF is governed by pension legislation, assets in the fund are protected from creditors, and a spouse or partner must provide written consent for the retiree to open a PRIF.

In Saskatchewan, money can be transferred into a PRIF either from another locked-in plan or directly from a pension plan; however, the plan holder must be of an age eligible to begin receiving his or her pension.

In Manitoba, the PRIF is used in more limited circumstances. Here, an individual who holds a LIF and is at least 55 years old can apply to unlock up to 50 percent of the value of his or her plan on a one-time basis. The PRIF has been established here for the sole purpose of holding these unlocked funds.

Early Access

As discussed above, funds in a locked-in account can be accessed in the event of serious financial hardship, shortened life expectancy, non-resident status, or if the assets in the plan are below a certain level as established by the jurisdiction in question. Specific rules differ from jurisdiction to jurisdiction and are outlined in Table 2 at the end of this chapter. It should be noted that, where "small amounts" can be unlocked, the amount in question usually applies to the total of all funds held in any locked-in account in that individual's name. It is not acceptable to divide the funds up into several locked-in accounts, and then apply to unlock them on the grounds that they now meet the small amount threshold.

In addition, some jurisdictions have introduced amendments that allow plan holders to unlock certain amounts of their funds on a one-time basis. For example, Alberta legislation allows workers who are at least 50 years old, and have written consent from their spouse or partner, to unlock up to 50 percent of their locked-in pension benefit when they are ready to access the funds as retirement income directly from the pension plan. Similarly, when funds are transferred from a LIRA to a life annuity or LIF, the plan holder will be able to transfer up to 50 percent of the value of the plan to a regular RRSP or take it in cash, subject to tax.

As discussed previously, Manitoba allows for the transfer of up to 50 percent of the funds in a LIF on a one-time basis, as long as the plan holder is over the age of 55. Unlocked funds must be transferred into a PRIF.

New Brunswick allows a one-time opportunity to unlock up to three times the maximum annual withdrawal of a LIF, with a cap of 25 percent of the value of the plan.

As of December 31, 2008, Ontario ceased to offer "old LIFs" and "LRIFs" and currently provides only "new LIFs" to those seeking to transfer funds from a LIRA. Individuals who buy a new LIF after December 31, 2009 can unlock up to 50 percent of the value of the funds on transfer into the plan.

In the federal jurisdiction, locked-in plan holders age 55 and older are entitled to a one-time conversion of up to 50 percent of their holdings into an RRSP or a RRIF.

These opportunities for unlocking lead to strategies that can be used for clients who have relatively small locked-in plans (less than the current YMPE or $52,500 in 2014). For example, Ann, age 56, is the holder of a federally regulated LIRA worth $50,000. Under the one-time conversion rule, she is eligible to unlock $25,000 of this amount and transfer it to her regular RRSP. This leaves her with $25,000 in the LIRA, which can then be unlocked under the small amount rule. The combination of these transactions allows her to unlock the full value of her LIRA and transfer the funds into a regular RRSP. If she chose to do so, she could also take the funds in cash or move them into a RRIF.

Pension Unlocking Scams

In recent years, the provincial securities commissions across Canada have received an increased number of complaints from investors about various pension unlocking scams. Unlike the legitimate opportunities outlined above, these scams are often promoted as unique investment opportunities. The types of investments may include shares in a company, bonds, cooperative shares, securities, mortgages in land or buildings, or other types of investments. As part of the investment, clients are often promised immediate access to their funds, sometimes without paying tax. The returns on these investments are usually described as far superior to other options.

Participation in these scams can have serious financial implications, including the loss of the previously locked-in funds and significant tax penalties.

Other Employer Sponsored Plans

Deferred Profit Sharing Plans (DPSPs)

A deferred profit sharing plan (DPSP) is a form of trust account to which an employer makes contributions on behalf of employees. While a DPSP must be registered with Canada Revenue Agency in order to establish and maintain its status as a tax-deferred plan, it is not regulated as a pension plan under federal or provincial pension legislation. There are limits to how much an employer can contribute in any given year, but unlike a pension plan, there is no requirement that the employer maintain a certain level of funding. The contributions may vary from year to year depending on the profits of the company. From the point of view of the participant employee, therefore, future contributions cannot be depended upon in the same way that a registered pension plan can.

The DPSP contribution limit is based on the earned income of the beneficiary employee. The limit is 18 percent of the employee's earned income up to a maximum of 50 percent of the money-purchase (defined contribution) pension plan limit for the year ($12,465 in 2014). Funds contributed to a DPSP are included in the employee's pension adjustment each year.

Employees are no longer allowed to contribute directly to a DPSP.

The *Income Tax Act* does not allow a DPSP to be set up for an owner-manager, controlling shareholder, or other non-arm's-length person.

Employee Stock Option Plans

The use of stock option plans has become an increasingly important component of employee compensation over the past several years. Many large companies in Canada now grant options to senior employees on an annual basis as an enhancement to the basic compensation package.

Essentially, an option is a right to purchase shares in the company at a future date at a fixed amount referred to as the exercise price. As the shares of the company grow over time, the options become more valuable to the holder.

On retirement, some clients may hold stock options that must be exercised within a certain number of years. If the client feels that there is considerable upside potential for the company, he or she may be tempted to hold the options as long as possible. However, the tax implications of exercising options must be considered as well.

There is no immediate tax implication when an employee is granted a stock option. However, the gain on the exercise of the option (difference between the exercise price and the fair market value of the shares at the time of purchase) is taxable as employment income. The timing of this taxation differs depending on whether the company qualifies as a Canadian Controlled Private Corporation (CCPC) or not. With stock options granted by CCPCs, taxation is deferred until the stock is sold.

If the employer is not a CCPC, taxation originally occurred when the option was exercised. However, as of the year 2000, option holders at arm's length from the corporation were allowed to defer tax on options granted by a non-CCPC until the shares were sold, bringing the tax treatment into line with that given to CCPC options. Option holders had to notify their employer of their intention to defer prior to January 16 of the following year. Taxation could have been deferred on shares with a fair market value at the time the options were granted of up to $100,000 each year.

In the federal budget of March 4, 2010, a number of changes regarding the tax treatment of stock options were introduced:

- The tax deferral election was repealed for employee stock options exercised after 4:00 p.m. Eastern Standard Time on March 4, 2010. As of January 1, 2011, employers are required to withhold tax at source on the exercise of stock options. These measures will prevent situations in which an employee is unable to meet his or her tax obligation as a result of a decrease in the value of these securities.

- To provide relief for taxpayers who deferred tax on stock options prior to the budget date, and these securities have since declined in value, a special elective tax treatment has been introduced. In effect, the special elective treatment ensures that the tax liability on a deferred stock option benefit does not exceed the proceeds of disposition of the optioned securities, taking into account tax relief resulting from the use of capital losses on the optioned securities against capital gains from other sources. Individuals who disposed of their optioned securities before 2010 had to make an election for this special treatment on or before the filing date for the 2010 taxation year. Individuals who have not disposed of their optioned securities before 2010 must do so before 2015. They then have until their filing date for the taxation year of disposition to make an election for this special treatment.

The stock option deduction (see below) will generally be available to employees only in situations where they exercise their options by acquiring securities of their employer. An employer may continue to allow employees to cash out their stock option rights to the corporation without affecting their eligibility for the stock option deduction provided the employer makes an election to forgo the deduction for the cash payment.

Stock options qualify for a special stock option deduction of 50 percent of the taxable benefit where the exercise price was equal to or greater than the fair market value of the shares at the time the option was granted. The stock option deduction is only available where the option holder is at arm's length from the employer.

There are other strategies that can be considered for reducing the tax impact of exercising stock options. Because the taxable benefit on the exercise of stock options is treated as employment income, it is therefore included as earned income for RRSP purposes. Clients should consider making an RRSP contribution to offset the tax associated with the exercise of the options. This can be done up until the end of the year the client reaches age 71, or even beyond if the client has a spouse who is still eligible for an RRSP by virtue of age.

Staggering the exercise of stock options over a period of several years after retirement can result in lower taxes. However, if clients expect to be impacted by the OAS clawback, they may wish to ensure they bring all options into income before they start to receive the OAS benefit.

Phantom Stock Plans

In recent years, other types of incentive programs based on the value of the employer's stock have become more popular. One of the reasons for this is that, with a phantom stock plan, no shares are actually issued; therefore, the plan does not dilute the outstanding capital stock in the same way that a stock option plan does.

With a phantom stock plan, the employee is granted a number of units (sometimes called deferred share units) with an entitlement date several years in the future. If the stock pays dividends between the grant date and the entitlement date, the dollar value of the dividends is added to the participant's account, to be paid out on the entitlement date along with the value of the share units themselves.

With this type of incentive program, the payment that is eventually made to the participant, while employed or in retirement, is taxed as ordinary income. Advisors need to ensure that they obtain full documentation on employer stock plans so that they understand when the payments will be brought into income, and how those payments will be taxed.

Supplemental Employee Retirement Plans (SERPs)

As discussed at the beginning of this chapter, the *Income Tax Act* sets limits on the maximum annual pension that can be paid out from a defined benefit pension plan. As a result, highly paid employees and executives often find that their earnings exceed the limit used to calculate maximum contributions into the plan. In these situations, employers often provide a SERP, which is an unregistered plan designed to provide additional retirement income to bridge the gap between the maximum benefit that can be provided from the pension plan, and the amount of income that would be expected in retirement, based on the employee's earnings and the pension formula. Because the SERP is unregistered, it has no impact on an employee's RRSP room.

A SERP that is unfunded relies on the employer's promise to pay the expected benefits once the employee retires. There is an element of risk here, in that future changes in senior management or at the Board level, as well as in the solvency of the employer, could jeopardize this future income.

A SERP that is funded provides the employee with a much higher level of security; however, there are some current tax implications for the employer. SERPs may be funded through Retirement Compensation Arrangements, as described below.

Retirement Compensation Arrangements (RCAs)

An RCA allows employers to pre-fund retirement arrangements without using registered pension plans. There are several different ways of funding an RCA, including cash contributions to an RCA trust, obtaining a letter of credit that allows the corporation to fund the RCA with future cash flow, and purchasing an exempt life insurance policy. However, funding with cash contributions has the drawback of the 50 percent refundable tax. Suppose the corporation has earmarked $60,000 to deposit into the RCA trust. Half of this amount must be sent immediately to CRA as payment of refundable tax. When the annual trust return is filed, half of the investment income and/or capital gains earned by the RCA must also be sent to CRA. The tax is refunded to the plan at the rate of 50 percent of benefits paid out during the year. While the RCA will recover 50 percent of any income payments made to the plan member down the road, the prepayment of tax ties up capital and limits the growth potential of the plan.

Refundable tax can be minimized if the employer provides enough cash for the trust to buy a letter of credit, which obligates the issuer (usually a bank) to pay the amount due when the time comes if the employer can't. The cost of this guarantee is based on the employer's financial standing, and is usually only a small percentage of the amount covered. Although this is a relatively inexpensive way to secure RCA payments, it's not perfect. Guarantees are typically issued for just one year at a time, and there is no assurance that a new letter of credit will be issued if the company has run into serious financial trouble in the meantime.

Exempt life insurance policies allow income to grow tax-deferred. In this case, the 50 percent refundable tax requirement does not apply to the growth in the plan. If the employee dies, the proceeds of the insurance policy are paid into the RCA tax-free. But when the income is paid out to the beneficiary, the money is taxable.

Regardless of how the plan is funded, employees report no income until they receive benefits from the plan during retirement, at which point the RCA payments are fully taxable.

Severance Payments

Retiring Allowance Treatment

The *Income Tax Act* defines a retiring allowance as an amount received on or after retirement from an office or employment in recognition of long service or in respect of loss of office or employment. In spite of the terminology, it is not necessary that the individual be retiring in the usual sense of the word - amounts received on termination of employment at any age fall within the scope of the definition. The full amount of the retiring allowance must be included in income under subparagraph 56(1)(a)(ii) of the *Income Tax Act*; however, there is an opportunity under paragraph 60 (j.1) to transfer the allowance or part of it to an RRSP to defer the tax owing on the payment. Retiring allowance payments are reported on line 130 of the income tax return as "other income". They are not considered to be employment income from the standpoint of CPP and EI contributions or regular RRSP contributions.

Canada Revenue Agency does point out, however, in *Interpretation Bulletin IT-337R4 (Consolidated) Retiring Allowances,* that retirement or loss of an office or employment does not include "termination of employment with an employer followed by re-employment with the employer (on a full or part-time basis) or employment with an affiliate of the employer pursuant to an arrangement made prior to the termination of employment". While many employees do, in fact, return to work for their previous employers after receiving a retiring allowance, it is most important that the arrangement to do so not be made in advance of the employee leaving their original position. If the arrangement is made ahead of time, CRA can deny the retiring allowance deduction.

Payments representing unused sick leave credits to which the employee was entitled also fall within the definition of retiring allowance. Payments representing accumulated vacation credits, however, are considered to be normal employment income.

The amount that can be transferred to the RRSP is calculated by the following formula:

- $2,000 for each full or partial calendar year of service with the employer up to and including 1995, plus

- $1,500 for each full or partial calendar year of service with the employer up to and including 1988, in which there was no vesting of pension or DPSP benefits

Note that the calculations are made on a calendar year basis, and that partial years of service qualify for the full amount. In other words, if a client had started work on December 20, 1995 and subsequently received a severance package, she would still be eligible to transfer $2,000 to an RRSP.

There are a number of "fine points" to consider when calculating the eligible amount of the rollover.

First, there is no requirement that the years of service with the employer be consecutive. Many employees, particularly in large organizations, will have breaks in service over the years when they left their employer for a period of time, only to return at some later date. Their entire employment history should be included in the calculation. This also applies to periods of part-time and/or summer employment prior to joining the organization as a full-time employee. The only exception would be where an employee already took advantage of a rollover provision on leaving his or her employer the first time. CRA's *Interpretation Bulletin IT-337R4 (Consolidated)* provides explicit clarification of this issue.

Second, periods of service with a related employer factor into the calculation as well.

Related employers include:

- those defined under section 251 of the *Income Tax Act*

- those whose business was acquired or continued by the current employer

- any previous employer of the retiree whose service therewith is recognized in determining the retiree's pension benefits

Contributions to an RRSP made as a result of a rollover of retiring allowance payments must be made to an RRSP in the employee's own name - such contributions cannot be made into a spousal plan.

The employer normally makes rollover contributions directly to the taxpayer's RRSP, with no tax withheld at source. However, it is possible for the taxpayer to take the retiring allowance in cash, minus the withholding tax, and subsequently contribute the eligible portion to an RRSP at a later date. In this situation, the contribution must be made within 60 days of the end of the calendar year the retiring allowance was received. There is no opportunity to carry forward these contributions to future years, as there is with regular RRSP contributions.

Any legal expenses that the taxpayer incurs in order to obtain or establish a right to the retiring allowance are deductible up to the limit of the payments received in cash in the year or in a preceding taxation year, i.e. not transferred to an RRSP. Note also that amounts received as an award or reimbursement of legal expenses paid by an individual to collect a retiring allowance must be included in the individual's income for the year received.

Financial counselling fees incurred by the taxpayer in order to make the decisions related to a severance package or offer of early retirement are fully deductible against income for the year paid.

Tax Planning Considerations

It is obviously in the employee's best interest from a tax planning point of view to shelter as much of the retiring allowance as possible from tax by making the maximum transfer allowable to an RRSP. However, it often happens that the retiring allowance is larger than the amount that can be transferred, and a certain portion must be taken in cash. The standard withholding rates that apply to a retiring allowance taken in cash in every province except Quebec are as follows:

- for amounts up to and including $5,000 – 10 percent
- for amounts over $5,000, up to and including $15,000 – 20 percent
- for amounts over $15,000 – 30 percent

In Quebec, the applicable rates are:

- for amounts up to and including $5,000 – 5 percent federal plus 20 percent provincial
- for amounts over $5,000, up to and including $15,000 – 10 percent federal plus 23 percent provincial
- for amounts over $15,000 – 15 percent federal plus 23 percent provincial

Clients should be advised that the withholding tax is similar to a preliminary tax instalment. Depending on their marginal tax rate, they may be eligible to get a refund of some of this tax when they file their return for the year, or they may have to pay more tax. Many clients are under the mistaken impression that the withholding tax is the only tax that applies to a retiring allowance.

It is also possible for an employee who has regular RRSP contribution room available to arrange to have money transferred from the retiring allowance directly to his or her RRSP without tax deducted at source. While the opportunity to receive an additional portion of the retiring allowance on a tax-deferred basis is appealing to many employees, problems can occur if the employee needs to withdraw these funds later to meet living expenses. Once funds are withdrawn from an RRSP, they cannot be replaced. In other words, a withdrawal does not open up additional contribution room. For this reason, most employees who plan to continue to work are better off to take their retiring allowance in cash, apart from the one-time opportunity for the $2,000 per year rollover, and fund their regular RRSP contributions once they are re-employed, with no likelihood of needing the funds in the short term. Of course, if the employee is transitioning into retirement, this is much less of a concern.

Retiring allowances that are paid in cash to non-residents of Canada are generally subject to a 25 percent withholding tax, although this rate may be reduced by a provision of a tax treaty. If the non-resident's income is low, they may also elect to pay tax on the retiring allowance at the rate they would be subject to if they were filing a Canadian tax return.

The receipt of a severance package towards the end of a calendar year affords some opportunities for tax planning. If the employer is willing, the departing employee can arrange to receive some or all of the severance payment in the following year, thus deferring and perhaps even reducing some of the tax owing on the payments. Factors that should be taken into consideration include:

- expectations re: taxable income for each of the two calendar years

- applicable federal and provincial tax rates in each of the two calendar years, i. e. is there a change in rates that would have a significant impact

- need for immediate income for cash flow purposes or for reducing high-interest debt

- ability to transfer some of the severance to an RRSP

Generally speaking, the portion that can be transferred to an RRSP should be taken immediately as there is no advantage to deferring this portion of the payment. If some cash is needed for the current calendar year, it may have to be taken as well, although consideration should be given to using other available cash resources when appropriate.

Salary Continuation versus Lump Sum Payment

In some situations, a departing employee has a number of choices as to how to receive his or her severance payment. If the employer is agreeable, lump sum payments may be spread over two or more years, or the company may offer to continue regular salary payments for a period of time.

A lump sum payment is characterized as a retiring allowance, and it qualifies for transfer to an RRSP as described earlier. Reported as "other income" on line 130 of the tax return, these amounts are not subject to any statutory deductions such as CPP and EI.

Regular salary payments are taxed as employment income, reported on line 101 of the tax return, and are subject to CPP and EI contributions. Other benefits such as medical and life insurance coverage normally continue throughout the salary continuation period[1], and the employee continues to maintain membership in the pension plan and accrue pension credit. The income earned while on salary continuation counts as earned income for RRSP purposes, and contributions may be made based on the normal contribution limits. These contributions can be directed towards the employee's own RRSP or to a spousal RRSP.

Some employers are willing to consider paying severance in a combination of methods that produces the best

---

[1] Long-term disability is the usual exception to this rule.

outcome for the employee. The financial advisor needs to analyse the options available to see how the best result can be achieved, keeping taxes in mind, as well as the impact on eventual pension payments. By definition, a retiring allowance does not provide for additional pension accrual. Benefits coverage for an extended period may also be an important issue, particularly where equivalent coverage is not provided for retirees.

TABLE 1

CONTACT INFORMATION FOR REGULATORS OF PRIVATE PENSION PLANS

Federally Regulated Pension Plans
Office of the Superintendent of Financial Institutions Canada 255 Albert Street Ottawa, Canada K1A 0H2 1 800 385 8647 613 943 3950 (local calls from Ottawa and Gatineau) www.osfi.gc.ca
Provincially Regulated Pension Plans
Alberta Treasury Board and Finance 9515-107 Street Edmonton, Alberta T5K 2C3 780 427 3035 www.finance.alberta.ca
Financial Institutions Commission Box 12116 2800-555 West Hastings Street Vancouver, British Columbia V6B 4N6 604 660 3555 www.fic.gov.bc.ca
The Manitoba Pension Commission Manitoba Labour and Immigration 1004 - 401 York Avenue Winnipeg, Manitoba R3C 0P8 204 945 2740 www.gov.mb.ca/labour/pension
Office of the Superintendent of Pensions Department of Justice and Consumer Affairs Frederick Square P.O. Box 6000 Fredericton, New Brunswick E3B 5H1 506 453 2055 www.fcnb.ca/PensionsIndustry

Provincially Regulated Pension Plans (cont'd)
Pensions Administration Division Department of Finance P.O. Box 8700 St. John's, Newfoundland A1B 4J6 707 729 3931 www.gov.nl.ca
Pension Regulation Division Department of Labour and Advanced Education 7th Floor 5151 Terminal Road Halifax, Nova Scotia B3J 1A1 902 424 8915 www.novascotia.ca/lae/pensions
Financial Services Commission of Ontario Pension Division 5160 Yonge Street P.O. Box 85, 4th Floor Toronto, Ontario M2N 6L9 416 250 7250 www.fsco.gov.on.ca/en/pensions
Régie des rentes du Québec Case postale 5200 Québec, Québec G1K 7S9 1 877 660 8282 www.rrq.gouv.qc.ca/en
Saskatchewan Financial Services Commission Pensions Division Suite 601, 1919 Saskatchewan Drive Regina, Saskatchewan S4P 4H2 306 787 7650 www.sfsc.gov.sk.ca/pensions

Source: www.osfi.gc.ca.

TABLE 2

SELECTED PENSION BENEFITS STANDARDS BY JURISDICTION

	Federal	Alberta
Website	www.osfi.gc.ca	www.finance.alberta.ca
Special Access	– Annual pension is < 4% of YMPE when transferred out of pension plan (access at that time only) – Shortened life expectancy – 2 yrs. after becoming non-resident – If age 55+, can unlock up to 50% of funds on one-time basis – Financial hardship – can unlock up to 50% of YMPE per year – FMV of LIF is <50% of YMPE if age 55+	– FMV is < 20% of YMPE – FMV is < 40% of YMPE if age 65+ – Shortened life expectancy – Non-resident – Financial hardship – If age 50+, can unlock up to 50% of funds on one-time basis when transferring from pension or LIRA into LIF or annuity (pension plan may restrict after certain age)
Post-retirement Survivor Benefits	Minimum 60% to surviving spouse.	Minimum 60% to surviving spouse.
LIRA	Locked-in until 10 yrs. prior to normal retirement age under plan. Surviving spouse continues to be subject to lock-in.	Locked-in until age 50. Surviving spouse continues to be subject to lock-in.
LIF	Maximum withdrawal determined by regulation. No requirement to annuitize at any age. Surviving spouse continues to be subject to lock-in.	No requirement to annuitize at any age. Surviving spouse not subject to lock-in.
LRIF	Not offered.	Discontinued.

	BC	Manitoba
Website	www.fic.gov.bc.ca	www.gov.mb.ca/labour/pension
Special Access	– FMV is < 20% of YMPE – FMV is < 40% of YMPE if age 65+ – Shortened life expectancy – 2 yrs. after becoming non-resident	– FMV estimated at age 65 < 40% of YMPE (estimate based on current value + 6% interest per year) – Shortened life expectancy – Non-resident – If age 55+, can transfer up to 50% of funds into PRIF on one-time basis
Post-retirement Survivor Benefits	Minimum 60% to surviving spouse.	Minimum 60% to surviving spouse.
LIRA	Locked-in until 55 or earliest retirement date allowed by plan. Surviving spouse continues to be subject to lock-in.	No minimum age for access to income. Surviving spouse continues to be subject to lock-in.
LIF	No requirement to annuitize at any age. Surviving spouse not subject to lock-in.	No requirement to annuitize at any age. Maximum withdrawal based on greater of prescribed annuity factors and investment income earned. Surviving spouse not subject to lock-in.
LRIF	Not offered.	Not offered.
PRIF	Not offered.	No maximum withdrawal limit. No requirement to annuitize at any agae. Surviving spouse not subject to lock-in.

Sources of Retirement Income — Employer Plans

	New Brunswick	**Newfoundland**
Website	www.fcnb.ca/PensionsIndustry	www.gov.nl.ca
Special Access	– FMV is < 40% of YMPE – Shortened life expectancy – 2 yrs. non-resident – One-time opportunity to unlock 3 times maximum annual withdrawal of LIF with cap of 25%.	– FMV is < 10% of YMPE – FMV is < 40% of YMPE if age 55+ – Shortened life expectancy if spouse has waived rights. – Temporary income withdrawal from LIF or LRIF if total pension income < 40% of YMPE and age < 65.
Post-retirement Survivor Benefits	Minimum 60% to surviving spouse.	Minimum 60% to surviving spouse.
LIRA	No minimum age for access to income. Surviving spouse not subject to lock-in.	Locked-in until age 55 or earliest retirement date allowed by plan. Surviving spouse not subject to lock-in.
LIF	No requirement to annuitize at any age. Surviving spouse not subject to lock-in.	Maximum withdrawal determined by regulation. Must annuitize by age 80. Surviving spouse not subject to lock-in.
LRIF	Not offered.	Maximum withdrawal based on investment earnings in previous year (limited to 6% in the first 2 yrs.). Surviving spouse not subject to lock-in.

The Boomers Retire

	Nova Scotia	Ontario
Website	novascotia.ca/lae/pensions	www.fsco.gov.on.ca/en/pensions
Special Access	– FMV is < 40% of YMPE – Shortened life expectancy – Financial hardship	– FMV is < 40% of YMPE and age 55+ – Life expectancy < 2 yrs. Pension plan provisions will override if more generous and funds are in LIF – 2 yrs. after becoming non-resident – Financial hardship – Can unlock up to 50% of funds of new LIF purchased after December 31, 2009.
Post-retirement Survivor Benefits	Minimum 60% to surviving spouse.	Minimum 60% to surviving spouse.
LIRA	Locked-in until age 55 or earlier if pension plan allows. Surviving spouse not subject to lock-in.	Locked-in until age 55 or earlier if pension plan allows. Surviving spouse not subject to lock-in.
LIF	Maximum withdrawal determined by regulation. No requirement to annuitize at any age. Provisions for temporary income withdrawals from 54 – 65. Surviving spouse not subject to lock-in.	Maximum withdrawal based on prescribed annuity factors. No requirement to annuitize at any age. Surviving spouse not subject to lock-in. Not available after Dec. 31, 2008.
LRIF	Not offered.	Maximum withdrawal based on investment earnings in previous year (limited to 6% in the first 2 yrs.). Where maximum not withdrawn in any year, amount carried forward and can be withdrawn in future years. No requirement to annuitize at any age. Surviving spouse not subject to lock-in. Not available after Dec. 31, 2008.
New LIF	Not offered.	Maximum withdrawal based on greater of LIF table and investment earnings in previous year. Carryforward of unused withdrawals no longer allowed. No requirement to annuitize at any age. Surviving spouse not subject to lock-in. Available as of Jan. 1, 2008.

Sources of Retirement Income — Employer Plans

	Quebec	Saskatchewan
Website	www.rrq.gouv.qc.ca/en	www.sfsc.gov.sk.ca/pensions
Special Access	– FMV is < 40% of YMPE and age 65+ – Shortened life expectancy – 2 yrs. non-resident – Temporary income withdrawals from LIRA where under age 54 and income is < 40% of YMPE. No income test for those aged 55 – 64.	– FMV is < 20% of YMPE – Annual pension is < 4% of YMPE – Shortened life expectancy
Post-retirement Survivor Benefits	Minimum 60% to surviving spouse.	Minimum 60% to surviving spouse.
LIRA	No minimum age for access to income. Surviving spouse not subject to lock-in.	Locked-in until age 55 or 10 years prior to normal retirement age under plan. Surviving spouse subject to lock-in.
LIF	No requirement to annuitize at any age. Surviving spouse not subject to lock-in.	Not offered.
LRIF	Not offered.	Not offered.
PRIF	Not offered.	No maximum withdrawal limit. No requirement to annuitize at any age. Surviving spouse not subject to lock-in.

Notes:

1. PEI has no pension benefits legislation.

2. Federal legislation applies to pensions in the three territories.

3. Pension plans are registered in the jurisdiction where most members are employed. Benefit standards, such as those listed above, are set by the jurisdiction where the employee works.

4. Maximum annual LIF withdrawal rates tend to be higher than maximums for LRIFs. LIF rates allow the plan holder to remove capital; LRIF rates only allow for the removal of earnings.

5. All jurisdictions except NB allow minimum withdrawals from locked-in plans to be based on the age of the younger spouse.

TABLE 3

MAXIMUM LIF WITHDRAWAL SCHEDULE 2014

Age as at January 1, 2014	New Brunswick, Newfoundland, Ontario, Saskatchewan	Alberta	British Columbia, Manitoba, Nova Scotia, Quebec	Federal
50	6.26996%	6.51%	6.10%	4.7680%
51	6.31073%	6.57%	6.10%	4.8043%
52	6.35454%	6.63%	6.10%	4.8433%
53	6.40164%	6.70%	6.10%	4.8854%
54	6.45234%	6.77%	6.10%	4.9308%
55	6.50697%	6.85%	6.40%	4.9799%
56	6.56589%	6.94%	6.50%	5.0330%
57	6.62952%	7.04%	6.50%	5.0905%
58	6.69833%	7.14%	6.60%	5.1529%
59	6.77285%	7.26%	6.70%	5.2208%
60	6.85367%	7.38%	6.70%	5.2947%
61	6.94147%	7.52%	6.80%	5.3754%
62	7.03703%	7.67%	6.90%	5.4637%
63	7.14124%	7.83%	7.00%	5.5604%
64	7.25513%	8.02%	7.10%	5.6668%
65	7.37988%	8.22%	7.20%	5.7841%
66	7.51689%	8.45%	7.30%	5.9139%
67	7.66778%	8.71%	7.40%	6.0580%
68	7.83449%	9.00%	7.60%	6.2185%
69	8.01930%	9.34%	7.70%	6.3983%
70	8.22496%	9.71%	7.90%	6.6006%
71	8.45480%	10.15%	8.10%	6.8294%
72	8.71288%	10.66%	8.30%	7.0900%
73	9.00423%	11.25%	8.50%	7.3888%
74	9.33511%	11.96%	8.80%	7.7344%
75	9.71347%	12.82%	9.10%	8.1378%
76	10.14952%	13.87%	9.40%	8.5988%
77	10.65661%	15.19%	9.80%	9.1340%
78	11.25255%	16.90%	10.30%	9.7585%
79	11.96160%	19.19%	10.80%	10.4977%

Sources of Retirement Income — Employer Plans

Age as at January 1, 2014	New Brunswick, Newfoundland, Ontario, Saskatchewan	Alberta	British Columbia, Manitoba, Nova Scotia, Quebec	Federal
80 *	12.81773%	22.40%	11.50%	11.3863%
81	13.87002%	27.23%	12.10%	12.4739%
82	15.19207%	35.29%	12.90%	13.8352%
83	16.89953%	51.46%	13.80%	15.5875%
84	19.18515%	100.00%	14.80%	17.9263%
85	22.39589%		16.00%	21.2035%
86	27.22561%		17.30%	26.1228%
87	35.29338%		18.90%	34.3266%
88	51.45631%		20.00%	50.7413%
89	100.00000%		20.00%	100.0000%
90 +			20.00%	

* A LIF must be converted to a life annuity by age 80 in Newfoundland.

Chapter 4: Sources of Retirement Income — Personal Savings and Employment Income

This chapter addresses the third component of retirement income – the personal resources that the retiree brings to the table. This can come in the form of income from registered savings, reverse mortgages, or continued employment, working for oneself or another employer. Many retirees also have non-registered savings and investments which can be used to provide additional income in the retirement years. Chapter 5, Investment Choices and Strategies for the Retirement Years, will discuss the efficient use of non-registered investment capital in retirement, as well as provide an overview of some of the investment choices that are most appropriate for the withdrawal stage of investment planning.

Registered Retirement Savings Plans (RRSPs)

Essentially, an RRSP is a contract between an individual annuitant and a plan issuer, which is registered under the *Income Tax Act*. The annuitant contributes funds to the plan, within certain parameters established by the *Act*, receives a tax deduction for his contributions, and at retirement, draws a taxable income from the plan. Clients who have earned income under the *ITA* definition can contribute to a plan in their own name, up to the end of the year they turn 71. An individual past this age who still has earned income can contribute to the plan of a younger spouse, up to the end of the year the spouse turns 71.

Contribution Limits

The current limit for calculating RRSP contribution room is 18 percent of the previous year's earned income, up to a certain dollar maximum each year. The maximum for 2014 is $24,270, and this is scheduled to increase to $24,930 for 2015. Thereafter, the limit will be indexed based on increases in the average industrial wage in Canada. Any unused room can be carried forward indefinitely and used in future years.

Earned income includes:

- employment earnings
- net income from a sole proprietorship or partnership
- disability payments from CPP, QPP, or taxable disability payments received from a group or private plan
- royalties for a work or invention of which the taxpayer was the author or inventor
- net rental income from real property
- taxable spousal support payments received
- net research grants
- employee profit-sharing plan allocations
- supplementary unemployment benefit plan payments (not including federal Employment Insurance benefits)

Minus:

- union or professional dues

- employment expenses claimed on the tax return
- current-year loss from a sole proprietorship or partnership
- current-year rental loss from real property
- deductible spousal support payments made

Where an individual belongs to an employer pension plan (RPP), pooled registered pension plan (PRPP), or deferred profit sharing plan (DPSP), the overall limit will be reduced by the Pension Adjustment (PA), which represents the value of the individual's participation in the employer's plan for the year.

Qualified Investments

The *Income Tax Act* has established rules that outline the types of investments that may be held in trusts governed by RRSPs and RRIFs.[1] Eligible investments include:

- securities listed on a designated stock exchange in or outside of Canada
- shares of small business corporations where the plan holder is not a connected shareholder of the corporation
- shares of venture capital corporations where the plan holder is not a connected shareholder of the corporation
- bonds, debentures, notes, or similar obligations (including stripped bonds or coupons) guaranteed by the Government of Canada or of a province, municipality, or Crown corporation
- guaranteed investment certificates issued by a Canadian trust company

---

[1] Interpretation Bulletin IT-320R3, CRA.

- debt obligations issued by a corporation whose shares are listed on a designated stock exchange inside or outside of Canada

- debt obligations issued by an authorized foreign bank and payable at a branch of the bank in Canada

- debt obligations issued by a mutual fund trust whose units are listed on a designated stock exchange in Canada

- any debt obligations which had an investment grade rating at the time of purchase from a prescribed credit rating agency, and were either issued as part of a single debt issue of at least $25 million, or where issued on a continuous basis, were issued by an issuer that has issued an outstanding debt of that type of at least $25 million

- mortgages in respect of real property situated in Canada. Where the mortgagor is not at arm's length from the annuitant, or where the mortgagor and the annuitant are one and the same, the mortgage must be administered by an approved lender under the *National Housing Act*, and must be insured. In addition, the mortgage interest rates and other terms of the mortgage must reflect normal commercial practice.

- amounts on deposit with a Canadian bank, a credit union, or a Canadian branch of a foreign bank

- units of a mutual fund trust or an exchange-traded fund

- annuity contracts

- warrants or rights that give the owner the right to acquire property that is a qualified investment. Note that this includes the purchase of call options that give the owner the right to acquire property that is a qualified investment. The purchase of a put option results in the acquisition of non-qualified property. Where a plan trust engages in short selling, or sells a call option on underlying property that it doesn't own (a naked call), it could be deemed to be carrying on business, in which case, it would be liable for tax on the business income.

- royalty units, listed on a designated stock exchange in Canada, and whose value is derived solely from Canadian resource properties

- limited partnership units listed on a designated stock exchange in Canada

- depository receipts listed on a designated stock exchange in or outside of Canada

- investment grade gold and silver bullion, coins, bars, and certificates on such investments

The Department of Finance maintains a list of designated stock exchanges on their website at www.fin.gc.ca.

Timing of Contributions

In order to be deductible for the current tax year, contributions to an RRSP must be made either during the year or up to 60 days after December 31 of the current year. Contributions made in the first 60 days of the next year must be reported on the tax return, and receipts must be submitted to Canada Revenue Agency, but the taxpayer has the choice of deducting them in the current year or a future year.

There is no obligation to deduct contributions in the year the contribution is made. The deduction can be carried forward indefinitely and used to offset income in a higher tax bracket in a future year. For example, a taxpayer who was concerned about the impact of the OAS clawback might want to make use of some RRSP deductions after he starts to receive OAS benefits.

Carryforward of Unused Room

Since 1991, unused contribution room can be carried forward indefinitely. Many clients are under the impression that, once they retire, they are no longer able to contribute to an RRSP. However, if they retire with unused contribution room, they can add to their RRSP at any time up until the end of the year they reach age 71 (or even beyond if they have a spouse under age 71), and the deduction can be applied to any source of income. Again, this could be a strategy that would be helpful to clients concerned about the OAS clawback.

Overcontributions

Rules for RRSPs introduced in 1991 allowed individual taxpayers to make a once in a lifetime overcontribution of up to $8,000. Effective in January 1996, this amount was reduced to $2,000. The overcontribution limit is designed to provide a buffer for estimated contributions that exceed allowable contributions. Contributions in excess of the $2,000 overcontribution limit will attract a penalty tax of 1 percent per month of the amount of the overcontribution, until they are either removed from the plan or used as a deductible contribution in future years.

A common planning technique involves deliberately making the $2,000 overcontribution, allowing it to earn tax-deferred income over the years, and using it as a deductible contribution at the point of retirement. If it is not used as a deductible contribution, it will effectively be double-taxed - no deduction is allowed for the contribution, and the contribution will be taxed again when it is received as retirement income. However, if the overcontribution was made early enough in the client's career, and the funds earned a good rate of return, the tax-deferred growth on the $2,000 could be enough to compensate for the double taxation that will be experienced.

Advisors need to be aware of which clients are in an overcontribution situation, and determine the best way of dealing with the overcontribution amount.

Use of Spousal Plans

A spousal RRSP is an RRSP that names the contributor's spouse as the annuitant. The contributor makes contributions from his or her own contribution room. It is important to keep spousal plans separate from those that the spouse may choose to set up for himself based on his own contribution room.

A spousal RRSP may be set up on behalf of a legally married, common-law, or same sex partner. As for all other income tax purposes, the *Income Tax Act* considers a common-law spouse to be a person of the same or opposite sex who cohabits with the taxpayer in a conjugal relationship and either:

- has cohabited with the taxpayer over the past 12 months, or

- is the biological or adoptive parent of a child of the taxpayer.

The amount which can be contributed to a spousal plan is the same amount as can be contributed to the taxpayer's own plan, according to the rules governing regular annual contributions. In other words, the taxpayer's own contribution room can be used to fund contributions to his or her own plan and/or a spousal plan, but he must stay within the limits of his own contribution room. Similarly, the deadline for making contributions to a spousal plan is the same as for contributions to the taxpayer's own plan. Special transfers such as the eligible portion of a retiring allowance or the commuted value of a pension plan cannot be contributed to a spousal plan.

Any contributions which are allocated to a spousal plan from the taxpayer's own contribution room do not affect the spouse's ability to contribute to his or her own plan, based on his or her own contribution room.

There are special anti-avoidance rules to prevent abuse of the spousal RRSP. If a spouse withdraws money from a spousal plan, and the taxpayer has contributed funds to any spousal plan in the year of withdrawal or the two preceding years, the withdrawal will be taxed back to the original contributor. Setting up a series of different spousal plans does not get around this problem - the rules apply to funds contributed to any spousal plan set up with the same annuitant spouse.

For example, consider the following contributions that George made to a spousal RRSP for his partner Suzanne.

Year	Contributions	Withdrawals
2012	$4,000	
2013	$4,000	
2014	$4,000	
2015	$4,000	$15,000

In this case, $12,000 of Suzanne's withdrawal will be taxed to George, since that is the amount he contributed in the year of withdrawal and the two previous years. The remaining $3,000 will be taxed in Suzanne's hands.

However, these attribution rules only apply to cash withdrawals made directly from an RRSP. If Suzanne were to transfer the RRSP funds into a RRIF in 2014, and make only the required minimum withdrawal in 2015, those funds would be taxed in her hands. If she withdraws more than the minimum required amount, the excess amount would be attributed to George, to the extent he contributed to the plan in the year of withdrawal and the two previous years. Similarly, if Suzanne buys an annuity with the spousal RRSP funds in 2015, and begins to draw an immediate income from the annuity, the total amount of the annuity payments will be taxed in her hands.

The goal of a spousal RRSP is to equalize retirement income as much as possible between the spouses, so as to reduce the overall tax burden in retirement. If neither one has a pension plan, or any other sources of retirement income apart from government benefits, RRSPs should be kept as equal as possible. If pensions are involved, an estimate of the commuted value of the plan should be factored into the eventual retirement assets.

The benefit of the tax savings derived from equalizing income depends primarily on the extent to which income would be taxed in a higher tax bracket if it were all received in the hands of one spouse. With the introduction of pension income splitting provisions, some advisors have questioned whether there is still a role for the spousal RRSP. However, remember that there is no opportunity to split RRIF or annuity income prior to age 65. Setting up a spousal RRSP still presents tax advantages for those who might wish to draw on registered funds prior to that age.

A Final Opportunity to Contribute

An RRSP must be collapsed by the end of the calendar year that the plan holder reaches age 71. However, this does not necessarily mean that contributions cannot be made beyond that age. Take for example Steven, age 75, who still has earned income from the royalties he receives as a writer. Since Steven's wife Stella is ten years younger than he is, she's still young enough to have an RRSP. Although Steven can't contribute to an RRSP in his own name, he can contribute to a spousal plan for Stella until she reaches age 71.

Another interesting opportunity for those who have reached age 71 and still have earned income is to make their final contribution to the RRSP one month in advance. Let's say that Martha turned 71 in September of this year and has to collapse her RRSP by the end of December.

But Martha is self-employed and has net business income of $50,000. This would normally entitle her to make an RRSP contribution of $9,000 the following year, but by then, she'll be over the age limit to have an RRSP. The way out of this dilemma is for Martha to contribute the $9,000 in December, before she collapses her RRSP.

By doing so, Martha is in an overcontribution situation for the month of December. The penalty for an overcontribution is 1 percent per month of the amount of the overcontribution. But remember that Martha is entitled to a $2,000 overcontribution without any penalties being assessed. If Martha has not already made an overcontribution, that would reduce her penalty to $7,000 x 1%, or $70. This penalty is a small price to pay for the benefit of reducing taxable income by $9,000 the following year.

Registered Retirement Income Funds (RRIFs)

Like an RRSP, a RRIF is a trust fund that is registered under the *Income Tax Act.* However, unlike an RRSP, funds must be gradually withdrawn from a RRIF beginning the year after the RRIF is opened. Usually, a RRIF is set up with funds transferred on a tax-deferred basis from an RRSP, although RRIFs can also accept funds from a registered pension plan, a deferred profit sharing plan (DPSP), or from another RRIF.

Note that eligible payments from a retiring allowance cannot be deposited directly to a RRIF – they must be paid into an RRSP first, and then transferred over.

Funds held in a RRIF can be invested in the same way as RRSP funds; in other words, they are subject to the same set of rules for eligible investments. A list of qualified investments for RRSP and RRIF purposes is presented earlier in this chapter. While there are no additional restrictions that apply to RRIF funds, the financial advisor needs to ensure that there are sufficient liquid assets in the RRIF to meet the minimum required withdrawal each year.

The minimum is calculated as a percentage of RRIF assets at the beginning of each calendar year, and the percentage increases with the age of the plan holder. When establishing a RRIF, plan holders can specify whether they want to use their own age or the age of their spouse to calculate the withdrawals. It's a good practice to base the withdrawal schedule on the age of the younger spouse. Doing so provides for a smaller required withdrawal each year, while still maintaining the flexibility to withdraw larger amounts.

Different withdrawal schedules apply, depending on when the RRIF was set up. RRIFs set up in 1992 or earlier, known as "qualifying RRIFs", are subject to the following rules:

- for plan holders under age 79 at the beginning of the year, the minimum withdrawal is calculated by dividing the value of the RRIF at the beginning of the year by (90 – the age of the plan holder)

- for plan holders age 79 or older at the beginning of the year, the minimum withdrawal is calculated according to the chart below

RRIFs set up in 1993 or later are known as "non-qualifying RRIFs" and are subject to the following withdrawal rules:

- for plan holders under age 71 at the beginning of the year, the minimum withdrawal is calculated by dividing the value of the RRIF at the beginning of the year by (90 – the age of the plan holder)

- for plan holders over age 71 at the beginning of the year, the minimum withdrawal is calculated according to the percentages in the following chart:

AGE AT BEGINNING OF YEAR	MINIMUM WITHDRAWAL % FOR NON-QUALIFYING RRIFS
71	7.38
72	7.48
73	7.59
74	7.71
75	7.85
76	7.99
77	8.15
78	8.33
79	8.53
80	8.75
81	8.99
82	9.27
83	9.58
84	9.93
85	10.33
86	10.79
87	11.33
88	11.96
89	12.71
90	13.62
91	14.73
92	16.12
93	17.92
94	20.00
95+	20.00

All RRIF withdrawals are fully taxable in the year received. However, withholding tax on RRIF withdrawals only applies to amounts in excess of the minimum.

The withholding tax on excess amounts in all parts of Canada except Quebec is calculated as follows:

- 10 percent if the withdrawal is not more than $5,000;

- 20 percent if the withdrawal is more than $5,000 but not more than $15,000; and

- 30 percent if the withdrawal is more than $15,000.

The rates for Quebec residents are 21 percent, 26 percent and 31 percent respectively.

Note, however, that where the RRIF holder has requested periodic payments throughout the year, say on a monthly or quarterly basis, CRA's policy is that the withholding tax is to be based on the total amount withdrawn for the year. So, if a retiree were to receive RRIF payments of $4,000 per month throughout the year, the withholding tax would be calculated as 30 percent of the amount of each payment above the minimum required.

Beneficiary Designations

Clients should be made aware of the importance of filling out a new beneficiary designation when they roll an RRSP into a RRIF. Under the *Income Tax Act*, the RRIF is treated as a brand new plan; therefore, the designation that was made on the RRSP does not automatically carry over to the RRIF.

On the death of a RRIF holder, payments may continue to the surviving spouse or partner as the successor annuitant, if the original annuitant so designated in the RRIF contract or in the will. Alternatively, where the surviving spouse or partner is designated as the beneficiary, he or she may transfer the remaining value of the RRIF on a tax-deferred basis into his or her own RRIF or RRSP, or to an issuer for the purchase of a registered annuity.

The *Income Tax Act* provides that amounts paid from a RRIF to a dependent child or grandchild will also be eligible for special treatment. As of 1993, "dependency" is defined in one of two ways:

- financial dependency is considered to exist when the dependent child or grandchild's net income in the year preceding the plan holder's death was less than or equal to the basic personal tax credit

- the dependent child or grandchild is physically or mentally infirm

If the dependency is strictly financial, the eligible amount can be used to buy a term annuity for the child, with income payments taxable in the child's hands. The maximum term for the annuity is calculated as 18 years, minus the age of the recipient at the time of purchase.

If the dependency is the result of physical or mental infirmity, the eligible amount may be transferred on a tax-deferred basis into an RRSP for the infirm dependent. Alternatively, for deaths occurring after March 3, 2010, a tax-deferred rollover of RRSP or RRIF proceeds into a Registered Disability Savings Plan (RDSP) may be made in the name of the beneficiary. Note that the rollover will be counted as part of the $200,000 limit of total contributions to the RDSP.

In all other cases, the fair market value of the RRIF will be reported as income on the deceased's final tax return.

Spousal RRIFs

Spousal RRIFs are those that are established with funds originating from a spousal RRSP. The income attribution rules for spousal RRSPs continue to apply to spousal RRIFs only to the extent that any withdrawals above the minimum amount are made from the spousal RRIF. As long as the withdrawals are limited to the minimum amount, they will not be attributed back to the contributor, even though contributions may have been made to a spousal RRSP within the past three years.

Creditor Protection

Since 2008, RRSPs and RRIFs, whether insurance-based or not, have offered protection from creditor claims on bankruptcy.

The only exception applies to property contributed to the RRSP or RRIF within 12 months prior to the date of bankruptcy.

For situations other than bankruptcy, for example if the plan holder is the subject of a lawsuit, there is no creditor protection for non-insurance-based RRSPs or RRIFs.

Insurance-based RRSPs and RRIFs have full creditor protection under provincial insurance regulations. In general, the designated beneficiary must be a family member specified in the relevant provincial insurance legislation. In most provinces, the family member must be a spouse, common law partner, child, grandchild or parent of the plan holder in order for the plan to provide creditor protection. In Quebec, the class of specified family members is wider, including all ascendants and descendants of the owner of the plan.

Creditor protection on death is a different issue again. Insurance-based RRSPs and RRIFs are protected from the creditors of a deceased annuitant's estate where there is a named beneficiary, as described above.

The protection for non-insurance based RRSPs and RRIFs on death varies from province to province. Saskatchewan, Prince Edward Island, Manitoba and Newfoundland have specific legislation in place that extends creditor protection to non-insurance based RRSPs and RRIFs with designated beneficiaries. British Columbia and Ontario have less specific provisions that may afford some protection to beneficiaries. For example, in Ontario, case law has established that, where the holder of a non-insurance retirement savings plan has designated a beneficiary to receive the proceeds of the plan on the holder's death, the proceeds do not form part of the estate and are protected from the holder's creditors[2].

When to Open a RRIF

A RRIF must be opened by the end of the calendar year that the client reaches age 71; however, there is no minimum age requirement for opening a RRIF. Once the RRIF is opened, annual withdrawals must be made, beginning the following calendar year. It is quite possible that the client may not require money from the RRIF in a particular year, but by law must bring a certain percentage into income.

Clients who have already opened a RRIF, and have discovered that they do not need the level of income produced by the minimum withdrawal requirement have the option of rolling the RRIF funds back into an RRSP, up until the end of the year they reach age 71.

Originally, financial planners were taught that the best approach to drawing funds from a RRIF was to wait until the last possible moment in order to allow for the maximum tax-deferred accumulation of funds. Clients were advised to draw on non-registered investments first until they reached the magic age of 71. The problem with this approach, however, is that it sometimes results in very low taxable income between retirement and age 71, followed by required RRIF withdrawals that are higher than the client needs. Since RRIF withdrawals are fully taxable, clients may find themselves in a higher tax bracket from age 71 onwards. Even worse, they may be subject to clawback of their OAS benefits and their age credit.

Today, most astute planners would agree that a more sensible approach is to create a level stream of income,

---

[2] *Amherst Crane Rentals Limited v. Perring*, Ontario Court of Appeal, June 16, 2004.

including both registered and non-registered sources, throughout the retirement period.

Pension Income Tax Credit

A client who has no employer pension income, and wishes to take advantage of the pension income tax credit at age 65, could consider transferring at least a portion of his or her RRSP into a RRIF or annuity at that age. Payments from a RRIF or annuity at age 65 or later qualify for the $2,000 pension income tax credit in situations where no employer pension payments are received. A transfer of approximately $40,000 at age 65 would provide for minimum withdrawals of $2,000 per year from age 65 to 71. Alternatively, approximately $16,000 could be transferred, with the intention of drawing down the bulk of the capital by age 71.

Minimizing Required Withdrawals

When opening a RRIF, the withdrawal schedule can be based either on the plan holder's own age or the age of the spouse or common law partner. Basing the withdrawals on the age of the younger partner means that the required withdrawal each year will be smaller. Where one partner is several years older than the other, this can make a substantial difference over the years.

Planners should be aware that this can be done, even where the partner has not been designated as the successor annuitant, entitled to receive payments after the original annuitant's death. Once the election is made, it cannot be changed, even if the spouse or common law partner dies. However, it is possible to establish another RRIF by transferring funds and then making a new election for the new RRIF. Note that, when transferring funds from one RRIF to another, the minimum required withdrawal must be made from the original RRIF before the transfer takes place.

Maximizing Tax-deferred Growth

Although clients must open their RRIF by the end of the year they reach age 71, there is no requirement to withdraw funds until the end of the following calendar year. Deferring the first withdrawal to the end of the year the client turns 72 allows for an extra year of tax-deferred growth. From that point on, a lump sum withdrawal can be made at the end of each calendar year to cover anticipated expenses for the following year.

Although this approach maximizes tax-deferred growth, it may create an unnecessarily high level of income past age 71. Depending on the client's overall situation, it may be better to withdraw registered funds earlier in order to create a more level income stream throughout the retirement years.

Registered Annuities

Today, annuities come in many different flavours. In recent years, the variable annuity with guaranteed minimum withdrawal benefits has become a popular investment option for retirees. These, and other variations on the theme, are treated in more detail in Chapter 5, Investment Choices and Strategies for the Retirement Years. What we will address in this chapter is the plain vanilla fixed-income annuity – a traditional option for registered funds when the holder is ready to draw income.

In the early years of the new millennium, many people saw the plain vanilla annuity as an old-fashioned product with little appeal in the markets of the day. However, the market volatility of recent years has encouraged many to look for a more secure form of retirement income. Today, although current interest rates are quite low by historical standards, annuities can be a very suitable choice for those who are looking for a guaranteed source of income, and who are not particularly concerned about estate protection.

The purchase of a registered annuity with RRSP funds can be done as an alternative to the purchase of a RRIF. This could be a suitable option for clients who have no employer pension, and whose registered funds are sufficient to provide them with the base income they expect to need throughout retirement. Another option would be to transfer some of the RRSP funds into a RRIF, and only use a portion to purchase an annuity. This strategy could be used for clients whose RRSP funds are more than what is needed to provide a base income, and who are looking for more flexibility than a fixed monthly income would provide.

A third option would be to transfer all RRSP funds initially into a RRIF, and, at some later date, into an annuity. This could be a suitable approach for clients who want to maintain control over their investments in the early years of retirement, and enjoy some flexibility, but become more concerned about a guaranteed income as the years go by. It also allows for the laddered purchase of more than one annuity over time, which means that retirees may be able to take advantage of increasing interest rates in future years. Another consideration is that, all other things being equal, the older the annuitant, the higher the income.

A registered annuity must provide payments either for the lifetime of the annuitant, or for a fixed term to age 90.

Fixed term (sometimes called term certain) annuities pay out instalments for a term of years that equals 90 minus the age of the annuitant at the time the annuity is purchased. Payments are normally level, but can be indexed for inflation. This type of annuity can be purchased from a wide variety of institutions, including banks, credit unions, and insurance companies. Clients purchasing fixed term annuities should be aware that many people today live beyond age 90. Basing the payments on a fixed term rather than life somewhat negates the benefits of having guaranteed income throughout retirement.

With life annuities, the payments may be based on the lifetime of the annuitant alone, or the annuitant and his or her spouse or partner. Single life or straight life annuities, where the payments continue only for the lifetime of the annuitant, provide the highest monthly income per dollar of premium. Joint and last survivor annuities, where the payments continue as long as at least one of the partners is still alive, provide protection for the surviving spouse, but will produce a lower monthly income from the beginning of the payment period. The amount of the reduction will depend to some extent on the age of the spouse or partner.

When a single life annuity holder or the last survivor of a joint annuity dies, the payments cease and there is nothing remaining for the estate. Some clients may be concerned about the possibility of premature death and the negative impact this would have on their estate. Purchasing insurance to provide a benefit to the estate would be one solution; however, it is also possible to buy an annuity with a guaranteed term. Payments can be guaranteed for a term of years that is not more than 90 minus the annuitant's age or spouse's age at the time the annuity is purchased. If death occurs before the guaranteed period is over, a lump sum equal to the value of the unpaid amounts for the remainder of the guaranteed term will be paid to the estate. For example, if Sonya purchases a single life annuity with a guaranteed term of five years, and dies at the end of year four, the total value of one year's worth of payments will be paid out to her estate in a lump sum.

This provides some level of estate protection, but, once again, comes at the expense of lower monthly income from the beginning of the payment period. The longer the guarantee period, the greater the impact on the monthly payments. See Table 1 at the end of this chapter for a comparison of current annuity rates.

As with fixed term annuities, payments can be increased each year in line with inflation, but this too will act to reduce the amount of the initial monthly payments.

Life annuities are sold only through life insurance companies. Some clients may be concerned about the safety of their monthly income should the insurance company become bankrupt. As long as the annuity issuer is a member of Assuris, annuity payments are protected up to $2,000 per month or 85 percent of the monthly payment, whichever is higher, in the event of bankruptcy of the insurer. For example, a monthly payment of $3,000 would be protected up to $2,550.

Planners should ensure that their clients purchase annuities only from reputable insurance companies that are members of Assuris. If annuity income is going to be higher than $2,000 per month, consideration should be given to dividing the amount invested between two or more insurers.

Annuities versus RRIFs – Making the Decision

Clients should be encouraged to consider the following factors before deciding how best to turn their registered funds into an income stream:

- A life annuity guarantees that the client will never outlive her money. This is particularly important for clients who have no guaranteed source of income such as an employer pension. The income stream provided by a RRIF is dependent on how successfully the funds are invested. While the flexibility of withdrawing larger amounts is an appealing feature, it can result in premature depletion of the fund.

- One of the drawbacks to an annuity is that the client no longer has access to the capital. A RRIF allows clients to draw on larger amounts as needed to cover extraordinary expenses.

- An annuity is an interest-rate-sensitive product. Buying an annuity when interest rates are low means that the client will be locked in to those rates for the entire payment period. If clients are likely to consider the purchase of an annuity, they need to monitor long-term interest trends several years in advance. There may be some benefit to staggering the purchase of two or three annuities as the clients get older.

- Annuities have very limited estate protection. With a single life annuity, there is no capital left for the estate after the annuitant dies. The same applies to a joint and last survivor annuity after both annuitants die. Choosing an annuity with a guarantee period, or purchasing life insurance to replace the lost capital, can alleviate this situation to a certain extent. On the other hand, clients without children may not view this as a concern.

- Tax deferral. The entire amount of the payment from a registered annuity is taxed as income. With a RRIF, the payments out of the plan are taxed as income, but the investments held in the plan continue to grow on a tax-sheltered basis.

The table below summarizes the advantages and disadvantages of the life annuity and the RRIF:

	Life Annuity	RRIF
Guaranteed lifetime income	Yes	No
Access to capital	No	Yes
Estate protection	Limited	Yes
Tax deferral	No	Yes

Tax-Free Savings Accounts (TFSA)

The Tax-Free Savings Account (TFSA) came into being at the beginning of January 2009. Introduced in the March

2008 federal budget, the TFSA is designed to encourage Canadians of all ages to save and invest their money. The plan originally allowed any Canadian resident over the age of 18, regardless of earned income, to contribute up to $5,000 per year in after-tax money. As of 2013, the annual limit was increased to $5,500.

There is no tax deduction for contributing to a TFSA, but the investment income accumulates on a tax-free basis. The funds can be withdrawn at any time, and no tax is payable on either capital or income on withdrawal. Unlike RRSPs, any amount withdrawn opens up an equivalent amount of contribution room as of the year following the withdrawal. As with RRSPs, there is a one percent per month penalty on any overcontributions made to a TFSA.

The contribution limit will increase in line with inflation; however, increased limits will be rounded to the nearest $500. For example, suppose inflation runs at three percent for the next several years. The limits would increase as follows:

	Inflationary Increase	TFSA Limit
Current Year	$5,500	$5,500
Year 2	$5,665	$5,500
Year 3	$5,835	$6,000
Year 4	$6,010	$6,000
Year 5	$6,190	$6,000
Year 6	$6,376	$6,500

As can be seen in the chart, even though there has been three percent inflation in Year 2, the TFSA limit does not change due to the rounding rule.

Any investment that is a qualified investment for RRSP purposes can be held in a TFSA. However, the greatest benefit will result from holding investments that would otherwise be taxed at normal rather than preferential rates: interest-bearing investments such as bonds and GICs. Some advisors suggest that it is more beneficial to hold growth investments in a TFSA, based on the argument that, although capital gains are taxed more favourably, equities have the potential to produce a higher return which should be tax-sheltered. While this may be true, the gain on an equity investment would have to be more than twice the gain on an interest-bearing investment for this argument to make sense. (Only 50 percent of an actual capital gain is taxable.) Also remember that any losses on equity investments inside a TFSA cannot be deducted against gains.

Investments can be transferred into a TFSA in kind, but the tax treatment on transfer will be the same as with RRSPs: capital gains will be reported for tax purposes, while capital losses will be denied.

If a client becomes non-resident, the TFSA can be paid out without any withholding tax. If the client wishes, the TFSA can still be maintained, but new contributions are not allowed, and no further contribution room accrues to the plan.

On death, the assets in the TFSA can be transferred into a surviving spouse or partner's TFSA without affecting the survivor's own contribution room. Alternatively, it is possible to name one's spouse or partner as a successor account holder on opening the TFSA. If there is no surviving spouse or partner, the value of the TFSA is paid into the estate on a tax-free basis. Only any income or gains that accrue after death are taxable.

There is no upper age limit for contributing to a TFSA. However, few clients in retirement are looking to save additional funds. There are, however, some valid reasons for retired clients to take advantage of this tax saving opportunity. To the extent that clients keep emergency funds, or set aside funds earmarked for a specific purpose such as replacing a car, or funding a child's wedding, these funds could be held within a TFSA. Since investments of this type are often held in fixed-income vehicles, clients will benefit from receiving interest income on a tax-free basis.

Many people over age 71 are in the position of having to withdraw more from their RRIFs than they need to cover expenses because of the minimum withdrawal rules. While there's no way of escaping tax on the withdrawal itself, depositing the unneeded funds into a TFSA will ensure there will be no further tax on any investment income earned.

But a more significant opportunity comes into play for clients who have already built up a substantial non-registered investment portfolio. Each year throughout retirement, they could transfer the maximum allowable from their existing portfolio into the TFSA in order to shelter future income. Given that many people will spend up to 30 years in retirement, they have the opportunity to shelter fairly large sums of money. The table below shows the projected accumulation, based on a two percent inflation rate and a four percent rate of return on the investments, assuming that the maximum TFSA contribution is made at the beginning of each year.

	Beginning of Year Value	TFSA Limit Based on 2% Inflation	4% Interest	End of Year Value
2009	$0	$5,000	$200	$5,200
2010	$5,200	$5,000	$408	$10,608
2011	$10,608	$5,000	$624	$16,232
2012	$16,232	$5,500	$869	$22,602
2013	$22,602	$5,500	$1,124	$29,226
2014	$29,226	$5,500	$1,389	$36,115
2015	$36,115	$5,500	$1,665	$43,279
2016	$43,279	$5,500	$1,951	$50,730
2017	$50,730	$6,000	$2,269	$59,000
2018	$59,000	$6,000	$2,600	$67,600
2019	$67,600	$6,000	$2,944	$76,544
2020	$76,544	$6,000	$3,302	$85,845
2021	$85,845	$6,500	$3,694	$96,039
2022	$96,039	$6,500	$4,102	$106,641
2023	$106,641	$6,500	$4,526	$117,666
2024	$117,666	$6,500	$4,967	$129,133

	Beginning of Year Value	TFSA Limit Based on 2% Inflation	4% Interest	End of Year Value
2025	$129,133	$7,000	$5,445	$141,578
2026	$141,578	$7,000	$5,943	$154,522
2027	$154,522	$7,000	$6,461	$167,982
2028	$167,982	$7,500	$7,019	$182,502
2029	$182,502	$7,500	$7,600	$197,602
2030	$197,602	$7,500	$8,204	$213,306
2031	$213,306	$7,500	$8,832	$229,638
2032	$229,638	$8,000	$9,506	$247,144
2033	$247,144	$8,000	$10,206	$265,349
2034	$265,349	$8,000	$10,934	$284,283
2035	$284,283	$8,500	$11,711	$304,495
2036	$304,495	$8,500	$12,520	$325,514
2037	$325,514	$8,500	$13,361	$347,375
2038	$347,375	$9,000	$14,255	$370,630
2039	$370,630	$9,000	$15,185	$394,815

Clients with a spouse or partner have yet another opportunity to build up their tax-free savings: amounts contributed to a TFSA are not subject to the attribution rules normally applied by the *Income Tax Act*. Therefore, in a situation where only one spouse or partner has accumulated significant capital, there is the opportunity to transfer some of that capital to the other partner by giving them funds to contribute to their own TFSA. That strategy would, of course, result in double the level of accumulation shown in the table above.

Reverse Mortgages

A reverse mortgage, sometimes known as a Home Equity Plan or a Reverse Annuity Mortgage, is a product designed to meet the needs of seniors who find that the bulk of their equity is tied up in the value of their homes, and who want to access that equity without selling the home. A reverse mortgage allows those over the age of 55 to take a loan for up to 50 percent of the value of their home (assuming the home is fully paid for), and take those funds as a lump sum, a monthly income, or a combination of the two.

The loan is essentially a lifetime loan with no fixed repayment schedule. Although borrowers can elect to make payments, no principal or interest payments are required until the home is sold, or both borrowers have moved out or died. At that point, the loan would be repaid from the proceeds of the sale of the home. If the amount of the loan exceeds the proceeds from the sale, the lender is responsible for the difference. In other words, repayment of the loan cannot be sought from other assets in the estate – the loan and the accumulated interest will be paid back up to the limit of the value of the property itself.

The reverse mortgage can be discharged early by paying the principal, accumulated interest and an interest rate differential, if mortgage rates have decreased. Planners should bear in mind that, because the term of the mortgage is very long (essentially the borrower's life expectancy) and assuming no payments have been made, even a small difference in interest rates could translate into a huge interest rate differential. There are also pre-payment penalties that apply within the first 36 months of the loan.

While some borrowers may choose to use part of the proceeds of the loan for home renovations or an extensive trip, the usual reason for obtaining a reverse mortgage is to create some regular monthly income. Therefore, most of the proceeds are typically used to purchase a life annuity or a joint and survivor annuity.

The *Income Tax Act* provides that the annuity payments are tax-free; however, the interest accruing on the loan is not tax-deductible, except in the event that the funds are used for investment outside of a registered account.

Although the reverse mortgage may seem appealing on the surface, there are several drawbacks that clients must consider. These include:

- Typically, the interest rate charged on the mortgage is about 1 percent higher than the interest rate paid on the annuity. This means that clients are borrowing money at a higher rate than the rate of return they are receiving.

- Early discharge of the mortgage can result in significant cost if mortgage rates have dropped even slightly. This can create problems for clients who may need to sell their home earlier than planned due to failing health or physical problems.

- The total amount owing on the loan compounds very quickly when payments are not made. For example, using the rule of 72, we can determine that the amount owing on a loan at 7.2 percent will double every ten years. Clients should be made aware of the impact this will have on their eventual estate.

- Clients should also be encouraged to consider that they may need the capital from the sale of their home to fund supported accommodation in future as they age. It's possible that, by the time they move into a nursing or retirement home, the reverse mortgage will have eaten away at the bulk of the equity they would have used for this purpose.

Continuing To Work

Part-time Employment and Contract Work

Many retirees today choose to continue to work on their own terms, seeking opportunities for part-time employment, contract work, or self-employment. Those from a professional background will often continue to be involved in their profession, but on a less demanding basis. Others will look at retirement from their primary career as a chance to try a completely different line of work.

Current demographics certainly work in favour of the retiree who is seeking a more gradual transition out of the workforce. As discussed in Chapter 1, many companies have recognized that they are starting to lose the knowledge base that has helped to build their success over the past decades, and are looking at ways to retain older employees so that they can mentor and pass their knowledge along to the next generation.

While there is no shortage of job opportunities advertised and promoted on-line, many of these turn out to be scams. However, there are a number of legitimate resources available for those seeking part-time or contract employment. The following websites link senior jobseekers with available opportunities across Canada and internationally:

- www.retiredworker.ca

- www.dinosaur-exchange.com

- seniorsforjobs.com

Launched in 2003 by Sarah Welstead and Max Stocker, Retired Worker claims to be the largest employment website in Canada for 50-plus job seekers. Dinosaur Exchange was founded by Martin Suenson in 2004, and operates out of the Channel Islands. While Dinosaur Exchange appears to have few listings for Canada, it could be a good source for clients looking for opportunities in the United States and abroad. Seniors for Jobs lists opportunities for 50-plus job seekers across Canada and the United States.

Self-employment

While some retirees may be interested in taking on various types of part-time or short-term contract work, others may want to run their own show and provide services to a variety of clients. Those who have been self-employed for many years have a good understanding of what it takes to make it work. However, retirees who have spent their career as employees, particularly if they have been long-term employees of a single organization, often find the transition to self-employment more challenging than they expected.

There is no shortage of opportunities for self-employment in retirement. Clients with professional skills often set themselves up as independent consultants, sometimes providing services to the organization they retired from, among others. Running a bed and breakfast operation is a business that appeals to many retirees, and has the advantage that it can be done on a seasonal basis. Many retirees choose to turn an interest or a hobby, such as gardening, woodworking or craftwork, into a small business.

Clients who are looking to create more balance in their lives should seek out opportunities that provide flexible work schedules, and perhaps the ability to work from home.

Working from home can be advantageous from a tax point of view because of the ability to deduct a portion of home-related expenses. These expenses can be deducted where the home office:

- is the principal place of business, or

- the space is used only to earn business income, and it is used on a regular basis for meeting clients.

The size of the home office determines the percentage of home-related expenses that can be deducted. For example, if the office occupies 10 percent of the floor space of the home, the business owner can deduct 10 percent of the operating costs of the home, including mortgage interest, property taxes, utilities, insurance, and maintenance. While capital cost allowance can be claimed, it is usually not recommended, since this will trigger the capital gain and recapture rules on that portion of the home when the home is sold in future.

In an unincorporated business, home office expenses cannot be used to create or increase a business loss. However, unused expenses can be carried forward to future years and be deducted against income at that time.

In general, business owners can deduct any reasonable expenses they incur in order to earn business income. These include advertising, fees for membership in trade or professional organizations, office supplies, legal and accounting fees, and travel. Only 50 percent of the cost of business-related meals and entertainment expenses is deductible. The costs of attending business-related conventions is deductible; however, business owners are limited to two conventions per year, and the conventions must be held in a location that falls within the scope of their business or profession.

Automobile expenses are deductible to the extent the vehicle is used for business purposes. Sole proprietors and partners will need to keep a log of business-related travel. The percentage of total travel that is related to business determines the percentage of vehicle-related expenses that can be deducted. Eligible expenses include license and registration fees, fuel, insurance, interest, leasing, maintenance and repairs, and depreciation (capital cost allowance). The *Income Tax Act* sets limits on the amounts claimed for interest and leasing costs, as well as capital cost allowance. Owners of an incorporated business can arrange to pay themselves a per-kilometre rate for business use of a personal vehicle. The federal budget sets the maximum allowable rate for each year. For 2014, the approved rate is 54 cents per kilometre for the first 5,000 business kilometres, and 48 cents per kilometre thereafter. An additional 4 cents per kilometre is added to the rates for the three territories.

Readers are directed to the Canada Revenue Agency publications *(T4002)(E) Business and Professional Income 2011* as well as *Interpretation Bulletin IT-514 Work Space in Home Expenses* for further details.

Income Splitting

A self-employed individual, whether incorporated or not, can hire his or her spouse and other family members to work in the business. Salaries paid to non-arm's length individuals must be reasonable; CRA interprets this to mean the equivalent of a salary that would be paid to an unrelated person for doing the same work. When family members are hired in this way, documentation of the hours they work and the tasks they perform is key. If the business income is substantial, paying salaries to family members can reduce the tax bill accordingly.

Sole Proprietorship versus Incorporation

Many clients who are starting a business wonder about the benefits of incorporation as opposed to operating as a sole proprietor. Here are some of the key factors to consider:

- Due to the nature of the business, is it reasonable to expect that there will be losses over the first couple of years of operations? In a sole proprietorship, losses can be deducted against other sources of income. In a corporation, the losses may be carried forward for up to ten years to be deducted against the income of the corporation at that time. However, sole proprietors should not expect to be able to deduct losses indefinitely. Claiming business losses for several years in a row may raise a red flag for CRA.

- Does the business owner plan to use all of the income of the business to cover personal expenses? If not, incorporation allows for the retention of earnings in the company, and provides greater flexibility in when and how remuneration can be received. The owner of an incorporated business can determine their desired level of salary or dividends each year. Dividends can also be paid to other shareholders, i.e. other family members. Sole proprietors must declare their earnings as net business income on an annual basis.

- Running a corporation entails legal fees for the initial set-up, as well as accounting fees for the annual corporate tax return. Operating a business as a sole proprietor is a less expensive approach.

- With a corporation, the potential for liability is limited to the assets owned by the corporation, unless the business owner has provided personal guarantees for business loans.

- Running a business as a corporation often provides a more desirable professional image.

TABLE 1

COMPARISON OF CURRENT ANNUITY RATES

The following comparison is based on registered life annuity rates current as of January 2014. The amounts shown represent average monthly payments based on $100,000 of premium.

	Age 65	Age 70	Age 75
Single life, male, no guarantee	$587	$681	$795
Single life, female, no guarantee	$533	$609	$709
Joint life, no guarantee	$475	$533	$599

Source: www.lifeannuities.com.

As a point of comparison, investing $100,000 in a GIC at 3% (the best available rate at the time of writing for a five-year term) would produce income of $250 per month. With the GIC, however, the capital is still under the control of the client.

Chapter 5: Investment Choices and Strategies for the Retirement Years

Introduction

For many years, the investment community focused on strategies to help clients accumulate the assets they would need to fund a comfortable retirement. But now, with ten million baby boomers in Canada hovering on the brink of retirement, more attention is being paid to strategies that will work while that pool of assets is being drawn down. There are a number of factors that work together to make investing *in* retirement a very different process from investing *for* retirement.

One major factor is the continuing increase in life expectancy, as discussed in Chapter 1, Retirement – What Does it Mean Today. Although some of us will continue to work part-time in the early years of retirement, many of us will be relying on income from our savings to cover our expenses for about 30 years at the end of our lives. This appears to suggest that retirees need to focus on growth investments in order to produce the level of returns that will sustain income for that length of time. But here's the problem. When money is being drawn out of an investment portfolio, stock market volatility can have a devastating effect. We will see, later in this chapter, how negative returns in the initial years of withdrawal can result in the depletion of a portfolio in fairly short order.

To compound the problem, the percentage of Canadians participating in registered pension plans has been declining over the past several years. In fact, Statistics Canada reported that, as of 2011, only 32.4 percent of the labour force were active members of an employer pension plan. The growing numbers of self-employed Canadians have no pension coverage at all. As a result, more individuals must rely on their own resources to a much greater extent than was the case in earlier years.

Moving from the accumulation phase to the distribution phase is a difficult transition for many. After so many years of saving and building up resources, it requires some mental toughness to take the plunge and start spending those hard-earned dollars. In fact, it's not uncommon to see retirees attempt to live strictly on an employer pension and government benefits, rather than enjoy a more comfortable lifestyle by dipping into some of their own capital.

Certainly, some of this reluctance to spend is based on fear – the fear of outliving the financial resources available, fear of declining health and the subsequent need for funds for medical care and a comfortable retirement home later on, and the fear of losing much-needed capital in a market meltdown. High tax rates represent another area of concern for retirees.

Financial advisors need to be aware of these concerns. Using highly conservative assumptions to show clients how much they can afford to spend will help to increase their comfort level. Running a Monte Carlo analysis to show clients the probability they will achieve their target income is also valuable. Some clients, particularly those without employer pension income, may want to look at creating their own guaranteed income through the use of annuities or other guaranteed vehicles.

The financial services industry has responded to these concerns by creating a number of new products that are geared either to provide tax-advantaged income or a certain level of protection against loss. This chapter offers a review of the specialized products currently on the market designed for those who are drawing on their investment capital, as well as a discussion of some of the investment strategies that may be appropriate for the retired client.

Bonds

Conventional wisdom used to be that, once a client reached retirement age, it was appropriate to move the investment portfolio from stocks to bonds and Guaranteed Investment Certificates (GICs) in order to protect the value built up over the years. In this way, funds could be drawn down without the risk of having to make a withdrawal at a time when stock prices had dropped. And returns were good. According to Sherry Cooper, Chief Economist, BMO Capital Markets, a portfolio of long-term government and corporate bonds returned a compounded annualized return of about 12.5 percent over the past 25 years, as compared to 9.5 percent for the TSX.[1]

But, in Cooper's words, "There is zero likelihood that the next 25 years will offer the same return for bond investors." With interest rates and inflation at historic lows, investors need to look for more diversified investment solutions in order to produce the required level of income throughout their retirement years.

Dividend Income

Preferred shares in Canadian companies that pay regular dividend income have long been considered a suitable investment for retirees. Although preferred shares technically are considered part of the equity asset class, they actually have characteristics of both equity and fixed income investments. Preferred shareholders rank behind creditors

---

[1] Cooper, Sherry. The New Retirement. P. 161.

but ahead of common shareholders in the event of failure of the company.

Common shares have, in general, a slightly higher risk profile than preferred shares. Depending on the particular company, the return on common shares tends to come more in the form of capital gain rather than dividend income.

In either case, dividends from Canadian companies, when held outside of a registered account, are eligible for favourable tax treatment due to the operation of the dividend tax credit. As of January 1, 2006, there are two classes of dividends in Canada. Eligible dividends are dividends paid after 2005 to Canadian residents by public companies, and by Canadian-controlled private corporations (CCPCs) out of income taxed at the federal general corporate rate. As of January 1, 2012, eligible dividends are grossed-up by 38 percent to calculate the taxable amount, and then a federal dividend tax credit of 15.02 percent of the taxable amount is applied. As of 2014, non-eligible dividends are grossed-up by 18 percent, and the federal dividend tax credit is calculated as 11.017 percent of the grossed-up amount. In both cases, additional provincial dividend tax credits apply. At the highest income tax bracket (using Ontario rates for 2014), eligible dividends have a preferential tax rate of 33.82 percent, compared to 40.13 for non-eligible dividends, and 49.53 percent for interest income.

However, for those over 65, dividend income may have some negative aspects. Because the grossed-up amount is the amount used to calculate taxable income, dividend income can increase a client's exposure to the clawback of the age credit and OAS benefits. While the tax tail should never wag the investment dog, this is a factor that should be considered when designing a non-registered portfolio for a client.

Passive Investments

There is ongoing debate within the investment community about the pros and cons of passive investment (tracking an index) versus an active approach, where managers attempt to identify undervalued securities. While some money managers claim that their skill and expertise in picking stocks and bonds has resulted in them outperforming their competitors, other financial professionals believe that it is impossible for any one manager or mutual fund to beat the index consistently over time.

In fact, for the three years ending in 2012, 85 percent of actively managed Canadian equity funds underperformed the S&P/TSX Composite Index, and 90 percent underperformed the index over the past five years[2]. Statistics comparing performance over longer time frames support these results[3]. However, there is also an argument that actively managed funds may perform better than their benchmark index in times of falling markets, as they are able to maintain some cash to cushion the fall. In rising markets, of course, the cash cushion serves as a drag on performance.

While the relative merits of passive versus active strategies are subject to debate, there is no question that the passive approach produces a more tax-efficient return when held outside of a registered plan. With an actively managed fund, the fund manager is buying and selling companies on a regular basis, resulting in capital gains for the fund that are passed along to the individual investors. Funds that follow a passive strategy mirror the stocks or bonds that are represented on a particular index, an approach that results in very little turnover within the fund, and therefore,

---

[2] Standard & Poor's "Index Versus Active Funds Scorecard for Canadian Funds", Year-end 2012.

[3] Morningstar Canada.

very little capital gain to be reported until the investor actually sells his or her units in the fund.

Investors can participate in a passive approach by buying index funds or exchange-traded funds (ETFs). An index fund is a type of mutual fund that is designed to replicate the performance of a particular stock or bond index. This is accomplished by selecting the same securities that are represented on the target index in the same proportions as they are weighted in the index itself. Like all other mutual funds, index funds are bought directly from the fund company.

An exchange-traded fund (ETF) is a security that tracks the performance of a market index or basket of assets. Although based on the same investment philosophy as an index mutual fund, an ETF trades like an individual stock on an exchange and is priced throughout the trading day. This feature also enhances the tax-efficiency of ETFs compared to index funds. Because investor redemptions can force index fund managers to sell stocks to meet liquidity demands, this can result in additional capital gains distributions to unitholders. With ETFs, transactions take place between buyers and sellers on the open market, so there is no need for managers to take any action to raise cash.

Investors pay brokerage commissions to buy and sell ETFs, but the management expense ratios (MERs) for ETFs and index funds are substantially lower than for actively managed funds. For example, most ETFs have MERs ranging from 0.10 percent to 0.50 percent. However, in 2013, the Morningstar Report on Global Fund Investor Experience showed that the average expense ratio of equity funds in Canada is 2.42 percent, while fixed-income funds come in at 1.50 percent, and money market funds at 0.5 percent. The report notes that Canada has the highest overall expense ratios of the 22 countries surveyed.

Although ETFs started out by replicating broadly based indexes such as the S&P/TSX or S&P 500, these products have evolved to include ETFs that track highly specialized sectors such as gold, as well as leveraged and inverse leveraged ETFs. However, as ETFs start tracking smaller subsets of various asset classes, management fees tend to rise. With a narrow focus and higher fees, these products are moving away from the features that made ETFs attractive in the first place. Another problem is that, if the ETF is small and thinly traded, the resulting lack of liquidity can lead to wide spreads between bid and ask prices, increasing the cost to clients.

Leveraged ETFs are a completely different type of investment. Usually based on futures contracts, leveraged ETFs aim to achieve daily returns that are double or triple the return of the underlying index, while inverse leveraged ETFs aim for returns that are double or triple the loss of the underlying index. These products are designed for clients who are speculators and are not recommended for an income-producing retirement portfolio.

While some advisors believe in using an indexed approach exclusively, others will suggest holding some passive investments as well as some actively managed investments. With a blend of approaches, consideration should be given to holding the more tax-efficient passive investments outside of a registered plan.

Income Trusts

Income trusts are commercial trusts that invest in one or more operating companies, with the objective of distributing cash flow to their unit holders in a tax-efficient manner. The units of income trusts trade on a stock exchange. While income trusts are designed to provide a regular income to unit holders, the investment belongs in the equity portion of a portfolio.

Income trusts tend to invest in properties that have little or no debt. This way, cash flow that would otherwise go to paying interest on debt can be distributed instead to the investor. The trust structure is most appropriate for a mature company with stable cash flows. Because trusts distribute all their profit instead of reinvesting profits back into the business, an attractive current yield can be provided to investors.

Income trusts can be grouped into the following categories:

- real estate investment trusts (REITs)
- royalty trusts
- business or specialty trusts

A real estate investment trust (REIT) invests in income-producing real estate properties, such as office buildings, shopping malls, retirement residences and apartment buildings, for the purpose of distributing rental income to unit holders.

A royalty trust purchases the royalty rights from companies that have productive natural resource properties, such as oil and gas. The royalty trust receives any royalty income generated by the natural resource company, which is the net cash flow generated by the company. Investors are essentially purchasing a share in the company's future profit from a specific pool of oil or gas, from a particular mineral reserve, or from a specific forestry location, until that resource runs out.

A business trust uses the proceeds from its initial public offering (IPO) to purchase all of the equity and debt of one or more companies. Any income generated by the assets of those companies then becomes the income of the trust, and the net cash flow is then distributed to investors.

The income that flows through from income trusts to unit holders as a distribution retains its nature, so interest income, rental income, and business income are fully taxed at the investor's marginal tax rate. Dividends from taxable

Canadian corporations are eligible for federal and provincial tax credits, and capital gains are subject to an inclusion rate of only 50 percent.

In addition, the income trust can distribute more than its net income to investors as a cash distribution. The amount of the distribution that is in excess of the net income is considered a return of capital, and this reduces the adjusted cost base (ACB) of the trust units. This creates a tax deferral for investors because they receive the cash now, but pay the tax later in the form of capital gains when they sell their units.

At the end of each taxation year, the income trust reports to unit holders how their cash distributions are to be treated for tax purposes.

It is most important that retired clients understand that the trust's continued income depends on the future performance of the underlying business. If profits decline in the underlying investment, distributions may have to be reduced. To understand the risks and returns inherent in any given income trust, the advisor must understand the purpose and structure of the underlying business.

Segregated Funds

Segregated funds are often referred to as the insurance industry equivalent of mutual funds. While the basic structure is broadly similar to a mutual fund, the insurance industry provides certain features and guarantees not found in regular mutual funds, and some of these features may be particularly appealing to retired clients.

One of the most significant benefits provided by a segregated fund is the maturity guarantee. This guarantee provides that a minimum amount of capital will be in the account at maturity of the contract (normally ten years after the initial deposit) and/or at various checkpoints during the life of the contract. The level of the guarantee ranges from 75 to 100 percent of the original deposit. However, advisors and clients should be aware that, when withdrawals are made, the guaranteed amount is reduced accordingly dollar-for-dollar. At the end of the ten-year period, the client is entitled to the greater of the actual account balance or the guaranteed amount.

The death benefit guarantee is also significant for many retired clients. Here, the guarantee provides that a minimum of all deposits, minus any withdrawals made, will be paid to the beneficiary when the investor dies. Of course, if the investment value is greater at that time, the full investment value will be paid. Note that some insurers may limit the guarantee based on the age of the investor when he or she purchases the segregated fund.

An investor also has the ability to name a designated beneficiary on a segregated fund, regardless of whether the fund is held in a registered or non-registered account. On the investor's death, the proceeds of the segregated fund are paid directly to the beneficiary, bypassing probate. This could be an important feature for clients who live in a jurisdiction such as Ontario, British Columbia, or Nova Scotia, where probate fees are high. In other jurisdictions, this would not be a major concern.

Those clients who continue to own a business in retirement may also appreciate the creditor protection offered by segregated funds where a spouse, child, or grandchild is named as the beneficiary.

Of course, these additional features and benefits do not come free of charge. In order to cover the cost of the reserves that must be established for providing guarantees, the management fees on segregated funds tend to be about 0.5 percent higher than those of regular mutual funds.

There is also an argument about the value of the maturity guarantee. If a segregated fund is invested in a balanced portfolio of Canadian stocks and bonds, how likely is it that the guarantee would ever be needed? For this reason, it is often best to consider using a segregated fund only for higher-risk investments such as emerging markets, which would normally represent a fairly small part of most retirees' investment portfolios anyway. There is little point in paying for a guarantee to protect less volatile investments.

Guaranteed Minimum Withdrawal Benefits

In the mid-2000s, guaranteed minimum withdrawal benefits (GMWBs) were introduced as an enhancement to segregated funds. The GMWB is an add-on feature that guarantees a monthly retirement income from a fund or portfolio of funds for life, regardless of how the underlying investments perform.

Manulife was the first firm in Canada to introduce this product, and many other insurers, including Standard Life, Sun Life, and Desjardins Financial Security, followed suit with a variety of product offerings.

GMWBs are designed to address the investor's fear of losing capital once he or she enters the retirement years. One of the major risks that retirees face is finding that their planned retirement date has coincided with a major market downturn. Withdrawing money during a bear market in the early years of retirement will deplete capital far more quickly than withdrawals made during a bull market. With a GMWB, the investor was originally guaranteed that she would get back at least five percent of the money invested each year from age 65 to death.[4] In addition, automatic reset provisions were introduced in order to lock in investment gains on a regular basis. These benefits applied in addition to the

---

[4] Beginning in 2012, several insurers have reduced the guaranteed payout for new purchasers.

death and maturity guarantees that are a component of the underlying investments.

An additional advantage is that, if the GMWB product is held inside a RRIF, the guaranteed annual withdrawal amount will increase, where necessary, to allow for the minimum required withdrawal from the RRIF.

While GMWBs offered substantial advantages when they were first introduced, changes over the past several years have made them less attractive. The poor investment climate as well as ongoing reserve requirements for these products has resulted in several insurers cutting back on features such as the guaranteed payout percentage and the income bonus. Other firms have raised their fees or limited policyholders to less volatile fixed income investments.

Across the range of GMWB providers, guarantee fees typically range from 0.35 percent to 0.85 percent, depending on the underlying investments in the fund. Of course, these fees are charged on top of the fund management fee, the insurance fee, and the costs of any selected riders. All in, the annual cost to the investor ranges from approximately three to four percent. As with segregated funds, the cost should be viewed in relation to the level of risk of the underlying investments. The more volatile the investment, the more it makes sense to pay to protect the retirement income.

Advisors should be aware that age limits apply to the purchase of GMWBs. Usually, purchasers must be under age 75, and reset provisions for death benefits do not usually extend beyond age 80. Also, some variations of this product provide income for a specific time period, usually 20 years, rather than a lifetime guarantee. Obviously, this variation is not a good choice for investors who want the guarantee of lifetime income.

Index-Linked GICs

Index-linked GICs appeal to clients who want to enjoy the growth potential of the stock markets while protecting their capital. Since these products vary considerably from one issuer to the next, advisors need to be extremely careful in their analysis of any particular GIC. In general, these products are designed to pay a guaranteed basic interest rate, with a premium amount, tied to the performance of a particular market index or group of indexes, paid at the end of the term. The premium amount may be based on a percentage of the growth of the index, and it may or may not be capped at a certain level.

Although index-linked GICs give investors the chance to participate in a rising market, they do have their drawbacks. The investor will receive only a percentage of the market gain, which will be fully taxable as interest income. Had the client invested directly in an index fund, they would get the full market return, taxable as capital gain on sale of the units. If the market drops, the client will receive only a minimal level of interest compared to what could have been obtained with a regular compound GIC or other fixed-income investments.

Principal Protected Notes

In some respects, a principal protected note (PPN) could be seen as a more sophisticated version of an index-linked GIC. Like the GIC, the PPN is an investment that guarantees the return of the capital invested when held to maturity, while providing an investment return based on a particular market index. However, where GICs are insured by the Canada Deposit Insurance Corporation (CDIC), PPNs are guaranteed by the issuer.

While PPNs may be appealing to some clients who would like to have the returns produced by equities in a bull market, but don't want to risk losing their capital, planners should ensure that clients also understand the drawbacks of these investments. For example, if clients want to redeem their investment before the maturity date (usually six to ten years from date of purchase), they may lose the guarantee on the principal and may also have to pay an early redemption fee. While some PPNs trade on the Toronto stock exchange, they are very illiquid and selling in the market will not likely provide a good return.

Because of the level of fees associated with PPNs, the returns are sometimes less attractive than clients expect.

Prescribed Annuities

An annuity is a guaranteed stream of income payments that is made up of a combination of principal and interest. Investors can purchase an annuity with either registered or non-registered funds. The source of the funds determines the tax treatment of the annuity payments. While the income from registered annuities is fully taxable, income from non-registered annuities can produce some significant tax advantages. Registered annuities are discussed more fully in Chapter 4; the discussion below is confined to non-registered annuities.

Many clients choose to buy annuities with non-registered capital as an alternative to GICs or other fixed-income investments. The payments received from a non-registered annuity are considered to be a blend of principal and interest. Only the interest portion is taxable; the balance is considered to be a non-taxable return of capital. With a regular annuity, the interest payments are much larger at the beginning of the period than at the end. This, of course, would result in higher taxable income in the early years.

On the other hand, the prescribed annuity has been developed in order to defer some of this tax liability to future years. With a prescribed annuity, the total interest paid out over the life of the contract (or estimated life in the case of a life annuity) is levelled out for each year of payment, creating a tax deferral for the annuitant. Under this structure, the investor receives the same amount of interest and tax-free return of capital for each year of payment, resulting in more tax-effective income in the earlier years. Prescribed annuities are specifically exempt from the interest accrual rules under Section 12.2(1) of the *Income Tax Act.*

The illustration below compares the after-tax income that could be received by a 70-year-old male retiree from a pre-scribed annuity with no guarantee period versus a GIC, using rates current as of May 2014.[5]

	GIC at 3%	Prescribed Annuity
Initial capital invested	500,000	500,000
Annual income	15,000	38,885
Taxable portion	15,000	2,653
Tax payable @ 40% rate	6,000	1,061
After tax income	9,000	37,824

Note that income from a prescribed annuity cannot be indexed to inflation, and, if the annuity has a guarantee period, payments cannot be guaranteed past age 90.

The factors that should be considered before buying a prescribed annuity are the same as those discussed for registered annuities in Chapter 4.

Insured Annuities

One of the concerns shared by many retired clients who are considering purchasing a prescribed annuity is the im-pact of this decision on their estate planning. With a life annuity, there is no capital remaining for the estate once the annuitant passes away. This factor can be a serious

---

[5] Annuity rates provided by FTL Consulting.

drawback for those who wish to leave an estate. One solution is to use part of the annuity income to purchase a term-to-100 life insurance policy designed to pay an amount equivalent to the original annuity investment. Let's extend the example presented in the previous section to illustrate how this would work.

	GIC at 3%	Prescribed Annuity
Initial capital invested	500,000	500,000
Annual income	15,000	38,885
Taxable portion	15,000	2,653
Tax payable @ 40% rate[6]	6,000	1,061
After tax annual income	9,000	37,824
Less insurance premium	0	22,585
Net after tax annual income	9,000	15,239

As seen in the example above, this strategy still produces more income than would be obtained through a fixed-income investment such as a GIC, even after accounting for the cost of the insurance premiums. In fact, the client in this example would need to earn over five percent on the GIC every year in order to match the net income from the insured annuity. Because the taxable income is lower with the annuity, there may be additional savings in the form of a reduced clawback on OAS payments or income-related credits such as the age credit.

Other insurance strategies, such as investing a lump sum up front in a universal life policy and purchasing a prescribed annuity for a smaller amount, could actually produce slightly higher income than the illustrated strategy above. Clients who are interested in this approach should explore a variety of alternatives.

---

[6] Based on non-smoker rates. Information provided by FTL Consulting.

Considering the purchase of an insured annuity is most suitable for clients in their early seventies. At this point, annuity income will be fairly strong, while the taxable portion will be quite low. In addition, insurance costs are still reasonable at this age, assuming the clients are in good health and are insurable. However, planners should bear in mind that once this strategy is implemented, there's no turning back. Clients will be locked in to a set income level for the rest of their lives.

Charitable Annuities

Combining regular guaranteed income with a gift to a charity is another possible option for at least a portion of non-registered retirement savings. A charitable gift annuity is a donation of a capital amount to a registered charity in return for regular payments at a specified rate for life. Payments are normally calculated so that at least 50 percent of the original principal goes to the charity following the death of the annuitant. Donors receive a charitable donation tax receipt of at least 20 percent of the annuity amount at the time the annuity is set up.

The value of the donation is calculated as the difference between the amount the client pays to the charity and the true cost of the regular payments the client is entitled to receive. For example, Barbara donates $75,000 to Memorial Hospital Foundation in exchange for a regular income of $500 per month. Based on her age and life expectancy, the cost of the annuity that the foundation must buy for Barbara is $50,000. The difference, $25,000, represents the amount of the donation receipt that Barbara will receive.

As with prescribed annuities, the older the client at the time of purchase, the higher the monthly income received. With charitable annuities, the amount of the donation receipt increases with age as well. The table below provides an illustration of the monthly income and approximate charitable donation receipt, based on rates in effect for annuities with the Salvation Army Canada as of June 2013.

SAMPLE RATES – Charitable Gift Annuities – revised June 27, 2013

Single Life Gift Annuity — Basic Amount of $100,000
Female Rates

Age at date of application	Effective Rate of Return	Monthly Income	Tax-Free Portion of Income	Donation Receipt (Approximate)
60	4.1%	$340.40	75.9%	$25,000
65	4.5%	371.84	83.6%	25,000
70	5.1%	428.72	90.5%	25,000
75	6.0%	500.24	100%	25,000
80	7.3%	606.52	100%	25,000
85	8.8%	730.20	100%	25,000
90	10.7%	891.76	100%	25,000

Illustration: A woman age 80 years, contributing $100,000 toward a gift annuity, would receive an annual income of 7.3 percent = $7,278 per year for life ($606.52 per month). This income would be 100 percent tax-free. She would receive an immediate one-time charitable tax receipt for the donation portion of $25,000

Notes:

1. These rates are for illustration purposes only and are subject to change.

2. Rates quoted for ages 60 to 70 may be higher on larger amounts.

3. The above rate table is based on female applicants; male rates may vary, especially at lower ages. Rates are also available for joint and survivor gift annuities, providing income to spouses or two siblings, with income continuing to the last survivor.

Source: The Salvation Army Canada. Reprinted with permission.

While some charitable organizations purchase the annuity from an insurance company, others have the ability to issue annuities directly. Where annuities are issued directly by the charity, advisors and their clients should ensure that the charity in question is a member of the Canadian

Charitable Annuity Association[7], a self-regulating agency. Gift annuity programs should be reviewed regularly by qualified actuaries. Advisors should review details of any gift annuity program carefully before making a recommendation to a client.

Systematic Withdrawal Plans

Investment advisors are familiar with the concept of dollar-cost averaging, whereby clients invest a set amount each month into the purchase of a mutual fund, and purchase a different number of units each month depending on the current price. A systematic withdrawal plan (SWP) operates the same way, but in reverse.

With a SWP, clients make regular periodic withdrawals from their mutual fund, usually monthly, although SWPs can be set up on a quarterly or semi-annual basis as well. The amount of the withdrawal can be calculated in a couple of different ways. The constant payment approach, where the same amount of income is drawn each time, is the most common approach. Payments may be increased from time to time in line with inflation adjustments; however, one drawback of this approach is that investment assets often decline in value during periods of high inflation. Increasing the amount of the withdrawal during these periods can put the capital at risk.

Another approach to determining the amount of the withdrawal is to maintain the income payments at a constant percentage of the value of the fund at the previous year-end. This approach helps to protect the capital by minimizing withdrawals during years of lower performance.

In either case, making fixed withdrawals at fixed intervals provides steady cash flow while minimizing risk by averaging out the redemption price of the units of the fund.

---

[7] www.charitableannuities.org.

From a tax point of view, there are some advantages to a SWP. The capital gain on the sale of the fund units is the difference between the redemption price and the purchase price, multiplied by the number of units sold. This will produce a tax bill far lower than might be expected, particularly in the early years of withdrawal. As withdrawals continue over the years, the adjusted cost base declines, and the amount of tax payable each year increases.

One possible disadvantage to the SWP is that it can be somewhat complicated when it comes to calculating the tax impact, due to the fact that capital gains must be calculated for each withdrawal made.

T-Series Investment Funds

In a sense, the T-Series fund is an enhancement of the systematic withdrawal plan, which is designed to improve the tax-efficiency of the payout. T-Series investment funds are designed to pay out a regular tax-advantaged monthly distribution that is set at a predetermined level based on the net asset value of the fund at the previous year-end. Currently, annual payout rates are typically in the range of five percent to six percent. For tax purposes, the monthly distributions are treated as a blend of investment income from the underlying securities and return of capital, the feature that provides their tax efficiency. When a distribution is considered to be return of capital, it is not taxed in the year received. Instead, it is applied to reduce the investor's adjusted cost base (ACB). Eventually, once all capital has been returned, investors will claim a capital gain that is based on the lower ACB.

Tax deferral is obviously the main advantage of the T-Series funds. However, another point to consider is that the lower taxable income they provide may reduce the impact of the OAS clawback as well as the clawback of the age credit for many clients.

Planners should consider, however, that depending on the performance of the fund itself, the distributions could substantially erode the capital base, or the net tax benefits may not be as significant as they initially appeared to be.

Corporate Class Funds

Many mutual fund companies have introduced corporate class funds that are designed to allow investors to move out of one fund and into another without incurring capital gains tax. This can be appealing for clients who have substantial non-registered investments and are looking for the flexibility to manage the asset mix without being concerned about triggering capital gains tax when they rebalance the account.

When a company creates a corporate structure, it groups versions of its most popular funds into a special corporate entity. Any transfers from one fund to another within that corporate entity will not create a potential tax liability. However, tax will be triggered when the investor moves out of the corporate class into another investment, or redeems his holdings for cash.

Corporate class funds tend to have management expense ratios that are slightly higher than the regular funds on which they're based. In order to offset the additional cost, they are best used for clients who expect to move frequently from fund to fund.

Summary of Products

Obviously, the financial services industry has been very respnsive to the needs of clients as they move into the withdrawal phase of their investment lives. The table below summarizes the current offerings discussed in this chapter, along with their major features and benefits.

	Tax-efficient Income	Guaranteed Lifetime Income	Other Special Features
Bonds	No	No	
Dividend income	Yes[8]	No	
Passive investments	Yes	No	Low cost
Income trusts	Yes	No	
Segregated funds	Depends on underlying investment	No	Death benefit guarantee, maturity guarantee, probate avoidance, creditor protection
GMWBs	Yes	Yes	Same as segregated funds, plus possible increases to income payments
Index-linked GICs	No	No	
Principal protected notes	No	No	
Prescribed annuities	Yes	Yes	
Insured annuities	Yes	Yes	Estate protection
Charitable annuities	Yes	Yes	Charitable donation tax receipt on purchase, provides support to charity on death of annuitant
SWPs	Yes	No	
T-series investment funds	Yes	No	

As more clients reach the withdrawal stage in the years to come, we expect that continued research and innovation in product development will take place. Advisors will need to investigate new products thoroughly to make sure that they fully understand both the benefits and the possible drawbacks to their use.

---

[8] Watch for impact on OAS clawback and age credit for clients 65 and older.

Planning Strategies

In addition to the issue of what investment vehicles are most appropriate for the retired client to hold, there is also the issue of the withdrawal strategy to be used throughout the retirement years. The traditional approach to retirement income planning would suggest that clients defer their tax liability to the maximum extent possible, usually by drawing on funds in this order:

- Non-registered cash

- Non-registered fixed income

- Non-registered equities

- Registered funds

However, for some clients with substantial registered holdings, this can create a dramatic, and unnecessary, increase in tax rates as they move through their retirement years. In some cases, drawing on a small amount of registered funds in the early years of retirement can be more tax-effective, particularly where the clawback of tax credits and OAS benefits is an issue. Note that, where the client is not receiving employer pension income, RRIF and annuity income is eligible for the pension income tax credit after the client reaches age 65. However, the decision to draw down on registered funds prior to the required age cannot be made without preparing detailed projections that take current tax rates and clawbacks of government benefits and credits into account.

Buckets of Money

An approach that many advisors have found effective is to start by creating a basic level of income that covers the client's day-to-day lifestyle needs. This income stream is typically based on guaranteed sources of income such as CPP and OAS benefits, and employer pensions. Where there is no employer pension, or the combination of pension and government benefits is inadequate to cover basic needs, other sources of guaranteed income such as pre-scribed annuities and registered annuity payments may be set up to cover the shortfall. Any income that is currently taxable, such as non-registered interest and dividend pay-ments the client currently receives, can also be used to cover expenses rather than being reinvested. Let's look at a simple example of how this would work.

Income Stream for Bob, Age 60

Income Source	Annual Amount
CPP	$ 7,000
Employer Pension	$30,000
Interest Income	$13,000
Total	$50,000

In the above illustration, Bob's income from CPP, his employer pension, and his interest income gives him a total of $50,000 per year. However, Bob, age 60, would like to be able to have income of $70,000 in order to be able to travel as he has planned. The remaining $20,000 per year must come from drawing down his investment portfolio.

Let's say that Bob has a non-registered portfolio of $500,000. Here is how it could be structured:

- First bucket: $20,000 in cash to supplement his in-come for the coming year.

- Second bucket: $100,000 in a bond or GIC ladder spread out over the next five years[9]. This allows Bob to roll $20,000 into cash each year to cover his planned spending for that year. Since these funds are invested in fixed-income vehicles, market vola-

---

[9] See the following section, Bond Laddering.

tility will not affect Bob's income during the five-year time frame.

- Third bucket: $380,000 invested in a balanced port-folio that meets Bob's risk tolerance requirements. Funds will be drawn from this portfolio as needed to make sure that the bond or GIC ladder stays topped up. If equities have gone up in value, they should be cashed in and the funds placed in the second bucket.

With this approach, Bob is working on drawing down his non-registered investments, while allowing his registered funds to grow until he has to draw on them at age 72. But suppose Bob also has $500,000 in his RRSP at age 60. By the time he reaches 72, this account may well be worth over $1,000,000. With a minimum withdrawal rate of 7.38 percent, Bob could be faced with taking an additional $73,800 into income that year on top of his CPP, employer pension, and non-registered investment income. Not only will this push Bob into a much higher tax bracket, he also stands to lose some or all of his OAS benefit to the claw-back.

On the other hand, with $500,000 in his RRSP at age 60, Bob could draw at least some of the funds he requires from here. For example, if he turned the RRSP into a RRIF at 60, his minimum required withdrawal for the first year would be $16,667. In that case, he would only need to reduce his non-registered portfolio by $3,000 to $4,000 that year. Once again, detailed projections must be carried out in order to verify that this approach would produce the best result for Bob.

The traditional approach to money management dic-tated that, where there is a difference in the overall income level of spouses, the higher-income spouse's non-regis-tered assets should be drawn down first, to reduce the in-come that is exposed to tax at a higher level. With the opportunity to split employer pension income, as well as

RRIF and annuity income after age 65, this approach may no longer be necessary for many clients. It will, however, still be effective for retired couples under age 65 who have no employer pension income. See Chapter 6, Tax Planning Tips and Strategies, for further discussion on this issue.

Bond Laddering

In our "buckets of money" illustration, we referred to funds in the second bucket being held in a bond ladder. This is a simple strategy for reducing interest rate risk, while providing the ongoing cash that the retiree needs to live on. With a bond ladder, bonds or GICs are spread evenly over the maturity spectrum. In the example of Bob on the previous pages, he needs to be able to cash in a $20,000 bond each year in order to meet his spending requirements. The bonds would be set up initially as a series, with a $20,000 bond maturing each year over the next five years. When a bond matures, the cash is moved into a money market fund for Bob to draw on. At the same time, another $20,000 bond is purchased with a maturity date at the far end of the spectrum, i.e. five years in the future in Bob's case. Replenishing the ladder in this way ensures that Bob will have a source of income over the next five years without having to cash in investments that could have gone down in value.

A bond ladder could also be used for a portion of the longer-term investments that Bob holds, i.e. the third bucket. Here, a longer maturity spectrum would likely be used.

Emergency Funds

Retired clients may also wish to ensure that they have access to emergency funds in order to meet unexpected expenses. A line of credit is an option for retirees with good financial discipline. Clients should be advised to establish the line of credit prior to retirement.

Where clients feel more comfortable maintaining their own emergency funds, a certain amount should be held in cash, over and above the requirements discussed above for planned expenses. The guidelines commonly used for working people (three to six months worth of expenses) are really designed to provide a cash cushion in the event of job loss or disability. In retirement, typically less is required, unless the savings are created for a specific need such as replacing a car or funding a child's wedding. Since the returns on short-term money in liquid accounts are relatively low, no more than necessary should be kept in cash.

If the client prefers to keep some funds available in cash, shop around to find the best possible rate of return. The premium savings accounts offered by institutions such as ICICI Bank, President's Choice Financial and ING Direct offer some of the best rates available at the time of writing (between one and two percent). Check www.ratesupermarket.ca for other ideas.

Sustainable Withdrawal Rates — How Much Can I Spend?

One of the common misconceptions held by many clients is that, if their investment portfolio is returning, on average, eight percent per year, they can afford to draw out eight percent of their initial investment, year after year, without the risk of running out of money. However, extensive research has shown that this is not the case. The volatility of the portfolio and the sequence in which returns occur are major factors in the portfolio's ability to preserve capital over time. Clients are particularly at risk when they experience negative returns in the first few years of the withdrawal period.

To illustrate this problem, Phillips, Hager & North Investment Management prepared an example based on data from the S&P/TSX Composite Index[10]. In their example, they assumed that a retiree invested $1 million in the TSX on retirement on January 1, 1981. Over the next 25 years, the index produced a compound annual return of 9.6 percent; therefore, it was assumed that the retiree withdrew 9.6 percent of $1 million, or $96,000, at the beginning of each year. As can be seen by the table below, the retiree would have run out of funds after 25 years.

	TSX Return	Year	Year-end Portfolio Value	Withdrawal Amount	Portfolio Value After With-drawal	Growth of $1
		0	$1,000,000	$0	**$1,000,000**	1.0000
1981	−10.3%	1	$897,000	$96,000	**$801,000**	0.8970
1982	5.5%	2	$845,055	$96,000	**$749,055**	0.9463
1983	35.5%	3	$1,014,970	$96,000	**$918,970**	1.2823
1984	−2.4%	4	$896,914	$96,000	**$800,914**	1.2515
1985	25.1%	5	$1,001,944	$96,000	**$905,944**	1.5656
1986	9.0%	6	$987,479	$96,000	**$891,479**	1.7065
1987	5.9%	7	$944,076	$96,000	**$848,076**	1.8072
1988	11.1%	8	$942,212	$96,000	**$846,212**	2.0078
1989	21.4%	9	$1,027,302	$96,000	**$931,302**	2.4375
1990	−14.8%	10	$793,469	$96,000	**$697,469**	2.0768
1991	12.0%	11	$781,165	$96,000	**$685,165**	2.3260
1992	−1.4%	12	$675,573	$96,000	**$579,573**	2.2934
1993	32.6%	13	$768,514	$96,000	**$672,514**	3.0411
1994	−0.2%	14	$671,169	$96,000	**$575,169**	3.0350
1995	14.5%	15	$658,568	$96,000	**$562,568**	3.4750
1996	28.4%	16	$722,338	$96,000	**$626,338**	4.4620
1997	15.0%	17	$720,288	$96,000	**$624,288**	5.1313
1998	−1.6%	18	$614,300	$96,000	**$518,300**	5.0492
1999	31.7%	19	$682,601	$96,000	**$586,601**	6.6497
2000	7.4%	20	$630,009	$96,000	**$534,009**	7.1418
2001	−12.6%	21	$466,724	$96,000	**$370,724**	6.2419

---

[10] Reprinted with permission of Phillips, Hager & North Investment Management Ltd.

	TSX Return	Year	Year-end Portfolio Value	Withdrawal Amount	Portfolio Value After With-drawal	Growth of $1
2002	−12.4%	22	$324,754	$96,000	$228,754	5.4679
2003	26.7%	23	$289,832	$96,000	$193,832	6.9279
2004	14.5%	24	$221,937	$96,000	$125,937	7.9324
2005	24.1%	25	$156,288	$96,000	$60,288	9.8441

For comparison purposes, Phillips, Hager & North then looked at what would happen if the sequence of returns throughout the 25-year period from 1981 to 2005 was changed. To do this, they reversed the returns experienced in 1981 (-10.3 percent) and 2005 (24.1 percent), so that our retiree now starts the withdrawal period with positive rather than negative returns. All other returns were held constant. As can be seen in the table below, instead of running out of money, the retiree's capital has more than doubled over the withdrawal period.

	TSX Return	Year	Year-end Portfolio Value	Withdrawal Amount	Portfolio Value After Withdrawal	Growth of $1
		0	$1,000,000	$0	$1,000,000	1.0000
1981	24.1%	1	$1,241,000	$96,000	$1,145,000	1.2410
1982	5.5%	2	$1,207,975	$96,000	$1,111,975	1.3093
1983	35.5%	3	$1,506,726	$96,000	$1,410,726	1.7740
1984	−2.4%	4	$1,376,869	$96,000	$1,280,869	1.7315
1985	25.1%	5	$1,602,367	$96,000	$1,506,367	2.1661
1986	9.0%	6	$1,641,940	$96,000	$1,545,940	2.3610
1987	5.9%	7	$1,637,150	$96,000	$1,541,150	2.5003
1988	11.1%	8	$1,712,218	$96,000	$1,616,218	2.7778
1989	21.4%	9	$1,962,088	$96,000	$1,866,088	3.3723
1990	−14.8%	10	$1,589,907	$96,000	$1,493,907	2.8732
1991	12.0%	11	$1,673,176	$96,000	$1,577,176	3.2180
1992	−1.4%	12	$1,555,096	$96,000	$1,459,096	3.1729
1993	32.6%	13	$1,934,761	$96,000	$1,838,761	4.2073
1994	−0.2%	14	$1,835,084	$96,000	$1,739,084	4.1989
1995	14.5%	15	$1,991,251	$96,000	$1,895,251	4.8077

	TSX Return	Year	Year-end Portfolio Value	Withdrawal Amount	Portfolio Value After Withdrawal	Growth of $1
1996	28.4%	16	$2,433,502	$96,000	$2,337,502	6.1731
1997	15.0%	17	$2,688,127	$96,000	$2,592,127	7.0991
1998	−1.6%	18	$2,550,653	$96,000	$2,454,653	6.9855
1999	31.7%	19	$3,232,778	$96,000	$3,136,778	9.1999
2000	7.4%	20	$3,368,900	$96,000	$3,272,900	9.8807
2001	−12.6%	21	$2,860,514	$96,000	$2,764,514	8.6357
2002	−12.4%	22	$2,421,715	$96,000	$2,325,715	7.5649
2003	26.7%	23	$2,946,680	$96,000	$2,850,680	9.5847
2004	14.5%	24	$3,264,029	$96,000	$3,168,029	10.9745
2005	−10.3%	25	$2,841,722	$96,000	$2,745,722	9.8441

Clearly, clients must be prepared to withdraw an amount that is less than the portfolio's expected compound annual rate of return. But how much is a safe amount?

A study conducted by three business professors from Trinity University in San Antonio, Texas was one of the first to look at how to determine a sustainable withdrawal rate in retirement.[11] Using data from the S&P 500 and high-grade U.S. corporate bond returns from 1926 to 1995, they concluded that a portfolio with an asset mix of 50 percent equities and 50 percent bonds would sustain a five percent withdrawal rate (not adjusted for inflation) over every 30-year period they studied.

Since the Trinity Study was published in 1998, much more work has been done in this area, particularly by William Bengen in the United States, and Moshe Milevsky and Jim Otar in Canada.

In a nutshell, most studies show that a portfolio of between 20 and 25 times the level of required pre-tax income is needed to generate income throughout the retirement

---

[11] Philip Cooley, Carl Hubbard, Daniel Walz, Journal of the American Association of Individual Investors, Volume 20. February 1998.

years. Put another way, a retiree could expect to withdraw between four and five percent of his or her portfolio during the first year of retirement. A couple of cautions are in order here. First, remember that the investment portfolio is not usually meant to provide every dollar of the retiree's income. Start by determining how much of the income need will be covered by CPP/QPP, OAS, employer pensions, annuities, and any other guaranteed sources of income. Only the balance needs to be covered by withdrawals from the investment portfolio.

Secondly, take the time to understand how the "four to five percent" calculation is applied. It applies to the balance in the investment portfolio at the beginning of the first year of retirement, and that dollar amount is then indexed for inflation over the retiree's remaining lifetime. For example, if Marybeth has $500,000 in her portfolio at the beginning of her first year of retirement, and has decided to work with a four percent withdrawal rate, she can draw $20,000 from her account for her first year. Assuming that inflation is running at three percent, she can draw $20,600 for the second year and $21,218 for the third year. Unlike RRIF withdrawal tables where the required percentage withdrawal increases each year, and is applied to the balance of the account at the beginning of each year, sustainable withdrawal rate calculations are based on a dollar figure that is established at the beginning of the withdrawal period, and increased each year for inflation.

The four to five percent withdrawal rate has been developed based on deterministic analysis using actual historical rates of return and Monte Carlo analysis which is based on a randomly generated pattern of returns. Because there is no way of accurately predicting the level and pattern of future investment returns, the four to five percent range is the most reliable guide we have available to estimating the level of income that will most likely be available to a retiree. According to Sherry Cooper, "Assuming markets behave in ways similar to what we have experienced since 1926, an initial withdrawal rate of 4.1 percent will assure *with virtual certainty* that you will generate your additional desired pre-tax income for a retirement period of 30 years."[12]

Of course, if the investment portfolio is kept in a bank account earning one percent interest, all bets are off. The assumption behind the above calculations is that the portfolio will earn a five percent average annual rate of return after adjusting for an average inflation rate of three percent (an eight percent nominal return). This presupposes that investments will be held in a diversified portfolio, fairly equally balanced between stocks and bonds.

Other factors that will come into play in determining where exactly a client sits in that four to five percent range include the following:

- proportion of equities held in the portfolio
- length of retirement period
- amount the client would like to leave at death

Obviously then, the four to five percent range is a guideline that advisors can use as a starting point, adapting it according to the client's age at retirement, their expected longevity, their asset mix, and their estate planning goals.

Conclusion

One of the key concerns of clients entering retirement is having enough money to live on. At this point, their accumulation years are over, and their employer pensions, if any, as well as government benefits, are already determined. While some will continue to produce a certain level of employment income in the early years of retirement, most will look to their investments to provide them with the lifestyle that they have dreamed of for many years.

---

[12] Cooper, Sherry. The New Retirement. P. 175.

Advisors now have many tools at their disposal to help clients make the best use of their available capital. Helping clients to understand realistic withdrawal rates is key, and introducing them to products designed to provide a guaranteed income stream can be invaluable for those who are risk-averse or who have not saved enough to fund their desired lifestyle.

Chapter 6: Tax Planning Tips and Strategies

Introduction

Most retirees find that their tax world changes dramatically once they leave the full-time workforce. Full-time employees, particularly those who have made regular RRSP contributions over the years, are generally accustomed to getting a tax refund each year – at least those who haven't applied to have their withholdings reduced at source. This very seldom happens in retirement – it's much more common that retirees must write a cheque to the Receiver General when they file a tax return.

There are two main reasons for this situation. First, some types of retirement income may not be taxed at source at all. This could apply to CPP/QPP and OAS payments, minimum RRIF withdrawals, and non-registered investment income. Clients have the opportunity to have taxes withheld at source from government benefits and RRIF withdrawals, but not all clients make this choice.

Second, when income arrives from a variety of different sources, as is typically the case in retirement, the source deductions that apply are often understated. Take the situation where Brenda is receiving employer pension income, government benefits, and salary from her part-time work with a small consulting firm. It's quite likely that each of these payers is withholding tax as if that particular source was Brenda's only source of income. If her total income pushes her up into a higher marginal tax bracket, CRA will be looking to her to make up the difference come tax time.

For that reason, advisors should work with their clients well in advance of that first tax return to ensure they have a good understanding of what the total tax bill will be, and what proportion of that tax bill has been covered by source deductions.

There are two approaches that can be taken to covering the required payment. Clients can request to have more tax taken off at source from employer pensions, government benefits, and RRIF income, or they can set the money aside in a savings account so that they will have the funds needed to pay the bill. Although deferring the payment of taxes as long as possible is generally the preferred strategy from a straight number-crunching point of view, advisors and clients need to keep in mind the possible impact on the requirement to pay tax by instalments. Many clients, particularly those who travel frequently, dislike the extra paperwork of paying taxes quarterly, although the advent of internet banking has made this process less painful for many.

Paying Tax by Instalments

Instalments must be made if the net tax owing is more than $3,000 in the current year, and in either of the two previous years. For Quebec residents, the net tax owing must be more than $1,800. Instalment payments are due March 15, June 15, September 15, and December 15 of each year.

There are three methods that can be used to calculate the amount of tax owing: the no-calculation option, the prior-year option, and the current-year option. CRA uses the no-calculation option on the instalment reminders they send to taxpayers in February and August of each year. However, taxpayers are free to base their instalments on either of the other two methods.

No-Calculation Option

In general, the no-calculation option is best for clients whose income, deductions and credits stay about the same from year to year. With this option, CRA will not charge instalment interest or penalties, even if the total of the payments turns out to be less than the total tax owing for the year.

Prior-Year Option

The prior-year option is suitable for clients whose income, deductions and credits for the current year, say 2014, are similar to the amounts for 2013, but significantly different from those amounts in 2012. For example, a client who retired at the end of 2012 may find that his or her income in 2014 is similar to that received in 2013, but considerably lower than in 2012 when he or she was still employed full-time.

Current-Year Option

The current-year option is recommended for situations where current (say 2014) income, deductions and credits are significantly different from those in both prior years. This could apply to a client who retired at the end of 2013.

The following chart can be used to estimate instalment payments using either the prior-year or the current-year option.

Calculation Chart for Instalment Payments[1]

The calculation chart below lists the items used to calculate **net tax owing** (line 13). It is also used to determine your **total instalment amount due** (line 15) when you choose either the prior-year or current-year payment option.

To complete the chart, see your *Notice of Assessment*, *Notice of Reassessment*, or a tax return and your prior-year or estimated current-year income information, depending on the option you decide to use. Then, enter the amounts that correspond to the lines in the chart.

Calculation Chart
The line references are from your tax return, *Notice of Assessment*, or *Notice of Reassessment*.

Net federal tax (line 420)		$ _____	1
Old Age Security (OAS) repayment (from line 422)	+	_____	2
Provincial or territorial tax (line 428)	+	_____	3
Yukon First Nations tax (line 432)	+	_____	4
Total payable (**add** lines 1 to 4)	=	_____	5
Total income tax deducted (line 437) (Quebec residents use line 439)		_____	6
Refundable abatements (line 440 plus line 441)	+	_____	7
Refundable medical expense supplement (line 452)	+	_____	8
Working income tax benefit (line 453)	+	_____	9
Refund of investment tax credit (line 454)	+	_____	10
Part XII.2 trust tax credit (line 456)	+	_____	11
Provincial or territorial tax credits (line 479)	+	_____	12
Total credits (**add** lines 6 to 12)	=	_____	13
Net tax owing (line 5 **minus** line 13)	=	_____	14
CPP/EI contributions payable (lines 421 and 430)	+	_____	15
Total instalment amount due (line 14 **plus** line 15)	=	_____	16

The *CRA Pamphlet P110, Paying Your Income Tax by Instalments,* is a useful source of further information.

---

[1] Reproduced with permission of the Canada Revenue Agency and the Minister of Public Works and Government Services Canada, 2008.

Note that CRA now has a system that allows taxpayers to set up pre-authorized payment of quarterly instalments, using either the no-calculation amount shown on the instalment reminders mailed out in February and August, or a fixed amount determined by the taxpayer. In order to initiate this system, taxpayers must complete Form T1162A-1 and mail it into CRA at least 30 days before they want the pre-authorized payments to begin.

Tax Planning

Advisors also have an important role to play in helping to create a tax-efficient income structure for their clients. Some of this can be done through the use of tax-efficient non-registered investments, such as those discussed in Chapter 5, Investment Choices and Strategies for the Retirement Years. The chapters on retirement income from government, employer and personal sources cover some of the tax aspects to be considered when planning how and when to receive payments from these sources.

The remainder of this chapter will focus on the proper use of non-refundable tax credits that may apply to clients in their later years, including the pension income amount, the age amount, and various medical/disability credits.

In addition, we will explore a variety of income splitting techniques that can help reduce the retired client's tax burden.

Definition of Common Law

When discussing tax planning, there are a number of techniques that apply to spouses and common law partners. Canada Revenue Agency defines a common law partner for tax purposes as one who lives in a conjugal relationship with the taxpayer and:

- has done so for at least 12 consecutive months, or

- is the parent of the taxpayer's child by birth or adoption, or

- has custody and control of the taxpayer's child and the child is wholly dependent on that person for support.

Canada Pension Plan defines a common law partner as one who has lived in a conjugal relationship with the taxpayer for at least one year. However, under the Quebec Pension Plan, the requirement is:

- living in a conjugal relationship for at least three years, or

- living in a conjugal relationship for at least one year where the couple has a child together either by birth or adoption.

QPP furthers stipulates that it is not possible for a taxpayer to have a common law spouse if he or she is legally married to another person at the same time.

Different definitions of "common law" may apply to employer pension plans and retiree benefits programs.

Tax Credits

Age Amount

The age amount, which is a non-refundable federal tax credit of $6,916 for the tax year 2014, is available to taxpayers 65 or older whose net income is less than $34,873. Above this level of income, the credit is gradually reduced at a rate of 15 cents on the dollar. The credit disappears at a net income level of $80,980. This credit, as well as the threshold net income amount, is indexed to inflation each year.

The provinces and territories have their own age amounts that eligible taxpayers must claim when they file their tax return. Note that the amounts and income thresholds are not necessarily the same as those used by the federal government. See Tables 2 and 3 at the end of this chapter for the most current information at the time of printing.

Pension Income Amount

The pension income amount is a non-refundable federal tax credit of up to $2,000 that applies to eligible pension income.

For recipients age 65 and older, eligible income includes:

- Pension payments under an employer pension plan

- Annuity payments from an RRSP or DPSP

- Interest payments from a prescribed annuity

- Payments from a RRIF, LIF, or LRIF

For recipients under age 65, eligible income includes:

- Pension payments under an employer pension plan

- Any of the above payments received as a result of the death of a spouse or partner

The provinces and territories have their own pension income amounts that eligible taxpayers must claim when they file their tax return. Note that the amounts and income thresholds are not necessarily the same as those used by the federal government. See Tables 2 and 3 at the end of this chapter for the most current information at the time of printing.

Advisors should be aware that payments from salary deferral arrangements, retirement compensation arrangements, or employee benefit plans are not eligible for the pension income amount.

Where employer pension income is not available, consideration should be given to buying an annuity or opening a RRIF at age 65 in order to produce at least $2,000 per year of taxable income, in order to take advantage of the pension income amount.

Disability Amount

Some retired clients may find that they are eligible for the non-refundable disability amount. The eligibility requirements are quite specific and relate to the client's ability to perform certain basic activities of daily living. These activities include speaking, hearing, walking, feeding, dressing, performing bowel and bladder functions, and "performing the mental functions necessary for everyday life".

In order to be considered eligible, a qualified practitioner must certify that the client has a prolonged impairment, such that he or she is significantly restricted in two or more basic activities of daily living, is blind, or is markedly restricted in one basic activity of daily living. "Prolonged" means that the condition has lasted, or is expected to last, longer than 12 months. The practitioner must complete CRA *Form T2201, Disability Tax Credit Certificate*. Advisors should be aware that, if a client intends to claim the disability amount, *Form T2201* should be completed and filed with CRA as soon as possible. It is not necessary to wait to file the form with the annual tax return, and doing so will only result in delays in processing the return.

The 2014 federal disability amount is a tax credit of $7,766. The provinces and territories have their own disability amounts that eligible taxpayers must claim when they file their tax return. See Tables 2 and 3 at the end of this chapter for the most current information at the time of printing.

Medical Expenses

There is a non-refundable federal tax credit for medical expenses incurred over and above a specific dollar threshold. For 2014, the threshold is $2,171, or three percent of net income, whichever is lower. A wide variety of expenses that are often incurred by older clients is eligible for this credit, including bathroom aids, power-operated chairs for stairway use, walkers, wheelchairs and scooters, eyeglasses and contact lenses, dentures, hearing aids, home care services, and premiums paid for private health services plans, including those purchased for out-of-country coverage. As of March 4, 2010, medical and dental procedures for strictly cosmetic purposes are no longer eligible.

Clients who mistakenly think that their medical expenses are too low to take advantage of this credit often miss out on some significant tax savings. Canada Revenue Agency maintains a detailed list of eligible medical expenses on their website (www.cra.gc.ca); this list should be consulted to make sure that all relevant expenses are taken into consideration.

Another point to consider is that, with a couple, one individual can claim for medical expenses incurred for both partners. In order to maximize the benefit of the tax credit, the lower income spouse or partner should consider claiming expenses for both. For example, if the lower income spouse has net income of $50,000, they can claim medical expenses over $1,500 ($50,000 x 3 percent) incurred for both partners.

Advisors and clients should also be aware that there is no requirement for expenses to be claimed on a calendar year basis. For example, in filing a tax return for the 2014 tax year, an individual can claim medical expenses for any 12-month period that ended in 2014. Therefore, a client could go back as far as February 2013 to see which 12-month period produced the highest dollar amount of expenses.

In some circumstances, the cost of attendant care is claimed as a medical expense. However, advisors should be aware that special rules apply in this area. The attendant must not be the spouse or common law partner of the claimant, and must be 18 years of age or older.

In general, the entire amount paid for full-time care in a nursing home may be claimed as a medical expense. For clients in retirement homes, homes for seniors, or living on their own, the fees claimed must be for salaries and wages paid for attendant care services, which include food preparation, housekeeping, laundry, health care, activities, salon services if included in the monthly fee, and transportation. Where an establishment such as a retirement home provides these services, the home must provide a detailed statement showing the amount paid for eligible services.

However, there are restrictions that relate to the claiming of the disability amount combined with medical expenses. Where medical expenses related to full-time care in a nursing home are claimed, the disability amount may not be claimed. If a client resides in his own home or in a retirement home, up to $10,000 of medical expenses can be claimed in addition to the disability amount. If more than $10,000 of medical expenses is claimed, the client is not eligible to claim the disability amount.

CRA has a number of useful publications that advisors may want to refer to, including *Guide RC4064, Medical and Disability-Related Information*, and *Interpretation Bulletin IT519R2 Consolidated, Medical Expense and Disability Tax Credits and Attendant Care Expense Deduction*.

Home Renovation Expenses

Although not available at the federal level, both British Columbia and Ontario offer refundable tax credits to those 65 and older who have incurred home renovation expenses that improve accessibility and/or make it easier for them to be more functional or mobile at home. In British Columbia, the BC Seniors' Home Renovation Tax Credit is calculated as 10% of eligible expenses, up to a maximum credit of $1,000 per year. In Ontario, the more generous Ontario Healthy Homes Renovation Tax Credit is based on 15% of eligible expenses, up to a maximum credit of $1,500 per year.

Claims can be made for a wide variety of expenses, including installation of comfort-height toilets, grab bars in a shower or bathtub, hand-held showers, improved interior and exterior lighting, pull-out shelving in the kitchen and bathroom, and the installation of wheelchair ramps and stair lifts.

Income Splitting

One of the ways that tax savings can be accomplished is by shifting income to another individual in a lower tax bracket, commonly referred to as income splitting. The attribution rules outlined in the *Income Tax Act* limit the number of situations where this can be accomplished effectively. In general, income earned by one individual must be taxed in that person's hands.

However, there are certain specific situations where the *Income Tax Act* sanctions income splitting. These include the sharing of CPP/QPP benefits and the pension income splitting provisions that were introduced by federal Finance Minister Jim Flaherty in October 2006. In addition, there are some strategies involving investment income that can effectively shift the tax burden from one spouse to another.

CPP/QPP

As discussed in Chapter 2, married or common law partners, who are both ready to receive their CPP/QPP retirement benefits, can apply to share the portion of their benefits that they earned during the time they were married or living together. If only one partner has contributed to CPP/QPP, the partners can share that one payment. Pension sharing can result in tax savings throughout retirement if one partner is in a higher tax bracket than the other.

Once a pension sharing application has been approved, the pensions will be divided at source and revised amounts sent out to each spouse accordingly. A copy of the application form for CPP (*ISP-1002-10-07E, Application for Pension Sharing of Retirement Pension(s) Canada Pension Plan*) is available on line at www.servicecanada.gc.ca.

Clients who are eligible for a QPP retirement pension can go to www.rrq.gouv.qc.ca for the application form. QPP procedures are slightly different. In the case of married spouses, only one spouse needs to apply for pension sharing, unless they lived together before marriage, in which case they must file a joint application. CPP requires an application from only one partner, regardless of marital status.

QPP also requires a joint written application from common law ("de facto") spouses, and stipulates that they must have been living together for at least three years at the time the pension sharing begins, or at least one year if they had or adopted a child during their time together.

Pension sharing may be started at any time (as long as both partners have reached age 60), and continues until either partner dies, or partners are no longer living together. It is also possible for recipients to cancel the pension sharing arrangement at any time if it is no longer to their advantage. At that point, each person will start to receive his or her original entitlement as determined before the pension sharing arrangement began.

When helping clients to decide if pension sharing is to their advantage, it is always best to ask CPP or QPP to do the calculation. Because it is only the portion earned during the time the couple was together that is eligible for sharing, the end result may be somewhat different from what the clients expect.

Consider the following example: Richard and Marilyn have been married since 1979. They are both over 60. Richard receives a CPP retirement benefit of $550 per month, while Marilyn receives $400. However, Marilyn earned some of her CPP credits before her marriage, while Richard only began working after they were married. Here is how the pension sharing arrangement would work for them:

	Richard	Marilyn
Amount of benefit earned before marriage	$ 0	$100
Amount of benefit earned after marriage (portion eligible for sharing)	$550	$300
New shared benefit ($850 / 2)	$425	$425
Total monthly payment under pension sharing (shared portion plus amount of benefit earned before marriage)	$425	$525

Note that the new Post-Retirement Benefit (see Chapter 2 for details) is not eligible for sharing.

Pension Splitting

Since 2007, taxpayers have been allowed to split income eligible for the pension income tax credit with a spouse or partner. For recipients age 65 and older, eligible income includes:

- Pension payments under an employer pension plan
- Annuity payments from an RRSP or DPSP[2]

---

[2] Note that cash withdrawals from an RRSP or DPSP are not considered eligible income.

- Interest payments from a prescribed annuity

- Payments from a RRIF, LIF, or LRIF

For recipients under age 65, eligible income includes:

- Pension payments under an employer pension plan

- Any of the above payments received as a result of the death of a spouse or partner

Unlike pension sharing with CPP/QPP, there is no need for clients to contact the source of this income to have different amounts paid to each spouse. Pension splitting is accomplished by assigning a certain amount of income to the spouse or partner, who must be a resident of Canada, at the time the annual tax return is filed. Both partners must file CRA *Form T1032, Joint Election to Split Pension Income*, with their tax return. If filing electronically, keep the completed form on hand in case CRA asks to see it.

Up to 50 percent of eligible income may be assigned to the spouse or partner. For those whose marital status changed during the year, the amount that can be allocated is prorated according to the number of months the couple lived together. The withholding tax that applies to this income must be assigned in the same proportion as the income itself. Clients can decide on an annual basis how much income they wish to split.

Note that there is no age restriction for the partner who receives the allocated income. Josh, age 55 and in receipt of employer pension income, could choose to assign up to 50 percent of that income to Mandy, his 40-year-old wife.

Income that is allocated to a spouse or partner retains its character, which creates an opportunity for both partners to take advantage of the pension income tax credit. In the example above, 40-year-old Mandy would be able to claim the pension income tax credit since there is no age restriction for employer pension income. However, let's say that

Steve, age 65, is in receipt of RRIF income, but has no employer pension. He is eligible to assign up to half his RRIF income to his wife Paula, age 58, but only Steve is entitled to the pension income credit. Paula will become entitled when she reaches age 65.

Benefits to Pension Splitting

There are several benefits to income splitting in retirement. First, of course, is the obvious reduction in overall taxes paid. In Ontario, for example, moving income from the highest tax bracket (49.53 percent) to the lowest bracket (20.5 percent) saves 29 percent of every dollar transferred.

In addition, there is the impact on certain tax credits and benefits to be considered. While benefits and credits that are calculated based on the total of the net incomes of both spouses or partners will not change, income splitting will affect any benefits or credits that are calculated based on one individual's net income. For example, there will be no impact on the GST/HST credit, but moving income from a higher tax bracket spouse to one in a lower tax bracket can have the effect of preserving some of the age credit as well as the OAS benefit for the higher tax bracket spouse.

Where pension income is transferred, there may be an opportunity for both spouses to claim the pension income tax credit. The original recipient can claim the lesser of $2,000 or the amount of eligible pension income that is left after subtracting amounts allocated to the spouse or partner. The partner receiving the allocated income can also claim the lesser of $2,000 or the amount of eligible pension income they receive, including the allocated income. Remember that eligibility for certain types of income depends on age. Therefore, income that is eligible for the original recipient might not be eligible for the partner, depending on the partner's age.

173

Here is an example of the effectiveness of pension income splitting. Tax rates in all subsequent examples are based on 2014 Ontario rates.

Before Income Splitting

	Bruce, Age 65	Judy, Age 60
RPP	72,000	0
Interest income	40,500	15,000
CPP	3,500	3,500
Total income	116,000	18,500
Tax payable	33,018	1,550
Total tax payable for both	34,568	
Couple's after-tax income excluding OAS	99,932	

After Income Splitting

	Bruce, Age 65	Judy, Age 60
RPP	36,000	36,000
Interest income	40,500	15,000
CPP	3,500	3,500
Total income	80,000	54,500
Tax payable	17,695	9,728
Total tax payable for both	27,423	
Couple's after-tax income excluding OAS	107,077	

In this example, Bruce's income before income splitting was high enough that it wiped out the age credit as well as his complete OAS benefit. Judy, on the other hand, is not eligible for the age credit or OAS because she is under age 65. After Bruce assigns 50 percent of his employer pension to Judy, he becomes eligible to receive a portion of the OAS benefit, while Judy is now eligible for the pension income credit. The end result is that this couple's after-tax income excluding OAS has increased by over $7,000. In addition, Bruce will now be entitled to receive an annual OAS pension of $5,357 pre-tax ($4,138 after tax), making a total difference after tax of over $11,000.

However, advisors should not assume that a 50 percent split is always the optimum way of assigning pension income. Remember that increasing income beyond certain levels can expose a client to the clawback of OAS and the federal and provincial age credits. Since these factors only affect clients age 65 and older, special care must be taken when assigning pension income to someone in that age bracket. Let's consider another example to illustrate this point. In the chart below, we have a couple, both age 65, with different levels of income.

Before Income Splitting

	Aaron, Age 65	Lola, Age 65
RPP	100,000	35,000
Interest income	60,000	0
CPP	11,520	11,520
Total income	171,520	46,520
Tax payable	58,176	6,315
Total tax payable for both	64,491	
Couple's after-tax income excluding OAS	153,549	

In this scenario, Lola would be entitled to full OAS benefits, while Aaron would be subject to a full clawback. This would increase their after tax-income by $5,413 (full OAS benefit of $6,618 minus $1,205 tax at Lola's average tax rate of 18.2%). After adding in OAS for Lola, this couple's total after-tax income would be $158,962.

Assigning 50 percent of Aaron's pension income to Lola would save $4,633 in tax, as seen below.

After Income Splitting, Version 1

	Aaron, Age 65	Lola, Age 65
RPP	50,000	85,000
Interest income	60,000	0
CPP	11,520	11,520
Total income	121,520	96,520
Tax payable	35,297	24,561
Total tax payable for both	59,858	
Couple's after-tax income excluding OAS	158,182	

What about OAS? Under the 50% split scenario, Aaron would still be subject to the full clawback, but now part of Lola's OAS would be clawed back as well. Lola would be entitled to receive $2,773 in after-tax OAS benefits. This increases their after-tax income to $160,955.

Can we improve the situation by assigning less of Aaron's pension income to Lola? The chart below shows the effect of assigning $25,000 of Aaron's pension income to Lola, just enough to take her up to the OAS clawback threshold.

After Income Splitting, Version 2

	Aaron, Age 65	Lola, Age 65
RPP	75,000	60,000
Interest income	60,000	0
CPP	11,520	11,520
Total income	146,520	71,520
Tax payable	46,574	14,832
Total tax payable for both	61,406	
Couple's after-tax income excluding OAS	156,634	

Because Lola is now entitled to receive the full OAS benefit of $6,618, her after-tax income increases by $5,128

($6,618 minus $1,490 at Lola's average tax rate of 21.55%). This couple's total after-tax income is now $161,762.

In all cases, Aaron's income is high enough that his total OAS benefit is clawed back. However, assigning a smaller percentage of Aaron's pension to Lola means that she is able to retain a greater proportion of her OAS benefit.

Most tax preparation software is designed to maximize the benefits of pension income splitting, taking federal and provincial tax rates into consideration. However, the impact on OAS must be considered separately. The website www.retirementadvisor.ca has a handy calculator that can be used to determine the amount of the OAS clawback for any level of income.

Other considerations to keep in mind include the impact of pension splitting on per diem rates charged in nursing homes, which are usually based on net income, and premiums paid or deductibles applied to provincial drug plans.

The CRA will not approve a reduction of tax withholding at source based on pension income splitting. However, it should be taken into consideration when helping clients calculate their instalment payments for the coming year. Using the current-year option, payments can be estimated based on the intention to split pension income. Advisors should be aware that, if instalment payments are insufficient, CRA may charge interest.

Proceeds of the Sale of a Principal Residence

When a home is sold, couples will need to consider how best to distribute the proceeds between them from an income splitting perspective. As long as it can be demonstrated that both of them did, in fact, contribute to the purchase, they may have some flexibility in this regard.

The proceeds of the sale of a principal residence will be tax-free, but the return on the invested capital will, of course, be taxed. If both spouses contributed to the purchase of the home, the financial advisor should consider how best to allocate the investment income between them.

For example, suppose that Doug and Kathryn sell their home for $500,000. They split the proceeds equally between them, and each adds $250,000 to their respective investment accounts. At a later date, they decide to purchase a home in the country for $300,000. Each one contributes $150,000 to the purchase. This works quite well if their other investment assets are fairly equal. But suppose that Doug started out with investments totalling $200,000, while Kathryn had none. They would still split the proceeds of the sale equally between them, but when it came time to buy the country property, Doug could contribute $250,000, while Kathryn contributed $50,000. They would each be left with investment capital of $200,000. They have effectively managed to split their investment income.

Careful documentation of these transactions is in order. If and when Doug and Kathryn sell the country property, it must be recalled that 83 percent of the proceeds now belong to Doug.

Investment Income

In general, income earned from property given or loaned to a spouse or common law partner will be attributed back to the donor and taxed in that person's hands. For example, if Bob were to give his wife Sue $10,000 to invest, he would be subject to tax on the interest, dividends, or capital gains that the investment produced.

However, compound income, or income-on-income, is not attributed back to the donor of the funds. For example, if Bob puts $10,000 in Sue's name to purchase bonds yielding three percent, the $300 of interest income is taxable in Bob's hands. In the second year, the income on the $300 of income that has already been attributed does not create "compound attribution". The planner can therefore structure the re-investment of the interest to avoid attribution: at the end of year one, utilize the income ($300 in this example) to purchase a separate investment vehicle, perhaps a $300 GIC. The income on this new separate investment vehicle will then be taxable in Sue's hands.

The advantage of this income-on-income or "second generation income" strategy is seen if we assume that the amount of funds transferred is large, say $100,000. At the end of ten years (assuming a three percent yield), Sue would have over $30,000 of second-generation income on which there is no future attribution.

Note that the transfer or loan of property to a spouse for use in a business does not give rise to attribution as long as the property is used to produce business income.

The attribution rules do not apply if funds are loaned to a spouse and interest is charged on the loan at CRA's prescribed rate, which is established on a quarterly basis. As of the second quarter of 2014, the prescribed rate is one percent, the lowest it has ever been and the lowest it can be due to the way it is calculated. It is important that the loan be documented in writing, and the interest payable must actually be paid within 30 days after the end of each year.

When the prescribed rate is low, the benefits of an interspousal loan should be considered. The low rate at the time the loan is made will be in effect throughout the life of the loan. As a demand loan, the principal can be paid off at any time, or it can remain outstanding on an indefinite basis.

Taxation of RRIF Withdrawals

As discussed in Chapter 4, once a RRIF is opened, a predetermined minimum amount must be withdrawn from the plan each year. No tax withholding is required on the minimum amount. However, any amounts above the minimum are subject to withholding tax according to the following schedule:

Amount Withdrawn	Federal	Quebec
$5,000 or less	10%	21%
$5,001 - $15,000	20%	26%
More than $15,000	30%	31%

Confusion arises because many clients are unsure how the amount of the withdrawal is determined. For example, if Beatrice arranges to withdraw $1,500 per month above the minimum for an annual amount of $18,000 above the minimum, is each withdrawal taxed at 10% or 30%? CRA's position is that, when a regular monthly (or quarterly or semi-annual) withdrawal is set up, each payment represents a portion of the total annual amount requested. As such, the 30% rate applies.

However, if Beatrice requested an additional lump sum payment of $4,000 partway through the year, the 10% withholding tax rate applies because this payment is seen as a separate request from the regular payments set up at the beginning of the year.

Clients who do not want to have to pay large amounts when they file their tax returns (or instalment payments) can ask their financial institution to increase the tax withholding at source.

Tax-Efficient Structuring of Income in Retirement

One of the challenges faced by clients with multiple streams of income in retirement is how and when to draw on each source in order to minimize the amount of tax payable and maximize the amount of after-tax income. At one time, advisors believed that the best approach was to defer tax as long as possible by continuing RRSP contributions and waiting until the last possible moment to convert an

RRSP into a RRIF or annuity. However, depending on the client's overall level of income, this can result in exposure to higher tax rates and the clawback of OAS benefits as well as the age credit in later years. In some situations, assuming the client is already retired or semi-retired, it can make sense to increase income slightly in the years prior to 65 in order to avoid this outcome.

Of course, every retiree's situation is different. The appropriate strategies will depend on the general level of income expected and whether the client has the opportunity to split income with a spouse. Income levels should be considered with regard to various clawback thresholds as well as the applicable federal and provincial tax brackets. Here are some benchmarks to keep in mind, using 2014 figures:

- Taxable income under $34,873 will not be affected by the clawback of the federal age credit.

- Taxable income under $43,953 is subject to the lowest federal tax rate of 15%.

- Taxable income under $71,592 will not be affected by the OAS clawback.

- If the taxpayer's net income is below $72,366, a lower threshold for the medical expense credit will apply[3].

- The age credit is completely clawed back when taxable income reaches $80,980.

- At taxable income of $87,907, the federal tax rate increases from 22% to 26%.

- At taxable income of $115,716, the OAS benefit is completely clawed back.

- When taxable income reaches $136,270, the federal tax rate increases from 26% to 29%.

---

[3] The medical expense credit is based on expenses that exceed 3% of net income or $2,171, whichever is less.

Whatever the client's level of income happens to be, it's important to manage taxable income from one year to the next to minimize unnecessary exposure to clawbacks and higher tax rates. This can be achieved through the various income splitting techniques discussed in this chapter, as well as:

- Taking CPP/QPP and OAS as early as possible to reduce the amount that comes into income each year.

- Starting RRSP withdrawals earlier than required. Where appropriate, funds could be transferred into a TFSA to shelter them from further tax exposure.

- Triggering capital gains or stock option benefits prior to age 65.

- Delaying RRSP deductions to years beyond age 65 where avoidance of OAS and age credit clawbacks is an issue.

TABLE 1

FEDERAL AND PROVINCIAL/TERRITORIAL TAX RATES AND BRACKETS FOR 2014

TAX REFERENCE TABLES
These tables provided by KPMG LLP, current to December 31, 2013

FEDERAL AND PROVINCIAL/TERRITORIAL INCOME TAX RATES, BRACKETS AND SURTAXES FOR 2014

	Tax Rates	Tax Brackets	Surtax Rate	Surtax Threshold
Federal[a]	15.00%	Up to $43,953		
	22.00	43,9544-87,907		
	26.00	87,908-136,270		
	29.00	136,271 and over		
British Columbia[b, c]	5.06%	Up to $37,606		
	7.70	37,607–75,213		
	10.50	74,214–86,354		
	12.29	86,355–104,858		
	14.70	104,859–150,000		
	1680	150,001 and over		
Alberta	10.00%	All income		
Saskatchewan[d]	11.00%	Up to $43,292		
	13.00	43,293–123,692		
	15.00	123,693 and over		
Manitoba[e]	10.80%	Up to $31,000		
	12.75	31,001–67,000		
	17.40	67,001 and over		
Ontario[f]	5.05%	Up to $40,120		
	9.15	40,121–80,242	20%	$4,331
	11.16	80,243–514,090	36	5,543
	13.16	514,091 and over		
Québec[g]	16.00%	Up to $41,495		
	20.00	41,496–82,985		
	24.00	82,986–100,970		
	25.75	100,971 and over		
New Brunswick[d]	9.68%	Up to $39,305		
	14.82	39,306–78,609		
	16.52	78,610–127,802		
	17.84	127,803 and over		
Nova Scotia[e]	8.79%	Up to $29,590		
	14.95	29,591–59,180		
	16.67	59,181–93,000		
	17.50	93,001–150,000		
	21.00	150,001 and over		
Prince Edward Island[e]	9.80%	Up to $31,984		
	13.80	31,985–63,969		
	16.70	63,970 and over	10%	$12,500

	Tax Rates	Tax Brackets	Surtax Rate	Surtax Threshold
Newfoundland & Labrador[h]	7.70%	Up to $34,254		
	12.50	34,255–68,508		
	13.30	68,509 and over		
Northwest Territories[d]	5.90%	Up to $39,808		
	8.60	39,809–79,618		
	12.20	79,619–129,441		
	14.05	129,442 and over		
Nunavut[d]	4.00%	Up to $41,909		
	7.00	41,910–83,818		
	9.00	83,819–136,270		
	11.50	136,271 and over		
Yukon[d]	7.04%	Up to $43,953		
	9.68	43,954–87,907		
	11.44	87,908–136,270		
	12.76	136,271 and over	5%	$6,000

Notes:

a   TThe federal tax brackets are indexed each year by a calculated inflation factor, which is based on the change in the average federal inflation rate over the 12-month period ending September 30 of the previous year compared to the change in the rate for the same period of the year prior to that. The federal inflation factor is 0.9% for 2014.

b   British Columbia indexes its tax brackets using the same formula as that used federally, but uses the provincial inflation rate rather than the federal rate in the calculation. The province s inflation factor is 0.1% for 2014. Residents of British Columbia are also required to make monthly payments under the province s Medical Services Plan.

c   British Columbia introduced a new temporary sixth bracket effective January 1, 2014 for individuals earning more than $150,000 in a taxation year. The new bracket has a tax rate of 16.80%. This two-year temporary measure will expire December 31, 2015.

d   Saskatchewan, New Brunswick and the territories (Northwest Territories, Nunavut and the Yukon) index their tax brackets using the same formula as that used federally. The inflation factor is 0.9% for 2014.

e   Manitoba, Nova Scotia and Prince Edward Island do not index their tax brackets or surtax thresholds.

f   Ontario indexes its tax brackets and surtax thresholds using the same formula as that used federally, but uses the provincial inflation rate rather than the federal rate in the calculation. The province's inflation factor is 1.0% for 2014. Ontario resident individuals with taxable income over $20,000 are also required to pay a Health Premium each year.

g   Québec indexes its tax brackets using the same formula as that used federally, but uses the provincial inflation rate, excluding changes in liquor and tobacco taxes, rather than the federal rate in the calculation. The province's inflation factor is 0.97% for 2014. Residents of Québec are required to pay a health contribution and to make payments to the province's Health Services Fund.

h   Newfoundland and Labrador indexes its tax brackets using the same formula as that used federally, but uses the applicable provincial inflation rate rather than the federal rate in the calculation. Newfoundland and Labrador's inflation factor is 1.5% for 2014.

TABLE 2

FEDERAL AND PROVINCIAL/TERRITORIAL TAX CREDITS FOR 2014

FEDERAL AND PROVINCIAL/TERRITORIAL **NON-REFUNDABLE TAX CREDIT RATES AND AMOUNTS** FOR 2014[a]

	Federal[b]	B.C.	Alta.[b]	Sask.	Man.[b, c]	Ont.
Tax rate applied to credits	15.00%	5.06%	10.00%	11.00%	10.80%	5.05%
Indexation factor[e]	0.90%	0.10%	1.10%	0.90%	n/a	1.00%
Basic personal	$11,138	$9,869	$17,787	$15,378	$9,134	$9,670
Spousal/partner and wholly dependent person[f, n]	11,138	8,450	17,787	15,378	9,134	8,211
Net income threshold	—	*845*	—	*1,538*	—	*821*
Dependants:[g, n]						
18 and over and infirm	6,589	4,318	10,296	9,060	3,605	4,558
Net income threshold	*6,607*	*6,879*	*6,802*	*6,428*	*5,115*	*6,478*
Child (max)[h, n]	2,255	—	—	5,834	—	—
Adoption[i]	11,774	11,774	12,165	—	10,000	11,797
Disability[j]	7,766	7,402	13,720	9,060	6,180	7,812
Disability supplement[k]	4,530	4,357	10,296	9,060	3,605	4,556
Pension (max)[l]	2,000	1,000	1,370	1,000	1,000	1,337
Age 65 and over[l, l]	6,916	4,426	4,957	4,684	3,728	4,721
Net income threshold	*34,873*	*32,943*	*36,898*	*34,873*	*27,749*	*35,146*
Medical expense threshold[m]	2,171	2,071	2,298	2,171	1,728	2,189
Caregiver[n]	4,530	4,318	10,296	9,060	3,605	4,557
Net income threshold	*15,472*	*14,615*	*16,371*	*15,473*	*12,312*	*15,593*
Employment[o]	1,127	—	Ref.*	—	—	—
Canada Pension Plan contributions (max)[p]	2,426	2,426	2,426	2,426	2,426	2,426
Employment Insurance premiums (max)[p]	914	914	914	914	914	914
Public transit pass costs[q]	Ref.*	—	—	—	—	—
Children's fitness (max)[r] and arts[s]	500	500	—	Ref.*	500	Ref.*
Home buyers (max)[t]	5000	—	—	10,000	—	—
Tuition fees and interest paid on student loans[u]						
Education and textbooks[u]						
Full-time — per month	465	200	691	400	400	520
Part-time — per month	140	60	207	120	120	156
Charitable donations[v]						
Credit rate on first $200	15.00%	5.06%	10.00%	11.00%	10.80%	5.05%
Credit rate on balance	29.00%	14.70%	21.00%	15.00%	17.40%	11.16%

Notes:

*   "Ref." indicates a refundable credit — see the applicable note.

a   See table preceding s. 118 for ITA section references to the above credits.

The table shows the dollar amounts of federal and provincial non-refundable tax credits for 2014 (except for Québec see table K-25). In order to determine the credit value, each dollar amount must be multiplied by the tax rate indicated, which is the lowest tax rate applicable in the particular jurisdiction. For example, the Ontario basic personal credit amount of $9,670 is multiplied by 5.05% to determine the credit value of $488.

Income earned by the taxpayer or dependant, as applicable, in excess of the net income thresholds shown in the table serves to reduce the availability of the credit on a dollar-for-dollar basis. The only exception to this is the age credit, which is reduced by 15% of the taxpayer s net income in excess of the threshold.

b   The spousal/partner and wholly dependent person amounts are calculated by subtracting the spouse/partner and wholly dependant s net income from the maximum amount.

c   In 2011, Manitoba enacted legislation to increase the basic, spousal and eligible dependant amounts by $1,000 over the next four years. The credits increased to $9,134 (from $8,884) in 2014.

d-v   See the Notes to table below.

FEDERAL AND PROVINCIAL/TERRITORIAL NON-REFUNDABLE TAX CREDIT RATES AND AMOUNTS FOR 2014[a] (cont'd)

	N.B	N.S.	P.E.I.[d]	Nfld.	NWT	Nunavut	Yukon
Tax rate applied to credits	9.68%	8.79%	9.80%	7.70%	5.90%	4.00%	7.04%
Indexation factor[e]	0.90%	n/a	n/a	1.50%	0.90%	0.90%	0.90%
Basic personal	$9,472	$8,481	$7,708	$8,578	$13,668	$12,567	$11,138
Spousal/partner and wholly dependent person[f, n]	8,043	8,481	6,546	7,009	13,668	12,567	11,138
Net income threshold	*805*	*848*	*655*	*702*	*—*	*—*	*—*
Dependants:[g, n]							
18 and over and infirm	4,473	2,798	2,446	2,724	4,530	4,530	6,589
Net income threshold	*6,347*	*5,683*	*4,966*	*5,854*	*6,428*	*6,428*	*6,607*
Child (max)[h, n]	—	1,200	1,200	7,000	—	1,200	2,255
Adoption[i]	—	—	—	11,576	—	—	11,774
Disability[j]	7,668	7,341	6,890	5,788	11,084	12,567	7,766
Disability supplement[k]	4,474	3,449	4,019	2,724	4,530	4,530	4,530
Pension (max)[l]	1,000	1,173	1,000	1,000	1,000	2,000	2,000
Age 65 and over[l, l]	4,625	4,141	3,764	5,476	6.686	9,425	6,916
Net income threshold	*34,431*	*30,828*	*36,898*	*28,019*	*30,007*	*34,873*	*34,873*
Medical expense threshold[m]	2,143	6,637	1,678	1,869	2,171	2,171	2,171
Caregiver[n]	4,473	4,898	2,446	2,724	4,531	4,531	4,530
Net income threshold	*15,277*	*13,677*	*11,953*	*13,313*	*15,472*	*15,472*	*15,472*
Employment[o]	—	—	—	—	—	—	—
Canada Employment (max)	—	—	—	—	—	—	1,127

	N.B	N.S.	P.E.I.[d]	Nfld.	NWT	Nunavut	Yukon
Canada Pension Plan contributions (max)[p]	2,426	2,426	2,426	2,426	2,426	2,426	2,426
Employment Insurance premiums (max)[p]	914	914	914	914	914	914	914
Public transit pass costs[q]	—	—	—	—	—	—	Ref.[*]
Children's fitness (max)[r] and arts[s]	—	500	—	—	—	—	500
Home buyers (max)[t]	—	—	—	—	—	—	—
Tuition fees and interest paid on student loans[u]							
Education and textbooks[u]							
Full-time — per month	400	200	400	200	400	465	465
Part-time — per month	120	60	120	60	120	140	140
Charitable donations[v]							
Credit rate on first $200	9.68%	8.79%	9.80%	7.70%	5.90%	4.00%	7.04%
Credit rate on balance	17.95%	21.00%	16.70%	13.30%	14.05%	11.50%	12.76%

Notes:

*   "Ref." indicates a refundable credit — see the applicable note.

a   See table preceding s. 118 for ITA section references to the above credits.

    The table shows the dollar amounts of federal and provincial non-refundable tax credits for 2014 (except for Québec see table K-25). In order to determine the credit value, each dollar amount must be multiplied by the tax rate indicated, which is the lowest tax rate applicable in the particular jurisdiction. For example, the Ontario basic personal credit amount of $9,670 is multiplied by 5.05% to determine the credit value of $488.

    Income earned by the taxpayer or dependant, as applicable, in excess of the net income thresholds shown in the table serves to reduce the availability of the credit on a dollar-for-dollar basis. The only exception to this is the age credit, which is reduced by 15% of the taxpayer's net income in excess of the threshold.

b,c   See the Notes to table above.

d   The amounts in the table referring to the "spousal/partner and wholly dependent person" only represent the spousal/partner credit. For purposes of the wholly dependent person, the amounts should read $6,294 and $629 respectively.

e   The indexation factors indicated in the table are used to index the credits in each jurisdiction. The calculation of these factors is based on the change in the average federal or provincial inflation rate over the 12-month period ending September 30 of the previous year compared to the change in the rate for the same period of the year prior to that. British Columbia, Alberta, Ontario and Newfoundland and Labrador use the applicable provincial inflation rate in their calculations, while New Brunswick uses the federal inflation rate. Manitoba, Nova Scotia and Prince Edward Island do not index their credits.

    The Northwest Territories, Nunavut and Yukon use the federal inflation rate.

f   The spousal/partner credit may be claimed for a common-law partner as well as for a spouse. Taxpayers who are single, divorced or separated, and who support a dependant in their home may claim the wholly dependent person credit. The credit can be claimed for dependants under the age of 18 who are related to the taxpayer, for the taxpayer's parents or grandparents, or for any other infirm person who is related to the taxpayer. If either the federal spousal/partner or wholly dependent tax credit is claimed for an infirm person, then the claim may be increased by $309 ($2,058 x 15%) (see note (n)).

g   The federal and Yukon infirm dependant tax credit amount reflects a $2,058 enhancement (or the family caregiver tax credit), which is generally available for dependants with infirmities. See note (n) for additional details.

h   The federal child tax credit may be claimed by parents for each child under age 18 at the end of the year. If the federal child tax credit is claimed for an infirm person, then the claim may be increased by $309 ($2,058 x

15%) (see note (n)). Unused credit amounts may be transferred between spouses. Nova Scotia, Prince Edward Island and Yukon provide a similar credit for children under the age of 6. If certain conditions are met, an individual can claim $100 per eligible month for a maximum of $1,200 per year.

Newfoundland and Labrador provides a non-refundable child care credit that allows for a maximum of $7,000 of child care expenses to be claimed for children up to seven years of age, for a maximum credit of $539, and $4,000 for children aged seven to sixteen, for a maximum credit of $308.

i The adoption credit is available on eligible adoption expenses incurred in the year and not reimbursed to the taxpayer, up to the maximum amount indicated in the table.

j The disability, pension and age credits are transferable to a spouse or partner. The amounts available for transfer are reduced by the excess of the spouse's or partner's net income over the basic personal credit amount. The disability credit is also transferable to a supporting person other than a spouse or partner; however, the amount of the credit is reduced by the excess of the disabled person's net income over the basic personal credit amount.

k The disability supplement may be claimed by an individual who is under the age of 18 at the end of the year. The amount in the table represents the maximum amount that may be claimed, and is reduced by certain child and attendant care expenses claimed in respect of this individual.

l Saskatchewan also provides an additional non-refundable tax credit for individuals aged 65 or older in the year, regardless of their net income amount. The amount for 2014 is $1,231.

Effective January 1, 2014 Nova Scotia introduced a new additional age tax credit. This non-refundable credit is $1,000 and may be claimed by individuals age 65 and over with taxable income of less than $24,000.

m The medical expense credit is calculated based on qualified medical expenses exceeding 3% of net income or the threshold shown in the table, whichever is less. Medical expenses incurred by both spouses/partners and by their children under age 18 may be totalled and claimed by either spouse/partner.

In Ontario, a taxpayer can also claim medical expenses in respect of a dependant who is 18 or older, but the expenses are reduced by the lesser of 3% of the dependant s net income or the medical threshold. This threshold on medical expenses claimed for a dependent relative is $11,797 for 2014.

n The caregiver credit is available to taxpayers who care for a related dependant in their home. The dependant must be over the age of 18 and infirm, or, in the case of a parent or grandparent, over the age of 65.

A new family caregiver tax credit of up to $309 ($2,058 x 15%) is available for caregivers of dependants with a mental or physical infirmity, including spouses and minor children. If eligible, you can claim this credit as an enhancement to one of the existing dependency-related credits: the spousal credit (see note (g)), child tax credit (see note (h)), wholly dependent person credit (see note (h)), caregiver credit or infirm dependant credit (see note (h)).

Yukon also offers a family caregiver tax credit of up to $143 ($2,040 x 7.04%) for caregivers of dependants with a mental or physical infirmity.

o The federal employment credit may be claimed by individuals based on the lesser of the amount indicated in the table and the amount of employment income earned in the year.

Alberta offers a refundable family employment credit for Alberta residents with children under the age of 18 who meet the income eligibility criteria. The credit is paid out in January and July of each year.

p Self-employed taxpayers can deduct 50% of their Canada or Québec Pension Plan contributions in calculating net income. The balance is claimed as a non-refundable tax credit. Self-employed taxpayers can also claim Employment Insurance premiums paid.

q Individuals can claim a federal credit in respect of the cost of monthly transit passes (or passes of a longer duration) incurred for travel by the individual, their spouse or partner, or dependent children under age 19. The costs of certain electronic payment cards and certain weekly public transit passes may also be claimed.

Yukon also offers a transit pass credit for individuals who meet the federal eligibility requirements.

r The federal children's fitness credit is available for fees paid for the enrolment of a child, under the age of 16 at the beginning of the year, in which the expenses are paid for an eligible program of physical activity to a maximum of $500 per child. If the child is eligible for the disability tax credit, the age limit increases to under the age of 18 and the claimable amount may increase to $1,000 when a minimum of $100 is paid on eligible expenses.

British Columbia and Manitoba also have a fitness tax credit similar to the federal children's fitness credit. However, in Manitoba this credit includes claims for fitness activities by young adults up to the age of 24.

Nova Scotia offers a Healthy Living Tax Credit for sport and recreational expenses incurred for an eligible child under the age of 18 to a maximum of $500 per child.

Ontario offers a refundable credit (Children's Activity Tax Credit) of up to a maximum of $55 per child under the age of 16 for eligible activities as defined by the province. Ontario's refundable credit increases to a maximum of $108 if the child is under the age of 18 and is eligible for the disability tax credit. Overall expenses claimed in 2014 cannot exceed $540.

Saskatchewan offers the Active Families Benefit, which is a refundable credit (up to a maximum of $150) for eligible children aged 6 to 18 as defined by the province.

Yukon also offers a children's fitness credit, to a maximum of $500 per child, for Yukon residents who meet the federal eligibility requirements.

s   The federal government provides an arts tax credit for eligible amounts up to $500 per year per child. The credit is available for fees paid for the enrolment of a child under the age of 16 at the beginning of the year in an eligible program of artistic, cultural, recreational or developmental activities. If the child is eligible for the disability tax credit, the age limit increases to under the age of 18 and the credit may be claimed on an additional $500 when a minimum of $100 is paid on eligible expenses.

Manitoba provides a children's arts and cultural activity tax credit for eligible amounts up to $500 per year per child. The credit is available for fees paid for the enrolment of a child under 16 years old at the beginning of the year in an eligible program of organized and supervised arts and cultural activities. If the child is eligible for the disability tax credit and is under 18 years old at the beginning of the year, the credit may be claimed on an additional $500 disability supplement amount when a minimum of $100 is paid on eligible expenses.

British Columbia provides a children's arts credit of up to $500 (or $1,000 for an individual eligible for the disability tax credit). The non-refundable tax credit mirrors the federal qualifications.

Yukon also offers a children's arts credit, to a maximum of $500 per child ($1,000 for a child eligible for the disability tax credit), for Yukon residents who meet the federal eligibility requirements.

t   First-time home buyers who acquire a qualifying home during the year may be entitled to claim a federal non-refundable tax credit up to $5,000 and worth up to $750 ($5,000 x 15%).

To qualify, neither the individual nor his or her spouse or common-law partner can have owned and lived in another home in the calendar year of the new home purchase or in any of the four preceding calendar years. The credit can be claimed by either the purchaser or by his or her spouse or common-law partner.

The credit will also be available for certain home purchases by or for the benefit of an individual eligible for the disability tax credit.

Saskatchewan's First-Time Home Buyers Tax Credit provides a non-refundable income tax credit of up to $1,100 (11% x $10,000) to eligible taxpayers. There are also provisions to allow persons with a disability to qualify for the purchase of more accessible homes, with eligibility rules similar to those for the existing federal incentive for first-time home buyers. The credit generally applies to qualifying homes acquired after December 31, 2011.

u   Amounts paid for tuition and mandatory ancillary fees in respect of the calendar year are eligible for federal and provincial tax credits.

Students may also claim for federal purposes a monthly amount in respect of the cost of textbooks, which is added to the monthly education amount. The monthly textbook credit amount is $65 for full-time students and $20 for part-time students.

The tuition, education and textbook credits are transferable to a spouse or common-law partner, parent or grandparent. The maximum amount transferable is $5,000 (indexed in some provinces) less the excess of the student s net income over the basic personal credit amount. Any amounts not transferred may be carried forward indefinitely by the student.

Interest paid on student loans is also eligible for both a federal and provincial tax credit. The tax credit must be claimed by the student, and can be carried forward for five years.

v   Charitable donations made by both spouses/partners may be totalled and claimed by either person. The maximum amount of donations that may be claimed in a year is 75% of net income. However, all donations may be carried forward for five years if they are not claimed in the year made.

The 2013 federal budget proposed a new temporary charitable donor s super credit to supplement the existing donation tax credit. A first-time donor would be entitled to a one-time 40% federal credit for money donations of S200 or less, and a 54% federal credit for donations between $200 and $1000. An individual would be considered a first-time donor if neither the individual nor the individual's spouse or common-law partner had claimed the charitable donations tax credit or first-time donor's super credit in any taxation year after 2007. This credit may be claimed once in the first-time donor's 2013 to 2017 taxation years.

TABLE 3

QUEBEC TAX CREDIT RATES AND AMOUNTS FOR 2014

QUÉBEC NON-REFUNDABLE TAX CREDIT RATE AND AMOUNTS FOR 2014	

Tax rate applied to credits[a]	20.0%
Indexation factor[b]	.97%
Basic personal amount	$11,305
Amounts for dependants:	
Child under 18 engaged in full-time training or post-secondary studies[c]	2,085
Child over 17 who is a full-time student[d]	
Other dependants over 17[e]	3,035
Person living alone or with a dependant[f, g]	
Basic amount	1,325
Single-parent amount	1,640
Age 65 and over[f]	2,435
Experienced workers (age 65 and over)[h]	3,000
Pension (max)[f]	2,160
Disability	2,570
Union and professional dues[j]	
Tuition fees[j]	8%
Interest paid on student loans[k]	
Medical expenses[l]	
Charitable donations[m]	
Credit rate on first $200	20%
Credit rate on balance	24%

The Boomers Retire

Notes:

a   Québec's credit rate is applied to the dollar amounts shown in the table to determine the credit value. For example, the basic personal credit amount of $11,305 is multiplied by 20% to determine the credit value of $2,261.

     The unused portion of all non-refundable credits may be transferred from one spouse/partner to another, but only after all credits have been taken into account in the calculation of the individual s income tax otherwise payable.

b   Québec indexes its tax credits each year by using an inflation factor that is calculated based on the provincial rate of inflation, excluding changes in liquor and tobacco taxes. The Québec inflation factor is 0.97% for 2014.

c   This credit is available for a dependent child who is under the age of 18 and is engaged in full-time professional training or postsecondary studies for each completed term, to a maximum of two semesters per year per dependant. It is also available for infirm dependants who are engaged in such activities part-time. The amount claimed is reduced by 80% of the dependant s income for the year, calculated without including any scholarships, fellowships or awards received during the year.

d   An eligible student is able to transfer to either parent an amount relating to an unused portion of their basic personal credit amount for the year (transfer mechanism for the recognized parental contribution). Each taxation year, the amount that can be transferred must not exceed the limit applicable for that particular year ($7,450 for 2014).

e   This credit is available if the dependant, other than the spouse, is related to the taxpayer by blood, marriage or adoption and ordinarily lives with the taxpayer. In order to be eligible for the tax credit, the taxpayer must also not have benefited from a transfer of the recognized parental contribution from this dependant. The amount claimed must be reduced by 80% of the dependant s income, calculated without including any scholarships, fellowships or awards received during the year.

f   The amounts for a person living alone or with a dependant for being 65 years of age or over and for pension income are added together and reduced by 15% of net family income. Net family income is the total income of both spouses/partners minus $32,795.

g   This credit is available if the individual lives in a self-contained domestic establishment that he maintains and in which no other person, other than himself, a minor person, or an eligible student lives. If the individual is living with an eligible student, for the purposes of the transfer mechanism for the recognized parental contribution (see note (d)), the individual may be able to add an amount for a singleparent family of $1,640 to the basic amount for a person living alone.

h   This tax credit became available in 2012 for workers who are 65 years of age or older. It applies to the portion of eligible work income in excess of $5,000. It is proposed that the eligible portion be $3,000. Any unused portion of the tax credit may not be carried forward or transferred to the individual's spouse.

     Eligible work income includes salary and business income, but excludes taxable benefits received for a previous employment as well as amounts deducted in computing taxable income, such as the stock option deduction.

i   The credit for union and professional dues is calculated based on the annual fees paid in the year. The portion of professional dues relating to liability insurance is allowed as a deduction from income and therefore not included in calculating the credit amount.

j   The tuition credit is calculated based on tuition, professional examination and mandatory ancillary fees paid for the calendar year. Québec announced in Information Bulletin 2013-3 that the province would decrease the tuition tax credit from 20% to 8%. The 20% rate applicable to such fees would be set at 8% following the winter 2013 session. The student may transfer the unused portion of the tuition credit to either one of his parents or grandparents. The portion of this credit that is not transferred will be available for future use by the student.

k   Interest paid on student loans is converted into a tax credit at a 20% rate. Interest not claimed in a particular year may be carried forward indefinitely.

l   The medical expense credit is calculated based on qualified medical expenses in excess of 3% of family income. Family income is the total income of both spouses/partners.

m   Charitable donations made by both spouses/partners may be totalled and claimed by either person. The maximum amount of donations that may be claimed in a year is 75% of net income. However, all donations may be carried forward for five years if they are not claimed in the year made.

QUÉBEC REFUNDABLE TAX CREDIT RATE AND AMOUNTS FOR 2014[a]

NOTE: © 2014 KPMG LLP, a Canadian limited liability partnership and a member firm of the KPMG network of independent member firms affiliated with KPMG International Cooperative ("KPMG International"), a Swiss entity. All rights reserved. Current to December 31, 2013. Reproduced by permission.

	Tax Rate	Maximum expense	Maximum credit
Medical expenses[b]	25%	certain eligible medical expenses	$1,141
Reduced by 5% of family income in excess of $22,080[c]			
Child care expense credit[d]	from 26 to 75%		
The lesser of the expenses incurred or:			
For a child who has a severe or prolonged mental or physical impairment		$10,000	
For a child under the age of seven		9,000	
For a child under the age of seventeen		4,000	
Adoption expense credit[e]	50%	20,000	10,000
Infertility treatment credit	50%	20,000	10,000
Informal caregivers of related adults[f]			
Basic amount			628[c]
Supplement			514[c]
Reduced by 16% of the eligible relative's income over $22,880[c]			
Respite of caregivers[g]	30%	5,200	1,560
Reduced by 3% of the caregiver's family income in excess of $55,320[b]			
Home support of elderly persons living alone[h]			
Not recognized as dependant seniors	32%	19,500	6,240
Recognized as dependant seniors	32%	25,500	8,160
Reduced by 3% of the individual's family income in excess of $55,320[c]			

The Boomers Retire

	Tax Rate	Maximum expense	Maximum credit
Short-term transition of seniors in rehabilitation centre	20%	costs incurred in maximum 60-day period	
Safety equipment for seniors	20%	costs incurred in excess of $500	
Youth activities	20%	$100	20
Écoreénov	20%	costs incurred in excess of $2,500 up to a maximum of 50,000	10,000

Notes:

a   Québec's credit rate, maximum expense eligible and method of calculation of the credit varies from one type of refundable credit to another. Québec's credit rate is applied to the dollar amounts in the table to determine the maximum credit value. For example, the adoption expense credit amount of $20,000 is multiplied by 50% to determine the maximum credit value of $10,000. Some refundable credits are reduced when thresholds are exceeded.

b   Québec provides a refundable tax credit equal to the total of 25% of medical expenses eligible for the non-refundable credit (see table I-7) and 25% of the amount deducted for impairment support products and services.

c   Québec indexes various tax credits each year by using an inflation factor that is calculated based on the provincial rate of inflation, excluding changes in liquor and tobacco taxes. The Québec inflation factor is 0.97% for 2014.

d   Unlike the federal treatment of qualifying child care expenses, which are eligible for a deduction in computing net income, Québec provides a refundable tax credit for such expenses. The rate of credit falls as net family income rises.

In general, the maximum amount of expenses eligible for credit is the lesser of:

- $10,000 for a child of any age who has a severe or prolonged mental or physical impairment, plus $9,000 for a child under the age of seven, plus $4,000 for a child under the age of 17, or
- the actual child care expenses incurred in the year.

The definition of eligible expenses includes costs incurred during the period an individual receives benefits under the Québec Parental Insurance Plan or the Employment Insurance Plan (see table I-16). The child care expenses are not limited by the earned income of the parent.

e   Qualifying expenses include court and legal fees paid to obtain the final adoption order, travel and accommodation expenses for foreign adoptions, translation expenses, and fees charged by foreign and domestic social agencies.

f   There are three components to this credit. The first component applies to caregivers who house an eligible relative in their home where the relative is 70 years of age or older or is an adult with a severe and prolonged mental or physical impairment.

Tax Planning Tips and Strategies

The second component applies to informal caregivers who live in an eligible relative's home and a physician has attested that the relative is unable to live alone due to a severe and prolonged mental or physical impairment. Finally, the third component applies to caregivers whose spouse is aged 70 years of age or older, or has a severe and prolonged mental or physical impairment, and the couple lives in their own home other than in a seniors' residence.

Note that caregivers caring for an elderly spouse are not entitled to the supplement amount, although the amount of the credit increased to $850 for 2014 in such cases.

For the purposes of this credit, an eligible relative is a child, grandchild, nephew, niece, brother, sister, uncle, aunt, great-uncle, great- aunt or any other direct ascendant of the individual or the individual's spouse.

g   Caregivers can also claim a refundable tax credit for respite services. Qualifying expenses include specialized respite services respecting the care and supervision of an eligible person. If the expense has been used in calculating another refundable or non-refundable credit, it cannot be claimed for this credit as well.

h   The home support tax credit can be claimed by persons age 70 and over living in their home. As of 2013, for seniors not recognized as dependant, and when this credit is determined in respect of a couple as soon as one of the members of the couple is recognized as dependant, no reduction based on family income applies. If the expense also qualifies for the non-refundable medical expense credit (see table I-7), it cannot be claimed for this credit as well.

i   The rehabilitation centre tax credit can by claimed by seniors age 70 or older in respect of costs incurred for the first 60 days of any given stay in a public or private "functional rehabilitation transition unit". There is no limit to the number of stays that can be claimed.

j   The safety equipment tax credit can by claimed by seniors age 70 or older for the purchase or rental of equipment used to improve their safety and security in their principal residence. The refundable tax credit is 20% of the amounts in excess of $500 paid for the purchase or rental of such equipment (including installation costs). Examples of qualifying equipment include remote monitoring systems, GPS tracking devices for persons, and walk-in bathtubs or showers.

k   The 2013 Québec budget (delivered on November 20, 2012) proposed a new refundable tax credit for certain expenses incurred to foster development of a child's aptitude and skills. The credit can be claimed by either spouse provided that the combined family income for 2014 does not exceed $131,260. The 2014 annual limit on eligible expenses for youth activities is $200 per child aged 5 to 15 years old at the beginning of the year. This annual limit will increase by $100 each year to $500 by 2017. If a child has a severe or prolonged impairment in mental or physical functions, the age limit is extended to 17 years old at the beginning of the year and the expenditure limit is doubled. Eligible expenses are for physical, cultural and artistic activities and mirror those of the federal children's fitness and arts nonrefundable tax credit (see table I-4).

l   Québec announced in Information Bulletin 2013-10 a new temporary refundable tax credit for green renovation. The EcoRenov Québec refundable credit will be generally available to individuals who have incurred green renovation expenditures to their residence after October 7, 2013 and before November 1, 2014. The refundable tax credit is 20% of eligible expenditures in excess of $2,500 for recognized work to a maximum credit of $10,000. The maximum credit can be claimed in 2013 and/or 2014.

TABLE 4

TAX TREATY WITHHOLDING RATES FOR NON-RESIDENTS

Current to January 1, 2014

Treaty Country	Interest[3]	Dividends[4]	Royalties	Pensions/ Annuities
Algeria	15	15	0/15	15/25
Argentina	12.5	10/15	3/5/10/15	15/25
Armenia	10	5/15	10	15/25
Australia[1]	10	5/15	10	15/25
Austria	10	5/15	0/10	25
Azerbaijan	10	10/15	5/10	25
Bangladesh	15	15	10	15/25
Barbados	15	15	0/10	15/25
Belgium	10	5/15	0/10	25
Bolivia	25% imposed under ITA			
Brazil	15	15/25	15/25	25
Bulgaria[5]	10	10/15	0/10	10/15/25
Cameroon	15	15	15	25
Chile[5]	15	10/15	15	15/25
China[1]	10	10/15	10	25

Tax Planning Tips and Strategies

NON-RESIDENT WITHHOLDING TAX RATES FOR TREATY COUNTRIES[a]				
Treaty Country	Interest[3]	Dividends[4]	Royalties	Pensions/ Annuities
Colombia[5]	10	5/15	10	15/25
Costa Rica	25% imposed under ITA			
Croatia	10	5/15	10	10/15
Cuba	25% imposed under ITA			
Cyprus	15	15	0/10	15/25
Czech Republic	10	5/15	10	15/25
Denmark	10	5/15	0/10	25
Dominican Republic	18	18	0/18	18/25
Ecuador[5]	15	5/15	10/15	15/25
Egypt	15	15	15	25
Estonia[5]	10	5/15	10	10/15/25
Finland	10	5/15	0/10	15/20/25
France[7]	10	5/15	0/10	25
Gabon	10	15	10	25
Germany	10	5/15	0/10	15/25
Greece	10	5/15	10	15/25
Guyana	15	15	10	25
Hong Kong	0/10	5/15	10	25
Hungary	10	5/15	0/10	10/15/25
Iceland	10	5/15	0/10	15/25
India	15	15/25	10/15/20	25
Indonesia	10	10/15	10	15/25
Ireland	10	5/15	0/10	0/15/25
Israel[1]	15	15	0/15	15/25
Italy	10	5/15	0/5/10	15/25
Ivory Coast	15	15	10	15/25
Jamaica	15	15	10	15/25
Japan	10	5/15	10	25
Jordan	10	10/15	10	25
Kazakhstan[5]	10	5/15	10	15/25
Kenya	15	15/25	15	15/25
Korea, Republic of	10	5/15	10	10/15/25
Kuwait	10	5/15	10	15/25
Kyrgyzstan	15	15	0/10	15/25
Latvia[5]	10	5/15	10	10/15/25
Lebanon[6]	[10]	[5/15]	[5/10]	[15/25]
Lithuania[5]	10	5/15	10	10/15/25
Luxembourg	10	5/15	0/10	25

NON-RESIDENT WITHHOLDING TAX RATES FOR TREATY COUNTRIES[a]			
Treaty Country	Interest[3]	Dividends[4]	Royalties	Pensions/ Annuities
Madagascar[1]	25% imposed under ITA		
Malaysia[1]	15	15	15	15/25
Malta	15	15	0/10	15/25
Mexico	10	5/15	0/10	15/25
Moldova	10	5/15	10	15/25
Mongolia	10	5/15	5/10	15/25
Morocco	15	15	5/10	25
Namibia[6]	[10]	[5/15]	[0/10]	[0/15]
Netherlands[1]	10	5/15	0/10	15/25
New Zealand[7]	15[10]	[5]/15	15 [5/10]	15/25
Nigeria	12.5	12.5/15	12.5	25
Norway	10	5/15	0/10	15/25
Oman	10	5/15	0/10	15/25
Pakistan	15	15	0/15	25
Papua New Guinea	10	15	10	15/25
Peru[5]	15	10/15	15	15/25
Philippines	15	15	10	25
Poland	10	5/15	0/5/10	15/25
Portugal	10	10/15	10	15/25
Romania	10	5/15	5/10	15/25
Russian Federation	10	10/15	0/10	25
Senegal	15	15	15	15/25
Serbia	10	5/15	10	15/25
Singapore	15	15	15	25
Slovak Republic	10	5/15	0/10	15/25
Slovenia	10	5/15	10	15/25
South Africa	10	5/15	6/10	25
Spain[1]	15	15	0/10	15/25
Sri Lanka	15	15	0/10	15/25
Sweden	10	5/15	0/10	25
Switzerland	10	5/15	0/10	15/25
Tanzania	15	20/25	20	15/25
Thailand	15	15	5/15	25
Trinidad & Tobago	10	5/15	0/10	15/25
Tunisia	15	15	0/15/20	25
Turkey	15	15/20	10	15/25
Ukraine	10	5/15	0/10	25
United Arab Emirates	10	5/15	0/10	25

Tax Planning Tips and Strategies

NON-RESIDENT WITHHOLDING TAX RATES FOR TREATY COUNTRIES[a]				
Treaty Country	Interest[3]	Dividends[4]	Royalties	Pensions/ Annuities
United Kingdom[1]	10	5/15	0/10	0/10/25
United States	0[2]	5/15	0/10	15/25
Uzbekistan	10	5/15	5/10	25
Venezuela[5]	10	10/15	5/10	25
Vietnam	10	5/10/15	7.5/10	15/25
Zambia	15	15	15	15/25
Zimbabwe	15	10/15	10	15/25

Notes:

The rates in the table apply to payments made by a resident of Canada to a person resident in the particular treaty country. The particular treaty should be consulted to determine if specific conditions, exemptions, etc. apply. For current information regarding the status and development of treaties, visit the Department of Finance website at www.fin.gc.ca/treaties-conventions/treatystatus_-eng.asp.

1   Under negotiation/re-negotiation.

2   Canada and the U.S. signed the Fifth Protocol to the treaty on September 21, 2007. The Fifth Protocol entered into force on December 15, 2008, and its provisions will have effect according to the rules specified in Article 27 of the Protocol. Generally, withholding tax on interest paid or credited on non-participating debt is eliminated as follows: where paid or credited to an unrelated person, the rate is nil after December 31, 2007, and where paid or credited to a related person, the rate is 7% in 2008, 4% in 2009, and nil after 2009.

3   Part XIII of the *Income Tax Act* (Canada) was amended to eliminate withholding tax on interest paid or credited to an arm's length nonresident on non-participating debt effective January 1, 2008.

4   The lower rate of withholding tax on dividends generally applies where the beneficial owner of the dividend owns a certain percentage of voting stock or voting power of the company paying the dividend.

5   The treaty currently in effect with these countries includes a Most Favoured Nation clause, which provides for reduced withholding rates if the other country signs a treaty with another OECD member country and that treaty includes a lower withholding rate. This clause allows the lower rate to apply to the Canadian treaty. The items of income to which the clause applies vary by treaty. The lower withholding rate in the other country's treaty will apply to Canada if that treaty is signed after the date that Canada's treaty with the particular country is signed.

6   A new treaty is signed but not yet ratified. Until ratification, the withholding tax rate is generally 25%. Rates that will apply once the treaty is ratified are indicated in square brackets.

7   A protocol or replacement treaty is signed but not yet ratified. Until ratification, the withholding tax rates are the rates specified in the existing treaty. New rates (if any) are indicated in square brackets.

Treaties signed but not yet in force: France, Lebanon, Namibia, and New Zealand.

Treaties under Negotiation/Re-negotiation: Australia, China (PRC), Israel, Madagascar, Malaysia, Netherlands, Spain and the United Kingdom.

199

Chapter 7: Where to Live

The choice of where to live in retirement is perhaps one of the most daunting decisions many retirees have to make. When your home location is no longer dictated by the demands of a job, you can live anywhere you want, at least in theory. In practice, there are many issues that must be taken into consideration.

This chapter will address these issues under three major headings. The first area, Staying Put, deals with the pros and cons of clients remaining in their current home, and discusses how to find the supports they may need, either now or in the future, to make staying put a feasible alternative.

Decisions around moving to another home can be grouped into two categories. The second part of this chapter, Moving to a Different Property, discusses the types of properties that are available for consideration, including condominiums, rental apartments, life lease facilities, retirement homes, and long-term care facilities. The third part of this chapter, Choosing a Location, addresses issues related to location of the property: moving to the cottage or a country property, living in a seniors' community, becoming a snowbird, and relocating permanently outside of Canada.

Staying Put

Many retirees are most comfortable staying in the homes they've lived in for the past several years. After all, moving is a lot of work, and unless there is a clear-cut reason to do so, it seems like unnecessary work. Besides, retirement itself is a major life change, so why complicate things by taking on another stressful change at the same time?

While this argument has a lot of merit, it must be remembered that the task of moving doesn't get any easier as one gets older. It's important for clients to keep monitoring the situation and avoid delaying a move until it becomes next to impossible.

Getting Help at Home

Clients who stay in their own homes in the early years of retirement experience many advantages. Being in a familiar setting means that they know their neighbours, they're familiar with local facilities and resources, and they've likely maintained or improved their homes to create the environment they want. However, with the aging process, they may find that, over the years, they need to arrange for additional support in order to be able to continue to live independently in that same home.

There are many services that have become available in recent years to support independent living, and with the growth of the senior population, more will come on stream in the years to come. Here are some areas to explore:

- Grocery delivery. Services range from small local shops to on-line services that cover a large metropolitan area, such as Grocery Gateway (www.grocerygateway.com) in the Greater Toronto Area.

- Delivery of prescription drugs. Again, many drug stores will provide this service on an individual basis, or clients can take advantage of on-line services such as Rexall Direct (formerly Meditrust), a national mail-order pharmacy that provides home delivery of prescriptions at no charge (www.rexalldirect.ca).

- Housecleaning. Many different individuals and agencies offer cleaning and housekeeping services on a regular or as-needed basis.

- Outdoor maintenance. Services range from eavestrough cleaning and window washing to snow shovelling, lawn and garden cleanup, regular lawn mowing, and weeding.

The services listed above are provided by competitive businesses, and, as such, they are relatively easy to locate. Unfortunately, this is not the case with more personal caregiving services, where some degree of funding may be provided through various levels of government. Figuring out what is available, and how to access the services, can be time-consuming and frustrating at best.

One place to start looking is the benefits plan the client may have through a former employer. If the employer offered an employee assistance program (EAP), there's a chance that this program continues to be available to retirees. EAP counsellors may be able to provide information and referrals to appropriate elder care services.

All provinces and territories provide an access point to home care support services, although not all services are provided free of charge. In Ontario, for example, the Community Care Access Centre (CCAC) is the point of contact for home care services such as nursing, personal support, physiotherapy, occupational therapy, speech and language therapy, and medical supplies and equipment.

Ease of access varies greatly from one jurisdiction to another. Table 1 at the end of this chapter, Contact Points for Home Care Support, lists the most up-to-date contact information at the time of writing, and should be used as a starting point for tracking down further information.

Similarly, the types of services provided can vary significantly between jurisdictions. In some areas, certain services may be provided free of charge, where in others, users pay at least a portion of the cost. Charges may or may not be geared to income. For those who can afford it, paying for services privately can mean bypassing lengthy waiting lists.

In all cases, however, these government contact points are a useful first step to finding out what is available in the local community.

Making the Home Accessible

One of the other challenges for clients remaining at home is ensuring that the physical environment continues to be appropriate to their needs as they age. Canada Mortgage and Housing Corporation (www.cmhc.ca) has an excellent checklist available to help clients evaluate the types of changes they might need to make, including the following:

- Widen the walkway to the house and install or repair handrails along the walkway

- Install motion detector lights outside the house

- Install lever-type door handles on exterior and interior doors

- Install two-way light switches at the top and bottom of interior stairwells

- Install or repair handrails on both sides of stairwells

- Install D-type handles on closets, kitchen cupboards, and drawers

- Install faucets with single levers in kitchen and bathrooms

- Add pullout storage units under kitchen counters

- Install pivoting or revolving shelves in corner cupboards

- Consider a shower stall separate from the bathtub

- Use grab bars and non-slip surfaces in the bath-rooms

- Install toilets with "comfort-height" seats

See Table 2 at the end of this chapter for a more complete list of suggestions reprinted with the kind permission of CMHC.

Once again, some governments may provide financial support to homeowners who need to make these types of improvements in order to remain in their homes. Although most financial support is targeted towards lower income families, both British Columbia and Ontario have introduced refundable tax credit programs that are available to seniors at all income levels.

The two provincial programs are similar in intent. In British Columbia, the BC Seniors' Home Renovation Tax Credit is calculated as 10% of eligible expenses, up to a maximum credit of $1,000 per year. In Ontario, the Ontario Healthy Homes Renovation Tax Credit is based on 15% of eligible expenses, up to a maximum credit of $1,500 per year. These credits are available to taxpayers who have reached the age of 65 by the end of the tax year and to qualifying relatives who live with them. The credit can be shared among the residents of the home, but the maximum amount applies per residence, not per individual taxpayer. The examples above from the CMHC checklist would all be considered eligible; however, both provinces offer detailed lists of eligible and ineligible expenses on their websites.

Moving to a Different Property

Condominiums

Condo ownership is becoming increasingly popular across Canada, not just with retirees, but with many age groups. However, the lifestyle it offers seems in some respects to be ideally suited to the retiree population. There are no worries about shovelling snow or mowing the lawn, and clients are less concerned about the security of their home while they're travelling. However, for seniors who may be relocating to a condo from a self-contained family home, there are important considerations to keep in mind.

Ownership of a condo includes the unit itself, as well as an undivided interest in the common elements of the building, such as lobbies, recreational facilities, and gardens. It is important to understand how the unit is defined, and where its boundaries end. For example, areas such as balconies, parking spaces and lawn areas adjacent to the unit are often considered to be "exclusive use common property elements". While they are designed for the exclusive use of the unit holder, they are considered part of the common elements of the building. As such, there may be restrictions on their use. For example, some condos will not allow unit holders to park an RV in their parking spot. Others may not allow bird feeders in front and back yards because of the additional maintenance involved.

Similarly, condo owners may not be able to paint their outside trim a different colour or change exterior light fixtures, as these details are determined and taken care of by the condominium corporation.

Even within individual units, condo owners will be subject to rules and regulations that may seem onerous to those who are used to setting their own agenda. Pets may or may not be allowed, and there may be restrictions concerning noise levels at certain times of day.

Many of the day-to-day decisions that must be made about maintenance and repairs, or the functioning of the building as a whole, are often handled by a committee of unit owners, especially in smaller buildings. While some residents may welcome the opportunity to be involved in committee work, others have no interest in spending their time this way. Nevertheless, in a condo, owners must choose between getting involved or living with the decisions made by others.

Most condos, particularly newer apartment-style and townhouse buildings, will be smaller than the fully detached family home many clients may be leaving. Decisions will have to be made about the furniture and appliances that will make the move, and those that will be given away. This process can be an emotionally charged one for clients who have a strong attachment to family heirlooms. On the other hand, some people look at this as a great opportunity to start over, with new furniture and a new decorating scheme to suit their new, freer lifestyle.

In general, it's important for prospective owners to ensure that the prevailing lifestyle in the condo development suits their own. Some complexes are marketed to seniors, although they may not be restricted to owners over a certain age. Others may be geared to families with young children, or young couples starting out.

Another issue to consider is whether the building is occupied primarily by owners or tenants. Some people feel that, where the units are mainly owner-occupied, there is more pride of ownership and a more stable feeling to the building. A high proportion of tenants can mean a higher turnover of neighbours and less chance to get to know those who live nearby.

Monthly condo fees are intended to cover the unit owner's share of the operating expenses of the common property elements, including an amount set aside in a reserve fund to cover major repairs that may be needed throughout the life of the building. Prospective owners should get a statement from the condominium corporation that clearly outlines the operating budget for the development, and specifies the expenses that are included as part of the fee. However, sometimes unexpected events occur, resulting in the immediate need for major repairs. If there is not enough money in the reserve fund to cover the work, the condo corporation may levy a special assessment charge in order to raise the funds. Canada Mortgage and Housing Corporation (CMHC) advises prospective owners to "review the financial statements, reserve fund level, building condition surveys, inspection reports, maintenance history and the estoppel or status certificate for the corporation"[1] before making a commitment to buy.

Table 3 at the end of this chapter presents a condominium selection checklist provided by CMHC.

Rental Apartments

While younger clients are often advised to buy a home in order to build up equity and invest for the future, for the retiree, the future is now. Selling a principal residence, investing the tax-free proceeds, and using a portion of the income to cover rent payments has many advantages for the older client. Rental accommodation can provide a care-free lifestyle, without the shared ownership drawbacks of a condominium. All maintenance concerns, even many of those related to the individual unit, are taken care of by building management.

If needs change, it is a relatively easy and inexpensive matter to move to a new location, compared to selling a property.

In evaluating the financial aspects of selling an existing home and moving to rental accommodation, the advisor should consider the capital that will be freed up by the sale of the home, and calculate the expected after-tax return on investment. This amount, plus the amount saved by eliminating or reducing household expenses such as property tax, home insurance, and maintenance costs, represents

---

[1] Canada Mortgage and Housing Corporation. Condominium Buyers' Guide. 2002.

the amount that can be devoted to rent without using any other resources.

For example, Molly and John expect to net $760,000 on the sale of their home, after real estate commissions, legal fees, and moving expenses. Using an estimated four per-cent rate of return, their investment capital produces an annual income of $30,400. Assuming this income is taxed at 33 percent, they will be left with $20,368 after tax. But, by leaving their home, let's assume that they are also saving an estimated $15,000 per year on property tax, home in-surance, maintenance, and utilities. This gives them $35,368 that can be applied toward their rent budget. If they are able to rent suitable accommodation for less than this amount, or if their investments produce a higher rate of return, they will be financially better off by renting rather than continuing to stay in their home.

However, the decision to give up home ownership in favour of rental accommodation is not to be taken lightly. Rental units need to be selected carefully to ensure there is a good management team in place that will keep the building properly cared for and will be responsive to tenant concerns.

Life Lease Facilities

A relatively new entry on the retirement living scene, life lease developments offer the opportunity for older people (usually 55-plus) to purchase the right to occupy a particular apartment or suite in a building designed for and limited to older adults. Often developed in conjunction with non-profit organizations, life lease developments share some similar-ities with condos as well as adult lifestyle communities. But there are important differences as well.

Many adult lifestyle communities are designed strictly for the younger, active retiree, featuring proximity to golf courses and country clubs. Life lease developments, on the other hand, are often located close to assisted living centres or retirement homes to allow for a continuum of care as the retiree "ages in place". The leasehold form of ownership also means a lower purchase price than many adult lifestyle communities, making it more attractive to the middle-income retiree. Despite the term "lease", these properties are acquired through a one-time purchase payment.

Some active seniors have moved into condos to take advantage of the freedom from outdoor maintenance they offer. But it's not a perfect solution. Even in buildings that are populated mainly by older people, there's no guarantee that a noisy family with a crying baby won't move in next door. While in most areas, condos can't legally restrict ownership to a particular age group, life lease developments don't have this problem. They can set their own membership criteria, which can include being older than a specified age, already living within the community, or being a member of a particular organization. Similar to condo living, life lease developments charge a monthly fee to cover the common elements and amenities provided.

When the life lease occupant moves out or dies, the tenancy generally reverts back to the sponsoring organization. The occupants or their heirs receive the amount redeemable at the end of the lease. The sponsor then resells the rights to the unit to another individual or couple meeting the age requirements. As described above, many non-profit life lease sponsors give preference to those who meet specific criteria.

There are many options available for determining the pricing of life lease units and the redemption value at the end of the lease. In general, for-profit developments charge close to the full market value for the unit, and the redemption value reflects the market value at the termination of the lease. Not-for-profit developments may provide their units at a lower price, but limit the redemption value to a lower level as well.

In general, life lease developments appeal to purchasers who are looking for a level of building quality similar to condo developments. They want the upgrades and features, and they don't want to be renting at this stage of their lives. They also like the fact that meals, medical care, home care, and housekeeping services can be made available as optional extras when the time comes.

In certain jurisdictions, it's not possible for a prospective buyer to obtain a mortgage to finance the purchase of a life lease unit because of the unique ownership structure. This factor makes a life lease property more suitable for someone who is selling the family home or cottage, or who has other sources of investment capital available.

Clients must realize that life lease developments vary widely in the services they provide. Because they are often developed by a community group, the properties offer the services that community members want. In some situations, meals, housekeeping and medical care are not provided, because the residents don't need or want this level of support. In some cases, a life lease arrangement can be terminated if the resident can't continue to live independently and requires more services than the development provides. In other situations, projects provide a continuum of care that allows for aging in place.

Retirement Homes

Many people confuse retirement homes with nursing homes, but they are targeted towards very different populations. Retirement homes are privately operated facilities that cater to active seniors who do not require day-to-day care, but are looking for an easier, maintenance-free lifestyle. Designed for those who want to enjoy life and let someone else take care of the cooking and housekeeping, top-end retirement home living closely resembles life in a luxury hotel, with the addition of on-site nursing care if needed.

Nursing homes, on the other hand, are licensed and regulated by provincial/territorial ministries of health, and provide accommodation and nursing care for those who are no longer able to live independently.

Retirement homes are considered to be a form of rental accommodation and, as such, fall under tenant protection legislation. There is wide variation in monthly fees across Canada, depending on factors such as location, size of rental unit, and the type of amenities included. The monthly fees, which can range from $2,000 to $7,000, typically include accommodation, meals, light housekeeping, and use of the building facilities. Extra charges are usually assessed for services such as hairdressing, massage, and health care or nursing. Some facilities do have special units for residents whose health has deteriorated to the point where ongoing care is required.

At present, retirement homes are not subject to government regulation in most provinces. However, a more proactive approach has been taken in Ontario, where the government created the Retirement Homes Regulatory Authority (RHRA) in 2012. Created under the *Retirement Homes Act 2010*, the RHRA is responsible for licensing and inspecting retirement homes in that province. Ontario and British Columbia have voluntary associations of retirement homes that set standards for their members. Contact the British Columbia Seniors Living Association (www.bcsla.ca) and the Ontario Retirement Communities Association (www.orcaretirement.com) for further information. A comprehensive list of retirement homes in all provinces across Canada (but not the territories) is published by The Care Guide and is available at www.thecareguide.com.

See Table 4 at the end of this chapter for a checklist of points to consider when evaluating retirement homes.

Long-Term Care Facilities

The term "long-term care facilities" encompasses both nursing homes and homes for the aged, both of which offer more care than can be provided through the other options discussed in this chapter. Long-term care facilities are licensed, regulated and funded through provincial governments, under the applicable Ministry of Health. A list of contact points for exploring and applying for long-term care is included under Table 5 at the end of this chapter.

Advisors and clients alike should be aware that most long-term care facilities have lengthy waiting lists, up to three years in some cases. Keep this in mind when making the decision to begin the application process.

Choosing a Location

Moving to the Cottage or a Country Property

Many retirees plan a permanent move to the cottage on retirement, while some consider the option of buying a property in a small town or rural location. Before making the decision to relocate permanently, clients should be advised test it out for a month or two at the least desirable time of year – maybe November. Many people don't consider the fact that the services and activities of summer often don't continue all year in cottage country. Clients should investigate what's available in other seasons, including shops, restaurants, theatre, movies, concerts, and fitness programs.

Access to medical care is another important issue for most retirees. Many smaller communities have limited medical services available, and local doctors may not be accepting new patients. There may be a hospital nearby, but specialized medical services such as cardiac care are usually available only in larger cities.

Most city dwellers have lots of options available for getting around town, including driving, taking public transit or taxis, or calling on the many services that deliver virtually anything right to the front door – groceries, prescription drugs, and dry cleaning. For those who live in the country, getting in the car and driving may be the only option – clients need to consider how they will feel about doing this on a regular basis on snowy roads that may or may not be ploughed regularly.

Living in a Seniors-only Community

There are many communities across Canada that are targeted specifically to those over 50 or 55. While the accommodations are usually designed as single-family dwellings (often bungalows), apartment and townhouse units may be available as well. In addition, there are often recreational facilities such as golf and tennis courts, swimming pools, and recreation centres situated within the complex. Some developments are in rural areas, with proximity to ski trails or water sports, while others are in suburban or small town locations.

Many of the issues discussed in the section above on moving to the cottage or a country property are pertinent for those considering a seniors-only community, since few of these communities are located in large urban centres, at least in Canada. In addition, the seniors-only community offers its own challenges and advantages.

On the plus side, many people find they enjoy the camaraderie and the opportunity to make new friends through shared interests and activities. However, others find that the lifestyle can be somewhat isolated from the local community at large. In some developments, there is a tendency for residents to keep to themselves rather than getting involved in activities that are based in the broader community.

Clients should be encouraged to consider this aspect before making a move.

Becoming a Snowbird

For many years, Canadians have dreamed of spending the winter in Florida or Arizona to escape the snow and blustery weather. More recently, popular snowbird destinations have expanded to include Mexico, Costa Rica, and Portugal. Like anything else, spending the winter in another, warmer location has its pros and cons.

Anyone contemplating such a move would be well advised to try it out first by renting before taking the plunge to buy property. Although, in the depths of winter, it can be hard to imagine the downside of living down south for several months, drawbacks do exist, and are sometimes discovered only through personal experience.

Clients should be advised to take the time necessary to do the research and develop a realistic budget for a second home. Who will look after the property when the client isn't there? It may be necessary to hire a property manager to keep an eye on things. Insurance coverage for an unoccupied property can be an issue, and costs have escalated dramatically in some areas (Sanibel and Captiva Islands in Florida, for example) following the hurricanes of recent years. Don't forget to factor in the possible cost of travel back and forth for holidays or special events over the winter months, and regular communications for keeping in touch with family and friends.

Health care outside of Canada is always a concern. While the provinces and territories continue their medical coverage to a certain extent, clients and advisors need to be aware that this coverage is very limited. The coverage provided is based on the cost that would be incurred in the client's home jurisdiction. For example, the Ontario Health

Insurance Plan (OHIP) reimburses up to $50 per day for an outpatient visit to a hospital emergency room. In the U.S., such a visit could cost hundreds, or even thousands, of dollars, depending on the severity of the situation. Travellers are always advised to purchase additional medical coverage whenever they leave the country, even for one day.

It's also important to realize that each ministry or department of health has its own rules about how long travellers can be outside of the country and still maintain coverage. See Table 6 at the end of this chapter for a summary of this information, and Table 7 for contact information.

Additional travel medical coverage can be purchased on a per-trip or year-round basis. In some cases, it might be included as one of the benefits of a premium credit card, or it could be provided by retiree medical coverage from a former employer. But all coverage isn't the same. Read the fine print and pay particular attention to the dollar limit of coverage provided by the policy. Many group policies, such as those offered by employers, cap out at $100,000 per incident. While this may be enough to handle some medical emergencies, be aware that insurers have paid single claims in the $300,000 to $500,000 range.

Another major feature to consider is whether the insurance provider arranges and pays for medical care up front, or expects the traveller to cover his or her own expenses and claim for reimbursement later. Most people would prefer to have the insurance provider take on the responsibility of locating the most appropriate services in a time of crisis.

See Chapter 8, Insurance Concerns, for more information about travel medical insurance.

Income Tax Issues

It is beyond the scope of this book to provide detailed information about tax issues affecting those who leave Canada, either on a temporary or permanent basis. What this section is intended to do is to make advisors and clients aware of the issues that need to be taken into consideration when a move is planned. The bibliography at the end of this book lists publications that provide more in-depth coverage of this area.

Since the U.S. is the most common destination for snowbirds, we will provide an overview of the tax issues that should be considered when a client decides to spend part of the year down south.

First is the possibility of having to file a tax return in the U.S. If your client is a Canadian resident who spends part of the year in the U.S., the Internal Revenue Service (IRS) considers him or her to be either a resident alien or a non-resident alien for tax purposes. Resident aliens are subject to U.S. tax on income from all sources throughout the world, whereas non-resident aliens are generally taxed only on income from U.S. sources.

There are two tests that can be used to determine the camp into which a snowbird falls – the lawful permanent resident test and the substantial presence test. Under the lawful permanent resident test, if your clients hold green cards, they are considered to be U.S. residents for tax purposes.

Under the substantial presence test, a formula is applied to calculate the number of days spent in the U.S. over a three-year period. The formula works as follows: number of days present in the U.S. during the current year, plus one-third of the number of days present in the U.S. in the immediately preceding year, plus one-sixth of the number of days present in the U.S. in the second preceding year. If the total is 183 days or more, and the client is present for at least 31 days in the current year, he or she is considered a resident alien. In general, if a client has spent at least four months per year in the U.S. over the past three years, he or she will normally meet the substantial presence test.

Even if a client meets the substantial presence test, it is possible to avoid being deemed a U.S. resident through the closer connection exception. This applies to those who meet the following requirements:

- They have spent less than 183 days in the U.S. in the current year and have neither applied for nor received permanent resident status (a green card).

- They own or rent a home in Canada that is available to them continuously throughout the year.

- They can demonstrate a closer connection to Canada than to the U.S., as evidenced by factors such as the location of their primary bank, investment accounts, other family members, and the jurisdiction where they vote and hold a driver's licence.

In order to claim the closer connection exception, *IRS Form 8840 – Closer Connection Exception Statement for Aliens* must be filed with the IRS by June 15 of the following year. Unless this is done on an annual basis, the IRS could subsequently determine that the snowbird meets the substantial presence test, and could levy penalties for nondisclosure. In order to complete this form, clients will also have to apply for a U.S. Individual Taxpayer Identification Number (ITIN) by completing *IRS Form W-7*.

Clients who are considering buying property in the U.S. will find that there are important differences in the purchase process, costs, acquisition of a mortgage, and ownership structure. Advisors should make sure that clients consult with professionals with expertise in this area prior to making a purchase, in order to avoid income tax or estate tax problems down the road.

Non-resident aliens who own real estate in the U.S. must consider the tax implications of renting and eventually disposing of their property. Those who receive rental income from their U.S. property should file *IRS Form 1040 NR, U.S. Non-Resident Alien Income Tax Return* to report their gross rental income, as well as the 30 percent withholding tax that is applied to the rents. While it is sufficient to remit the 30 percent withholding tax on gross rents, clients can reduce their taxes by filing a return, reducing the gross rental income by operating expenses and depreciation, and paying tax at the marginal rate. Any tax paid may be claimed as a foreign tax credit on the Canadian tax return.

Capital gains on the sale of U.S. real estate must also be reported on *Form 1040 NR*, even if no tax is payable as a result of the capital gains exemption. While American residents can sometimes defer tax on the sale of a property if they are buying another U.S. property, this benefit is not extended to non-resident aliens.

Non-residents who transfer U.S. real estate as a gift to another person may be subject to U.S. gift tax. Between spouses who are not U.S. citizens, gift tax only applies to gifts valued at over $143,000 (2013 threshold). However, for other recipients, gift tax applies over a threshold amount of $14,000 in 2014.

Estate Tax Issues

Individuals who are residents of the U.S. for estate tax purposes are subject to U.S. estate tax on their worldwide assets, whereas non-residents are subject to U.S. estate tax only on their U.S. assets.

U.S. estate tax is based on the fair market value of the U.S. assets on the date of death. U.S. assets include U. S. *situs* real estate, shares of U.S. corporations, U.S. treasury bills, and U.S. money market accounts. However, the client's estate can now claim foreign tax credits on U.S. estate tax paid against deemed disposition capital gains taxes owed in Canada on death. In addition, the Canada/U.S. Tax Treaty provides for a "unified credit" that exempts a certain amount from estate tax. The unified credit is equal to the greater of:

- $13,000

- $2,081,800 x (the value of US assets / worldwide assets)

The estate tax regime in the U.S. currently provides for a maximum tax rate of 40% in 2014 and an individual exemption of $5,340,000 in 2014.

Many strategies are available for reducing the impact of U.S. estate tax, including joint ownership of property with a spouse or other family members, holding the U.S. property in a sole purpose Canadian holding corporation, or taking out a non-recourse mortgage on the U.S. home. These strategies should be reviewed with a Certified Financial Planner and/or tax accountant who is thoroughly familiar with cross-border issues. As some strategies can be expensive to implement, it is wise to undertake a cost/benefit analysis before proceeding.

Estate Planning Issues

A will that is properly drafted in Canada should be valid in the U.S. as well, and specific clauses can be used to cover U.S. assets. This should be done in conjunction with a U.S. lawyer to ensure that the wording meets the requirements of the snowbird state. It is not necessary, and can even be problematic, to have a Canadian will and a U.S. will. A (potential) beneficiary could challenge the will in one jurisdiction, but not the other, or there could be a risk that one will revokes the other.

Advisors should be aware that, if assets are located in both the U.S. and Canada, probate will be required in both jurisdictions, and the estate will require a lawyer in each country. Probate fees in the U.S. are not just an administrative charge as they are in Canada; they refer to the fees that a lawyer charges for probating the estate. For example, in California, the court filing fee for an estate of $100,000 would be $320, but the probate fee for the lawyer is $4,000.

Power of attorney can be a thornier issue for snowbirds. In most jurisdictions in Canada, we have a general power of attorney, an enduring power of attorney, and a power of attorney for personal care. Not all forms of power of attorney are recognized in all states, and may not be readily accepted. It is recommended that a power of attorney should be drawn up in the snowbird state, dealing specifically with the property and assets held in that state.

With power of attorney for personal care, it is also a good idea to have a document drawn up in Canada as well as one drawn up in the snowbird state in order to comply with the appropriate legislation. Almost all U.S. states now have some form of legislation dealing with living wills, so that clients can convey specific wishes in the event that there is no reasonable expectation of recovery from physical or mental disability.

Money Management Issues

At one time, U.S. securities laws restricted the ability of Canadians living or spending time in the U.S. to manage the investments in their Canadian accounts. However, in 2000, the laws were relaxed to allow Canadians to manage registered accounts (RRSPs and RRIFs) from outside of the country, when they are living in a state that has adopted special registration requirements. At the time of writing, most U.S. states provide for special registration for Canadian firms and investment advisors who deal with clients who are snowbirds or permanent residents.

Moving Permanently Outside of Canada

Leaving Canada permanently in retirement is a major decision not to be undertaken lightly. Some people do this in search of a lower tax jurisdiction or lower cost of living, but those who focus strictly on the financial benefits can lose sight of the emotional and psychological factors that can make or break a successful retirement. Detailed research and planning is required, and it is always best to test the waters by spending an extended period in the chosen location (perhaps three months in the off-season) before making any long-term commitments.

Some of the factors to consider in choosing a location are as follows:

- Safety and political stability of the country.

- The social milieu. Does the client want to socialize primarily with other expatriates or to blend in with the local community?

- Language. Even if the client is seeking a largely expatriate community, the ability to speak another language may be important in dealing with the local people.

- Local property laws. Not all countries allow expatriates to buy property, and some impose restrictions. Check with a local real estate lawyer rather than relying on the assurances of real estate agents. In addition, it can be difficult for retired foreigners to obtain conventional mortgage financing in some countries.

- Estate planning implications. Check into the death or inheritance taxes that might apply to real estate in the foreign country. It may make more sense to rent than to own.

- The health care system. Is there a comprehensive health care plan that provides coverage to expatriates after a certain waiting period? Are private health care facilities available, and at what cost? Is insurance available, based on pre-existing medical conditions and the age of the client?

- The tax system. Some countries are more tax-friendly than others. In the U.S., consider the implications of state and municipal as well as federal tax. Does the country have a tax treaty with Canada? If not, clients could be subject to double taxation, since tax withheld in Canada would not be creditable against tax in the foreign jurisdiction.

- Citizenship regulations. Some countries require immigrants to take out citizenship in order to live full-time and/or own property, and dual citizenship may not be permitted in some cases. While many people are prepared to give up Canadian residency status, few want to relinquish their Canadian citizenship.

The website for Foreign Affairs and International Trade Canada (www.international.gc.ca) has links to travel and immigration information, as well as country profiles, for many different destinations around the world.

Giving up Canadian Residency

When moving permanently to another country, clients must sever their ties with Canada in order to avoid being deemed a resident of Canada for tax purposes. There is no one single factor that is used to determine residency. Rather, CRA looks at a number of factors to determine if the clients have, in fact, given up Canadian residency status. According to CRA's *Interpretation Bulletin IT-221R3 (Consolidated) Determination of an Individual's Residence Status,* "The most important factor to be considered in determining whether or not an individual leaving Canada remains resident in Canada for tax purposes is whether or not the individual maintains residential ties with Canada while he or she is abroad."

IT-221R3 as well as CRA Form *NR 73 Determination of Residency Status (Leaving Canada)* are useful documents that describe many of the factors that CRA will consider as indications that clients have or have not maintained residential ties. The following list summarizes the most important actions that clients can take in order to demonstrate that they have severed their residential ties to Canada:

- Sell the principal residence in Canada or lease it through an agency to an individual on an arm's length basis.

- Take all valuable personal possessions out of Canada.

- Terminate Canadian bank accounts, investment accounts and credit cards.

- Give up a provincial or territorial driver's licence and health card.

- Terminate Canadian car insurance and vehicle registration.

- Discontinue memberships in professional associations, recreational clubs, civic and cultural organizations.

- Terminate all addresses in Canada, including post office boxes.

- Close all Canadian safe deposit boxes.

- Terminate subscriptions to magazines and newsletters, or have them mailed directly out of country.

- Sell or wind up any business interests.

- File a Canadian exit return.

- Plan not to return to Canada for at least two years after leaving.

- Establish residential ties in the new country.

Departure Taxes

When an individual becomes non-resident, Canada captures its share of capital gains on certain assets. Just like on death, an exit return must be filed, showing the client's income for the year, up to the date of departure, plus the capital gains on the deemed disposition of certain assets. CRA Form *T1161 List of Properties by an Emigrant of Canada* must be filed along with the tax return if the fair market value of all of the client's property exceeds $25,000.

Properties that are taxable on departure include investments held in non-registered brokerage accounts, foreign real estate, and personal use property valued at over $10,000.

Other properties, such as funds held in registered accounts, Canadian real estate, life insurance policies or annuities, and employee stock options granted while in Canada, are not subject to departure tax. However, income from these items continues to be taxable in Canada, even after the holder becomes non-resident.

Obviously, clients who are considering a permanent move from Canada in retirement would do well to consult with an advisor who specializes in this area, not only to become familiar with the requirements, but also to develop planning strategies to minimize the tax costs.

Government Benefits

Clients will continue to receive OAS benefits as non-residents, provided they were resident in Canada for at least 20 years after reaching age 18. CPP/QPP benefits will continue to be paid, without any residence requirement. Withholding tax may apply to these payments, as well as any employer pension payments or annuity payments, depending on the tax treaty in effect between Canada and the country where the client is now resident. The normal rate of withholding tax is 25 percent, but this can be reduced where there is a tax treaty in effect. See Table 3 in Chapter 2, Sources of Retirement Income – Government Benefits, for a listing of non-resident withholding tax rates on government benefits applicable to countries that have a tax treaty with Canada.

TABLE 1

CONTACT POINTS FOR HOME CARE SUPPORT

Province or Territory	Organization	Website
Alberta	Regional Health Authorities (RHA)	www.seniors.alberta.ca
British Columbia	BC Health Authorities	www.health.gov.bc.ca/socsec
Manitoba	Regional Health Authorities (RHA)	www.gov.mb.ca/health/homecare/index.html
New Brunswick	Family and Community Services (Extra Mural Program)	www2.gnb.ca/content/gnb/en/departments/social_development/seniors.html
Newfoundland	Regional Integrated Health Authorities	www.health.gov.nl.ca/health/personsdisabilities/fundingprograms_hcs.html#phsp
Northwest Territories	Health and Social Services (HSS) Authorities	www.hss.gov.nt.ca/hss-authorities
Nova Scotia	Continuing Care	novascotia.ca/dhw/ccs/
Nunavut	Health and Social Services	www.gov.nu.ca/health
Ontario	Community Care Access Centres (CCAC)	healthcareathome.ca
Prince Edward Island	Home Care and Support	www.healthpei.ca/homecare
Quebec	Santé et Services Sociaux Québec	msss.gouv.qc.ca/en
Saskatchewan	Regional Health Authorities (RHA)	www.health.gov.sk.ca/home-care
Yukon	Yukon Home Care Program	www.hss.gov.yk.ca/homecare.php

TABLE 2

CHECKLIST FOR MAKING A HOME ACCESSIBLE

Getting In and Out of the Home:

☐ Repair holes or uneven joints in walking surfaces that could cause tripping

☐ Widen walkway

☐ Add steps to remove steep slope

☐ Add a ramp to bypass existing steps

☐ Install or repair handrails along walkway, ramp, and steps

☐ Provide non-slip finish on walking surfaces

☐ Install light fixtures or floodlights to illuminate entrances, steps, and walkways

☐ Install easily accessible light switches or sensors to control outside lights

☐ Remove screen door

☐ Reduce height of door threshold and adjust or replace door as necessary

☐ Add a grab bar or handle near step or threshold

☐ Install a delayed action door closer

☐ Replace locks to make operation easier

☐ Install lever-type door handles

☐ Install small shelves inside and outside entrances at elbow height to hold parcels while opening doors

☐ Use colour contrast on door, door frame, handle, and doorbell

Using the Stairs:

☐ Improve lighting in stairs

- [ ] Install two-way light switches at top and bottom of stairs
- [ ] Install or repair handrails on both sides
- [ ] Maintain a consistent handrail height above floor
- [ ] At the top of the stairs, extend handrail horizontally by the length of one tread
- [ ] At the bottom of the stairs, extend handrail the length of one tread beyond the bottom step, then extend horizontally at least 300 mm
- [ ] Replace worn stair coverings
- [ ] Mark steps permanently if they are not distinctly visible
- [ ] Relocate bedroom to main floor level
- [ ] Relocate washers and dryers to a more convenient place
- [ ] Add a toilet on all levels

Moving Around the Home:

- [ ] Reduce height of, or eliminate, door thresholds at room entrances
- [ ] Use colour contrast or changes in floor texture whenever there is a change in floor level
- [ ] Install handrails or grab bars where there are significant changes in floor levels
- [ ] Replace door knobs with lever-type door handles
- [ ] Install sliding, bi-fold or accordion doors on closets
- [ ] Install D-type handles on sliding, bi-fold, and accordion doors
- [ ] Install phone jacks or cordless phones in convenient locations around the home

☐ Install additional electrical outlets as needed to avoid the use of long extension cords

Using the Kitchen:

☐ Install lever-type faucets, a single lever faucet, or a faucet with an electronic sensor

☐ Install pivoting or revolving shelves in corner cupboards

☐ Add a vertical cupboard or pantry

☐ Add pull-out storage units under the counter

☐ Install D-type handles on cupboards and drawers

☐ Provide electrical outlets for small appliances in more convenient locations

Using the Bathroom:

☐ Install lever-type faucets, a single lever faucet, or a faucet with an electronic sensor

☐ Install additional light fixtures near mirror or medicine cabinet

☐ Install a vertical and a horizontal or angled grab bar by the tub

☐ Install non-slip flooring throughout the bathroom

☐ Install a non-slip surface in the bathtub

☐ Install a separate shower stall with a floor of non-slip tiles

☐ Install a hand-held shower on an adjustable rod

☐ Install a waterproof light fixture in the shower stall

☐ Build permanent or flip-up seating into the shower stall

☐ Replace the toilet with a "comfort-height" model

Using Closets and Storage Areas:

☐ Install bi-fold or accordion doors

☐ Install lights in closet

☐ Add or lower rods

☐ Add or lower shelves

☐ Install hooks or drawers in closets

☐ Install an easy-access storage closet for household tools and appliances such as vacuum cleaners, ironing boards, etc.

TABLE 3

CONDOMINIUM SELECTION CHECKLIST

Here is a list of questions to ask yourself before you buy. You can use the chart below to "score" each condominium you consider. First, give each question below an importance rating based on your wish list, with **10 being very important and 0 not important at all**. Then, put a check mark under **yes** or **no** for each question. For each **yes** answer, the condominium will receive the number of points you gave the question for importance. You can total the points at the end to help you rank the different condominiums you look at. But remember, this exercise is to help you make sure that you have considered all the factors before you sign on the dotted line.

Questions	Importance (1-10)	Yes	No	Score
Location:				
Is the condominium in the neighbourhood I want?				
Is it accessible by public transit?				
Is it close to amenities (shops, theatres, restaurants, etc.)?				
Amenities:				
Does the condominium have recreational facilities?				
Does it have an exercise room?				
Does it have a pool?				
Does it have a party room?				
Does it have a convenience store?				
Does it have parking available? Indoor or outdoor? Guest parking?				
Does it have suitable storage available?				

Where to Live

Questions	Importance (1-10)	Yes	No	Score
Rules and Regulations:				
Are the condominium rules and restrictions clearly defined and understandable?				
Are the condominium rules and regulations reasonable? Can I live under these rules?				
Are there rules about the numbers of occupants permitted?				
Can I rent out my unit?				
Does the Board of Directors or developer seem helpful in explaining the rules?				
Can I take my pet?				
Can I operate a business from the condominium?				
Does the management fit my lifestyle (property manager vs. self-managed)?				
Affordability:				
Is the purchase price of the condominium within my budget?				
Can I afford the monthly condominium fees along with my taxes, insurance and other expenses?				
Does the price seem reasonable for what I am getting?				
Are there upgrades available that I need or want and how much would they cost?				
Are finishes included in the purchase price?				
Is cable/satellite and/or internet access included in the monthly condominium fees, and if not, how much would they cost?				
How is the condominium heated / cooled / ventilated?				

The Boomers Retire

Questions	Importance (1-10)	Yes	No	Score
Is the building energy and water efficient?				
Are utilities included in the monthly condominium fees, and if not, how much can I expect to spend each month?				
The Building:				
Is the condominium the type that I want (high-rise, low-rise, townhouse, freehold, loft)?				
Will the construction be finished on time, and if not, can I wait?				
Is the building attractive?				
Is the condominium in good physical condition?				
Does it seem well built and well maintained?				
Will the condominium be durable?				
Are the grounds attractive and well maintained?				
Is the unit attractive?				
Is it the right size?				
Does it have the features I want (fireplace, number of bedrooms, balcony)?				
Does it have enough storage space?				
Does it have enough light?				
Does it have fire protection systems (smoke detectors, sprinklers)?				
Does everyone in the family like it?				
The Condominium Corporation:				
Is the condominium corporation in good financial condition?				
Is all documentation for the condominium accessible and in good order?				

Where to Live

Questions	Importance (1-10)	Yes	No	Score
Are there any legal claims or judgements against the condominium corporation?				
Community and Lifestyle:				
Does the condominium community seem to match my lifestyle (older adults vs. families with small children)?				
Is the condominium strictly residential or is it mixed use?				
What is the proportion of owner-occupied to rented units?				
Is it accessible for people with special needs?				
Do the current occupants seem friendly and happy?				
Are there any noise implications (roadways, neighbours, garbage chutes, elevators)?				
Total Points:				

TABLE 4

CHECKLIST FOR EVALUATING RETIREMENT HOMES

☐ Is the home a member of the provincial retirement communities association, if applicable?

☐ Are there individual temperature controls in each suite?

☐ Is the building air-conditioned?

☐ Does the building seem secure? Is there an alarm system? Is there a concierge at the reception desk 24/7?

☐ Is the building clean, attractive and well maintained?

☐ Is there a patio or garden area with adequate shade and comfortable seating?

☐ Are guest parking facilities adequate? Are they supplied free of charge?

☐ Are there TV cables and phone outlets in all suites?

☐ Is storage space, either in the suite or somewhere else in the building, adequate?

☐ What amenities are available in the facility?

☐ Do the recreation programs appeal to the prospective resident?

☐ Can friends and relatives accompany residents on trips and outings?

☐ What is the quality of the meals like? The best way to test this out is to join the residents for lunch or dinner.

☐ Are there a number of choices available at each meal, or is there a set menu each day?

☐ Are residents able to enjoy a glass of wine with their meals?

☐ Do the staff members treat residents respectfully?

☐ What decorating, painting, and wallpapering is done before the resident moves in?

☐ Are there any restrictions about overnight guests or daytime visitors?

☐ Is there easy access to public transit?

☐ Is transportation provided for medical or other appointments?

☐ What local community resources (banks, libraries, bookstores, convenience stores, and pharmacies) are available?

☐ Are there regular fire drills and inspections?

☐ Is there an option of a temporary or trial stay?

TABLE 5

CONTACT POINTS FOR LONG-TERM CARE

Province or Territory	Organization	Website
Alberta	Regional Health Authorities (RHA)	www.seniors.alberta.ca
British Columbia	BC Health Authorities	www.health.gov.bc.ca/socsec
Manitoba	Regional Health Authorities (RHA)	www.gov.mb.ca/health/rha/contact.html
New Brunswick	Family and Community Services (Extra Mural Program)	www2.gnb.ca/content/gnb/en/services/services_renderer.10115.Long-Term_Care_Services_for_Seniors.html
Newfoundland	Regional Integrated Health Authorities	www.health.gov.nl.ca/health/seniors/residentialoptions.html
Northwest Territories	Continuing Care Unit – Territorial Integrated Services	www.hss.gov.nt.ca/health/long-term
Nova Scotia	Continuing Care	novascotia.ca/dhw/ccs/long-term-care.asp
Nunavut	Department of Health and Social Services	www.gov.nu.ca/health
Ontario	Ministry of Health and Long Term Care	www.health.gov.on.ca/en/public/programs/ltc/default.aspx
Prince Edward Island	Department of Health	www.healthpei.ca/longtermcare
Quebec	Santé et Services Sociaux Québec	msss.gouv.qc.ca/en
Saskatchewan	Special Care Homes	www.health.gov.sk.ca/special-care-homes
Yukon	Residential Care Programs	www.hss.gov.yk.ca/residentialcare.php

TABLE 6

EMERGENCY MEDICAL COVERAGE
OUTSIDE OF CANADA

Province or Territory	Minimum Residence Requirement per Year	Coverage for Extended Absence	Notification Required if Away Longer than:
Alberta	183 days	Up to 2 years	183 days
British Columbia	6 months	Up to 24 months once every 5 years	
Manitoba	183 days	Up to 24 months	90 days
New Brunswick	183 days	An extra 12 month period once every 3 years	30 days
Newfoundland	4 months	Up to 12 months once per lifetime	Any extended absence
Northwest Territories	6 months	Up to 12 months	3 months
Nova Scotia	183 days	Up to 12 months	3 months
Nunavut	183 days	Up to 12 months. Frequency determined by Health Services.	
Ontario	153 days	Up to 5 years	
Prince Edward Island	6 months plus 1 day	Up to 12 months	1 month
Quebec	182 days	Up to 12 months once every 7 years	182 days
Saskatchewan	6 months	Up to 12 months	6 months
Yukon	6 months	Decided on a case-by-case basis.	2 months

Readers should note that these are general guidelines only that would apply to most retirees. Different rules may apply to students and full-time employees. Consult with the relevant provincial or territorial department of health for specific information.

TABLE 7

CONTACT POINTS FOR EMERGENCY MEDICAL COVERAGE OUTSIDE OF CANADA

Province or Territory	Website
Alberta	www.health.alberta.ca/AHCIP/outside-coverage.html
British Columbia	www.health.gov.bc.ca/msp/infoben/ leavingbc.html#absence
Manitoba	www.gov.mb.ca/health/mhsip/index.html#Q13
New Brunswick	www.gnb.ca/0394/leaving-e.asp#temp
Newfoundland	www.health.gov.nl.ca/health/mcp/ outofprovincecoverage.html
Northwest Territories	www.hss.gov.nt.ca/health/nwt-health-care-plan/ health-coverage-outside-nwt
Nova Scotia	novascotia.ca/DHW/msi/moving_travel.asp
Nunavut	www.gov.nu.ca/health
Ontario	www.health.gov.on.ca/en/public/publications/ohip/ travel.aspx
Prince Edward Island	http://www.healthpei.ca/ index.php3?number=1020795&lang=E
Quebec	www.ramq.gouv.qc.ca/en/citizens/temporary-stays-outside-quebec/health-insurance/Pages/eligibility-during-stay.aspx
Saskatchewan	www.health.gov.sk.ca/ph_med_services.html
Yukon	www.hss.gov.yk.ca/insured_services_ outsideyukon.php

Chapter 8: Insurance Concerns

Maintaining good health throughout the retirement years is a major concern for most Canadians. Good health not only means that retirees will be able to enjoy their remaining years to the fullest, it also translates into less of a drain on financial resources.

There are two reasons to be concerned about future health expenses. The first is that the cost of medical care is increasing much more rapidly than the general rate of inflation[1], leaving many seniors to wonder if they will be able to afford the care they may need as they get older. The second factor is that traditional sources of medical coverage such as governments and employers may be reducing the level of coverage they offer. With less than half of employers now providing medical coverage for their retirees[2], many of us will be on our own when it comes to covering these expenses, relying either on our own savings or on insurance policies to foot the bills.

This chapter will address some of the major insurance needs of retired Canadians, including basic medical care, travel medical insurance, critical illness, long-term care, and life insurance.

---

[1] Buck Consultants Canadian Health Care Trend Survey 2013 cites 11.79% inflation for prescription drugs, medical plans, and hospital coverage.

[2] Watson Wyatt survey of 500 major Canadian employers.

Basic Medical Care

All provinces and territories in Canada provide basic medical care for their residents, including hospital accommodation, visits to the doctor's office, and emergency care. In addition, some jurisdictions provide extra coverage for those over 65, regardless of income. Most often, this includes coverage for prescription drugs included on the provincial/territorial formulary, although some jurisdictions provide dental and/or vision care as well. Other jurisdictions provide programs to help those with high drug costs in relation to income. Table 1 at the end of this chapter outlines the additional medical coverage provided for seniors by each jurisdiction. Advisors should be aware that, even where a province or territory provides prescription drug coverage for seniors, not all drugs are listed on the formulary. There is often a time lag between the introduction of a new drug and its addition to the formulary. For example, many drugs for the treatment of cancer have not been covered until several years after their introduction.

There is an excellent website, www.drugcoverage.ca that provides up-to-date detailed information on drug benefit programs across Canada, including listings of the drugs covered by each provincial formulary. The site is run by Plasmid Biocommunications Inc., a wholly-owned subsidiary of Shoppers Drug Mart Corporation. Readers are directed to this website for current information on drug coverage in their jurisdiction.

Extended medical coverage provides insurance for services that are not provided by government. These could include prescription drugs, dental benefits, vision care, and services provided by licensed practitioners such as chiropractors, physiotherapists, massage therapists, and optometrists.

Retirees who can arrange to continue extended medical coverage through a former employer are very fortunate.

Where many employers once covered the cost of providing a retiree benefits program, today's retirees are more frequently being asked to contribute to the cost, or, in some cases, to absorb the cost completely. Even where retirees are asked to pay the total cost of benefits coverage, there is still an advantage to this type of coverage. Not only is the cost of such coverage much lower than private insurance, the coverage limits are typically much higher, and coverage can be obtained without the need to pass a medical exam. Remember that passing a medical exam becomes more of a challenge with increasing age.

If extended medical coverage is not available through a former employer, consideration should be given to purchasing it from a private insurer.

Remember that any premiums paid for medical coverage may be eligible for a tax credit as a medical expense. See Chapter 6, Tax Planning Tips and Strategies, for further details.

Advisors should also ensure that clients understand that, even if they have retiree benefits today, specific provisions can change down the road. Retirees may be asked to contribute at a higher rate for their coverage, or certain types of coverage could be reduced. Factor these expenses into the future cost of health care.

Travel Medical Insurance

One of the most important types of insurance for retired clients to have, even if their travel outside their home province is minimal, is travel medical coverage. Many people make the mistake of thinking that medical expenses for illnesses and injuries sustained while travelling in another part of Canada will automatically be covered by their home province or territory. Such is not the case. While basic medical costs, including hospital stays, are covered up to the home province's maximum fee schedule[3], special expenses such as ambulance services, prescription drugs, transportation home, or bringing a family member to the injured person's bedside will not be. This may not be a major issue under most circumstances; however, situations where the client must be airlifted to a hospital can run up bills of thousands of dollars. Retirees whose interests take them into remote areas for skiing, hiking, or canoeing may be particularly at risk for this type of occurrence.

Some retirees have travel medical insurance included as part of an employer benefit package. However, advisors and clients should review the terms of this type of coverage carefully. In many cases, the coverage is capped at a low level such as $100,000 per incident, or may only cover the retiree up to a certain age. Since some insurers have handled single claims in the $300,000 to $500,000 range, a limit of $100,000 may be inadequate. In the southern U.S., for example, basic coronary bypass surgery without any complications can cost a minimum of $100,000 U.S. Private travel medical policies can be obtained with coverage limits of up to $5,000,000 U.S.

Another consideration is the currency on which the coverage limits are based. Although the Canadian and U.S. dollars have recently been close to par, it is important to ensure that coverage limits are based on the U.S. dollar, since most travel claims are settled in U.S. dollars.

How should travel medical policies be evaluated? Obviously, cost is a concern. The cost of a travel medical policy will be determined by three major factors: the client's age, the length of the trip, and the client's state of health. As clients get older, travel for longer periods, or their health deteriorates, their costs will go up. With some insurance providers, choosing a higher deductible can reduce costs.

---

[3] Daily maximums for hospital coverage range from $75 to $952 for the provinces and $1,261 to $1,297 for the territories.

Another major feature to consider is whether the insurance provider arranges and pays for medical care up front, or expects the client to look after himself and claim for reimbursement later. Learning one's way around the medical system in a foreign country is an unwelcome challenge when a family member is in a life-threatening situation. Where the insurance provider offers a medical emergency call service, determine whether calls are handled by call centre clerical staff or by licensed medical personnel.

Travel medical insurance can be purchased on an annual or per-trip basis. Clients who travel away from their home province more than once per year are usually better off to arrange for annual coverage. Where clients live close to the U.S. border, and can be expected to make occasional day or weekend trips stateside, this is particularly important, since few people think to take out travel medical coverage for this type of trip.

Table 2 at the end of this chapter provides a checklist that can be used to evaluate travel medical policies.

As with all types of insurance, clients should be cautioned about making incomplete or inaccurate statements when filling out health questionnaires as part of the application process for travel medical coverage.

Clients should be advised that any premiums paid for travel medical insurance may be eligible for a tax credit as a medical expense. See Chapter 6, Tax Planning Tips and Strategies, for further details.

Critical Illness Insurance

Critical illness (CI) insurance is designed to provide a lump-sum cash benefit if an insured client is diagnosed with any one of the critical illnesses defined in the specific policy and survives the illness for a stated period of time, usually 30 days. The lump sum is paid to the beneficiary, who is free to use the funds as he or she sees fit. Depending on the circumstances, funds could be used for home renovations, medical treatment outside of Canada, in-home nursing care, or a trip around the world.

Virtually all critical illness policies provide coverage for heart attack, stroke, and life-threatening cancer (usually defined as stage three). However, specific definitions can vary from policy to policy and must be examined carefully. For example, permanent heart damage may have to be sustained before a specific policy will pay out based on heart attack. Similarly, brain damage may be required before a policy pays out based on stroke. Non-critical conditions such as first stage breast cancer, prostate cancer, and angioplasty are typically not covered, or are subject to a limited payout. Some policies will cover conditions such as multiple sclerosis, kidney failure, major organ transplant, and Alzheimer's disease. If a client has concerns about a specific illness, the advisor should shop the market carefully to find a policy that covers that condition.

Although critical illness insurance must usually be purchased by age 65, coverage can continue during retirement, usually up to age 75. Coverage is generally available in amounts ranging from $10,000 to $1,000,000. While many Canadians feel that critical illness insurance is very expensive, costs in Canada are far lower than in other countries with longer experience with this type of insurance. Typical monthly premiums for a 65-year-old non-smoking female for $100,000 of coverage are in the range of $260. For a 55-year-old non-smoking female, the same amount of coverage would be approximately $175[4]. Corresponding estimated rates for men are $430 for a 65-year-old non-smoker and $235 for a 55-year-old non-smoker.

---

[4] These rates are based on level premiums to age 75 for a non-cancellable policy. Rates have been provided by FTL Consulting.

While the *Income Tax Act* does not deal specifically with critical illness insurance, some tax aspects have been well established in practice over recent years. Where the CI policy is personally owned, the premiums paid are not tax-deductible, but the lump-sum benefit that may be received is tax-free.

However, some CI policies offer a return of premium (ROP) feature, and the tax treatment of this benefit is less clear. With return of premium, clients who do not make a claim under the CI policy are entitled to receive a refund of 100 percent of the premiums paid on death or expiry of the policy. While the cost for ROP on death is only marginally higher, ROP on expiry increases the premium cost substantially, so it is important for applicants to be sure that they will be able to keep the coverage in effect until the expiry date if they choose this option. A recent sample quote from a major insurer showed the annual cost of $100,000 coverage for a 55-year-old female non-smoker (level payments to age 75) at $1,931 without ROP, $2,022 with ROP on death and $4,412 with ROP on expiry[5]. Although it is assumed that a return of premium would be tax free, Canada Revenue Agency has not yet made a ruling in this regard.

While many retired clients may feel that they would be able to deal with the costs associated with a critical illness by drawing on their investment capital, it is wise to consider the impact that this could have on retirement lifestyle both for the affected individual and for the spouse or partner. The funds may indeed be there to cover the expenses of the illness, but at what cost to other retirement goals?

The Insurance & Investment Journal regularly publishes tables comparing the critical illness insurance products offered by the major Canadian insurance companies.

---

[5] Rates provided by FTL Consulting.

Long-Term Care Insurance

Long-term care (LTC) insurance is designed to help finance care at home or in a long-term care facility when the client is no longer capable of caring fully for him- or herself. Having sufficient insurance in place allows a client to control his or her own care and decide between home health care and moving into a long-term care facility if and when the situation arises. If the insurance benefits are high enough to cover actual charges, the client will not need to draw on investment assets in order to pay health care costs. On the other hand, coverage can be purchased to cover only a portion of expenses, with the knowledge that individual resources will be used to self-insure to a certain extent.

Policies provide a monthly benefit when the individual's doctor indicates that care is medically necessary as a result of injury or sickness, chronic illness, cognitive impairment, or the inability to perform two or more activities of daily living (bathing, toileting, maintaining continence, eating, getting out of a bed or chair, and dressing).

There are many different variations of long-term care policies on the market. Income policies provide a monthly or weekly income benefit that can be used as the client sees fit. Reimbursement policies provide a designated level of reimbursement for care provided by a qualified care provider. Sometimes, this includes skilled care only (licensed nursing personnel), while other policies include non-skilled care (home health aides). Some policies cover only facility care, while others cover either facility or home care.

The length of time that benefits continue can range from 250 weeks to lifetime. (Studies have shown that the average stay in a long-term care facility is about three years.) There is usually an elimination period that applies before benefits begin to be paid, and choosing a longer elimination period will reduce the costs of coverage. Some benefits may be indexed to inflation.

While the costs of long-term care insurance increase with the age of the applicant, this type of coverage can still be taken out when clients are in their seventies. However, they must be in good health to obtain coverage. If they already need assistance with any activity of daily living, or have been diagnosed with cancer, Alzheimer's, Parkinson's, multiple sclerosis, kidney or heart disease, they may not qualify for coverage.   Note that, in order to qualify for coverage, the applicant must successfully pass a memory test. If this is a concern, it is probably best to apply sooner rather than later.

As with critical illness, the premiums paid for personally owned long-term care policies are not tax-deductible, and the benefits received are tax-free.

Clients with very low income levels may not be good candidates for long-term care insurance simply because the premiums may be unaffordable. Also, should they need to move into a long-term care facility, they may qualify for subsidized rates. At the other end of the spectrum, clients with net worth of $2,000,000 or more may be tempted to self-insure, feeling that they have the personal resources to cover the costs of long-term care. While this may be the case, a requirement for long-term care for an extended period of time can deplete an investment portfolio fairly quickly. For example, the cost of a private long-term care facility in major urban areas can be as high as $7,000 per month. Comprehensive in-home nursing care can cost up to $100,000 per year. Clients who reason that they could sell their home to pay for the cost of long-term care must consider the possibility that only one partner may require such care. If the healthy partner wants to maintain the current home, other resources will have to be used to pay for the long-term care expenses.

Particularly where the client wishes to leave assets to a surviving spouse or to other family members, consideration should be given to purchasing insurance coverage.

As an example of the cost of coverage, a $3,000 per month benefit for a maximum of five years with a 90-day elimination period would cost approximately $3,400 per year for a 65-year-old female and $2,600 per year for a 65-year-old male.[6]

Since the risk of needing long-term care is less at younger ages, many people wait until they are retired to consider the purchase of long-term care insurance. However, insurers do not accept applicants after a certain age, usually age 80, and, of course, the premiums go up as the applicant gets older. In addition, clients run the risk of developing conditions that would preclude them from coverage. Individuals who have policies in force before reaching the cut-off age will continue to qualify for benefits regardless of age.

See Table 3 at the end of this chapter for a list of factors to be considered when shopping for long-term care insurance. *The Insurance & Investment Journal* regularly publishes tables comparing the long-term care insurance products offered by the major Canadian insurance companies.

Life Insurance

In addition to private insurance, many clients have group life insurance through an employer plan while they are employed. The major financial changes that take place at retirement provide an excellent opportunity to review the need for continued life insurance coverage.

Some employer plans extend coverage into retirement, often up to age 65 at the same level of coverage, and then declining annually from that point on. At a certain age, the coverage either disappears, or drops to a minimal amount of $10,000 or so. Other plans cease on retirement, with the opportunity to convert the policy to private coverage, usually within a 30-day period, without undergoing a medical exam.

---

[6] Sample rates provided by FTL Consulting.

Many clients find that, beyond a minimal amount to provide for some immediate cash at death, there is no particular need to maintain life insurance into the retirement years. After all, the main purpose of insurance is to provide support to beneficiaries in the event of the client's untimely death. Usually, by the time the client retires, any beneficiaries are self-supporting, either through their own income, in the case of grown children, or through other financial resources built up over the years, in the case of a surviving spouse.

Nevertheless, there are some valid reasons for maintaining life insurance in the later years, particularly for providing a source of funds to pay for anticipated capital gains taxes on death, or for funding a donation to charity. The use of life insurance for these purposes is discussed in Chapter 9, Estate Planning.

TABLE 1

ADDITIONAL MEDICAL COVERAGE PROVIDED FOR SENIORS[7]

Province or Territory	Additional Benefits
Alberta	Seniors and their spouses/partners are eligible for premium-free Alberta Blue Cross coverage, which provides some coverage for prescription drugs, ambulance services, prosthetics, and limited psychological and nursing services.
British Columbia	Routine eye exams for seniors.
Manitoba	One complete routine eye exam is covered every two years.
New Brunswick	No special benefits for seniors.
Newfoundland	No special benefits for seniors.
Northwest Territories	Additional benefits are provided to Métis and non-native residents 60 years of age or older[8]. Benefits include dental care, eyeglasses, medical supplies and equipment, medical travel, and prescription drugs.
Nova Scotia	Seniors who do not have drug coverage through any other private or public plan may pay premiums to join Seniors' Pharmacare. This program pays for a portion of the cost of prescription drugs listed on the Nova Scotia Formulary.
Nunavut	Additional benefits are provided to Métis and non-native residents 60 years of age or older[9]. Benefits include dental care, eyeglasses, medical supplies and equipment, medical travel, and prescription drugs.

---

[7] Seniors are defined as those age 65 and older, except where noted. This table summarizes additional services that are available to all seniors, regardless of income. Additional premium subsidies and special programs may be available for lower income seniors.

[8] The Federal Government's Non-insured Health Benefits (NIHB) Program provides benefits to Inuit and Registered Indian seniors.

[9] The Federal Government's Non-insured Health Benefits (NIHB) Program provides benefits to Inuit and Registered Indian seniors.

Insurance Concerns

Province or Territory	Additional Benefits
Ontario	Routine eye exams are covered for seniors once every 12 months. Physiotherapy services are available for seniors. People 65 years of age and older are eligible for the Ontario Drug Benefit Program, which pays for a portion of the cost of prescription drugs listed on the Ontario Formulary.
Prince Edward Island	No special benefits for seniors.
Quebec	One complete eye exam per year is covered for seniors 65 years of age and older. Prescription drug insurance is mandatory for all residents of Quebec. Retirees who do not have access to a private plan must register and pay premiums for the Public Prescription Drug Insurance Plan.
Saskatchewan	The Seniors' Drug Plan is available to seniors who are eligible for the federal age credit, which indicates a net income of less than $80,980 in 2014. The Seniors' Drug Plan covers most of the cost of prescription drugs listed on the Saskatchewan formulary.
Yukon	The Pharmacare and Extended Benefits Program helps with the cost of dentures, vision care, and medical supplies and equipment. The total cost of prescription drugs listed in the Yukon formulary is covered. Seniors 65 and older, as well as their spouses/partners aged 60 and over, are covered.

TABLE 2

CHECKLIST WHEN SHOPPING FOR TRAVEL MEDICAL COVERAGE

☐ What is the maximum amount of coverage available? Is it sufficient? Is it quoted in US dollars?

☐ Does the policy cover air ambulance transportation back to Canada after the client's condition has stabilized?

☐ Does the policy cover the cost to return a travelling companion home? Does it pay for any required medical escort?

☐ Does the insurance provider arrange and pay for medical care up front, or is the client expected to submit receipts for reimbursement after the fact?

☐ Are there specific exclusions that apply to sports or other activities, such as scuba diving or skydiving?

☐ Are there certain locations or countries that are not covered under the policy?

☐ Can coverage be extended if the clients decide to extend their trip?

☐ Consider purchasing an annual multi-trip plan rather than individual coverage for each foray outside the home province or territory.

☐ Is there a worldwide emergency hotline to call when medical assistance is needed? Is it available 24/7? Are the operators multilingual? Are nurses or doctors on staff?

☐ Does the policy provide for cash advances if a hospital only accepts such payment?

☐ If a client dies while travelling, does the policy cover the return to Canada of the body?

☐ Is there a deductible or co-payment clause?

TABLE 3

LONG-TERM CARE INSURANCE CHECKLIST

Company issuing policy _____ Rating? _____

	Yes	No

1. What is the insurance company's rating? _____

2. What types of care does the policy cover (e.g., nursing home, alternative care facility, home health care, adult day care)? _____

   _____

   The policy should cover both skilled (e.g., professional care such as those provided by nurses and therapists) and nonskilled (e.g., personal care such as those provided by home health aides) care.

3. What events trigger benefits (e.g., medical necessity, disability due to functional impairment, cognitive impairment, or prior hospitalization? _____

   _____

   The policy should use activities of daily living (ADLs) in determining when care is covered by the policy. Benefits should be payable when the insured cannot carry out a specific number of ADLs (e.g., two out of six). The policy should also provide that coverage applies for a cognitive impairment (e.g., Alzheimer's).

4. Must the insured have a prior hospital stay prior to entering a long-term care facility?　　　　☐　　☐

   The answer should be "No".

5. Must the insured have prior long-term facility coverage to obtain home health care coverage?　　☐　　☐

   The answer should be "No".

6. Does the policy cover home health care?　　　　☐　　☐

	Yes	No

While most policies require in-home health services to be provided by individuals hired through a licensed home health care agency, some allow free-lance professionals or relatives to provide the services. However, if premiums are a consideration and the individual has no one to live with, a nursing home or assisted living facility may be the best option. Home health care benefits are designed primarily to augment an existing support structure that includes family, because 24-hour care generally costs much more than nursing home care. Typically, professional home care is economically viable only if paid care is limited to roughly half the day.

7. Does the policy cover adult day care? ☐ ☐

Most policies cover it if they provide for home care benefits.

8. Is respite care covered? ☐ ☐

Respite care is a short-term inpatient stay in a facility or some home health care used to give temporary relief (i.e., a vacation) to the individual who regularly assists with home health care. Some policies only pay respite care in the home; it is better when respite care is paid at home or in a facility. The elimination period should not apply to respite care.

9. What is the annual premium? $ _____

Caution: Often companies with the lowest rates are at a greater risk for rate increases.

10. Are any discounts available? For example, a discount is often offered if both spouses purchase a policy. Discounts may also exist for preferred health. ☐ ☐

11. Can the policy be renewed regardless of the insured's age or physical or mental condition? ☐ ☐

The answer should be "Yes"; the only reason for canceling, terminating, or not renewing the policy should be for non-payment of premiums.

	Yes	No

12. Can premiums increase as the insured ages? ☐ ☐

   Premiums may increase in certain policies if benefits increase because of inflation. The premium should remain level including inflation coverage except for class increases.

   A few policies (called noncancelable) cannot raise premiums. A few policies also have rate guarantees for a specific time period such as 3, 5, or 10 years.

13. Can premiums be waived? ☐ ☐

   Most policies waive premiums after the insured has been in a nursing home for a certain amount of time (e.g., 90 days). However, premiums might be waived if the insured is receiving assisted living, home, or adult day care.

14. How much does the policy pay and how much are local providers currently charging for the services?

	Policy	Local Charges
Amounts for various components:	$	$
a. Nursing home	$_____	$_____
b. Alternate care facility	$_____	$_____
c. Home health care	$_____	$_____
d. Adult day care	$_____	$_____

   The policy generally will pay a certain benefit amount for each day or month the insured is covered under the benefit. Some policies pay no more than the actual charges. When selecting a daily or monthly benefit, consider the usual average of an additional 20% in charges above room and board costs for nursing homes due to miscellaneous charges such as non-prescription drugs and care-related supplies. A client should consider these extra charges if he or she is trying to self-insure part of the costs. The decision may depend on whether the insured has coverage for prescription drugs.

Yes   No

15. What are the policy's maximum lifetime limits? _____

_____

These may be measured by a dollar limit (e.g., $200,000, $500,000, unlimited) or a certain time limit (e.g., three years, five years, lifetime), or both. After the dollar or time limit is reached, no further benefits are payable under the policy.

16. Can benefits be restored?   ☐   ☐

For example, assume the insured uses $10,000 of long-term care benefits on a policy with a lifetime maximum of $100,000. If the insured no longer requires long-term care for a specific period (usually six months), is his or her lifetime coverage now $90,000, or can it be restored to the $100,000 original coverage. However, after two to three years the probability of utilizing this benefit is small.

17. Does the policy have inflation protection?   ☐   ☐

If not, can additional coverage be purchased at a   ☐   ☐
later date?

There are two types of policies: (a) automatically increases benefits annually without increasing premiums, and (b) allows future purchase options. The amount of increase on the second type may be based on the consumer price index (CPI) or may be based on CPI with a minimum 5% compound, or may be a specific amount such as 3% or 5% compounded. Whatever the basis for calculating the future purchase offer, the premium for the increase is based on attained age. However, with most policies of this type, once the individual is claiming benefits, he or she cannot purchase more benefits under the future purchase option.

The authors recommend that inflation protection be purchased by most clients.

Insurance Concerns

	Yes	No
18. Does the policy have a guaranteed insurability rider?	☐	☐

This allows the insured to increase coverage without providing proof of health. This rider typically refers to a policy that allows the future purchase offer (see question 17) regardless of health. However, most policies stop short of giving the individual the offer if he or she is claiming benefits.

| 19. Is the policy guaranteed renewable? | ☐ | ☐ |

As long as the premiums are paid, the policy cannot be canceled.

| 20. Can the policy be automatically upgraded if the insurance company offers an improved policy? | ☐ | ☐ |

If the policy can be upgraded, the insured can acquire an improved policy without having to meet the health requirements of a new policyholder and without having to pay a larger premium because of current age. However, a larger premium will likely be charged to pay for the enhanced benefits.

21. What is the waiting or elimination period? _____

_____

The insured may have only one waiting period during his or her lifetime. Alternatively, a new waiting period may begin each time the insured enters a long-term care facility or requires care at home. Most policies require formal charges to be incurred to satisfy the waiting period, which means a family member cannot take care of the elderly person to satisfy the waiting period. A few policies, however, allow the waiting period to start on the first day of disability as certified by a physician.

	Yes	No

In addition, some policies have accumulation periods, meaning the waiting period may only have to be satisfied once in a lifetime, but only if it is accumulated within a certain time period (e.g., 730 days).

23. Does the policy limit benefits for pre-existing conditions?   ☐   ☐

Some policies provide that pre-existing conditions are not covered for a specific period of time (e.g., six months). The definition of a pre-existing condition should also be included in the policy.

24. What conditions are specifically excluded from coverage? _____

Policy exclusions may include alcoholism and drug dependency, attempted suicide, and intentionally self-inflicted injuries. However, the policy should cover Alzheimer's and similar organic brain disease or dysfunction (e.g., senility). A growing number of policies include coverage for mental and nervous conditions, which alleviate confusion (particularly with older individuals) over whether mental dysfunction is organic or psychological.

Chapter 9: Estate Planning

Overview

Even clients who have not previously been concerned about estate planning begin to think about it more seriously once they reach their retirement years. This chapter addresses the basic tools of wills and powers of attorney, the use of trusts, and planning strategies such as techniques for reducing probate, supporting charitable causes, passing the cottage on to the next generation, and ensuring equal distribution of assets to children.

The Basic Tools

The Will

The will is the most basic tool available for ensuring that a client's personal wishes for the disposition of his or her estate on death are carried out as quickly and as inexpensively as possible. For smaller estates, the will may be the only estate planning tool needed, apart from the power of attorney, which is effective during the client's lifetime. A will serves the following purposes:

- A will is the vehicle for naming an executor, the individual who is charged with distributing property according to the wishes of the client.

- A will outlines the client's wishes for distributing his or her money and property following death. Without a valid will in place, provincial/territorial intestate succession law will be used to determine how assets are to be divided. Typically, where there is a surviving spouse and children, the spouse is not entitled to the full value of the estate.

- A will can provide for tax planning strategies to minimize taxation at death.

- In some cases, clients may specifically choose not to leave assets to certain children. As long as the children are non-dependent adults, it is possible to make this stipulation in a will. Making one's intentions clear in this manner reduces the chance of a claim that the child was simply forgotten.

- Most jurisdictions require administrators of an intestate estate to post a performance bond with a guarantee by a surety company. A will can avoid this requirement.

Clients who have property outside Canada should consider drawing up a will according to the laws of the other country. Where more than one country is involved, or the client travels frequently, an international will should be considered. Note that not all jurisdictions in Canada accept the concept of international wills. See Chapter 7, Where to Live, for additional comments on estate planning for snowbirds.

Wills generally follow a common structure. The clauses outlined below are included in many, if not most, wills that are drafted today by legal counsel.

- *Identification and Revocation.* This clause serves to identify the testator and his or her domicile. The testator declares this to be his or her last will and testament and invalidates all prior wills.

- *Appointment of Executor.* This clause identifies the individual who will serve as executor of the estate. It may also name co-executors, alternates, and successors, as appropriate. The use of co-executors is recommended in situations where specialized knowledge of a business is required, or where the client wants to name the spouse as executor, but recognizes that the spouse will need some assistance in carrying out the duties. In cases where several children are named as executors, the testator needs to decide whether any decisions must be unanimous, or whether majority rule is acceptable. This clause can also be used to waive the posting of a performance bond by the executor, and may provide for payment to the executor for his or her services. Being an executor is a lengthy and time-consuming task, and compensation should be considered. Where the estate includes complex and extensive business interests, the client may want to consider the appointment of a corporate executor. See Table 1 at the end of this chapter for a listing of the general duties of an executor.

- *Payment of Debts.* This clause allows for the direction of payment of debts, including funeral expenses and administration costs. This clause should also identify the source from which the debts and any obligations that are not apparent, such as a loan from a relative, will be paid.

- *Payment of Taxes.* This clause authorizes the payment of any and all indebtedness for taxes payable pursuant to the *Income Tax Act.* If a spousal trust is involved, it is especially important to specify from what part of the estate the taxes are to be paid. If the taxes are paid from the trust assets, this will serve to taint the trust, rendering it ineffective.

- *Specific Bequests.* In this clause, the testator identifies the recipients of specific personal property, real estate and heirlooms such as vehicles, clothing, jewellery, and furniture. Assets such as registered investment accounts or cash legacies may also be covered in this clause. Another, perhaps better, way of approaching the disposition of personal property is for the testator to write a separate informal memorandum to be given to the executor. If any changes are required in future, it is a much simpler task to revise an informal memorandum than to draft a codicil to the will.

- *Residual Estate.* This clause provides for the transfer of assets remaining after all other dispositions have been accounted for. The residual estate may be disposed of by transfer to one or a number of beneficiaries in stated proportions, to a testamentary trust, or to an existing *inter vivos* trust. Although clients can name anyone they wish as a beneficiary, advisors should be aware of the restrictions imposed by most provincial Family Law Acts. These Acts typically state that, on death or marriage breakdown, the net value of the property that the spouse acquired during the marriage is to be divided equally between them. Therefore, on death, a surviving spouse can choose to take his or her entitlement under the will or elect the statutory equalization of net family property. However, planners in Alberta should be aware that, under a proposed amendment to the *Wills and Succession Act* in that province, a surviving spouse would be entitled to make a claim against the estate for matrimonial property division in addition to what is specifically gifted under the will. Although the new *Wills and Succession Act* came into force on February 1, 2012, this particular section will not be proclaimed until further review has taken place.

- *Trusts.* If any trusts are created by the will, this clause serves to set out the terms, such as how and when income and capital will be distributed. Trusts will be discussed in more detail later in this chapter.

- *Common Disaster Clause.* This clause usually stipulates that one spouse must survive the other by a certain period of time, usually 25 to 30 days, before he or she can inherit under the other spouse's will. Without this clause, the estate of the spouse who died first would be settled, probate fees would be paid, and the assets transferred to the estate of the spouse who died second. Probate fees would then be payable again on the same assets, even though one spouse may have died only a few days after the other.

- *Powers.* This clause allows the executor to exercise various powers, such as managing and selling property, borrowing and lending, investing and re-investing assets and making elections under the *Income Tax Act* without the approval of the probate court.

- *Mutual Funds.* Generally, executors and trustees are not allowed to delegate their responsibilities. Without specific power to do so, many trustees will not invest in mutual funds for this reason.

- *Testimonium and Attestation.* These clauses are at the end of a will. They establish that the testator had knowledge that the instrument was a will and provide for compliance with other requirements, such as signatures of witnesses.

Clients who have what appear to be simple estates may be tempted to draw up their own wills. This is seldom a recommended strategy. Advisors need to emphasize the importance of giving this task to a lawyer, so that the will is professionally prepared and signed in front of two witnesses who are not beneficiaries under the will. In rare cases, a client may need to prepare a holograph will, in situations where death is imminent, and there is no time to consult a lawyer. In order to be valid, a holograph will must be written entirely in the handwriting of the testator. Some jurisdictions require the testator's signature, while others do not. Witnesses are not required. Note that holograph wills are not considered valid in all jurisdictions.

A will review checklist has been included as Table 2 at the end of this chapter. This checklist includes questions designed to help the advisor evaluate the adequacy of the will. At retirement, it is not uncommon to find that clients have not updated their wills in many years. This is a good opportunity to review the will and update it as needed to cover changes in tax and other laws, as well as changing family circumstances. The family's financial position may be quite different now than when the will was originally drafted. The original executor or beneficiaries may have died, executors may have moved away, or the needs and circumstances of beneficiaries may have changed.

Also, with increasing life expectancy, many retirees will have parents who are still living. Don't let clients make the mistake of assuming that their parents will die first. If a client is providing financial support for an elderly relative, the will should address this issue in the event that the client predeceases the parent.

The Power of Attorney (POA) for Property

A POA for property is a formal legal document in which a client (the donor or principal) gives to another person (the donee or attorney) the authority to act on behalf of the donor in conducting his or her financial affairs. A POA may be structured in many different ways. It could be used on a temporary basis to assist a client who will be travelling over an extended period, so that the attorney can handle financial transactions in the client's absence. It could also be limited to specific acts, such as the conduct of banking business, the sale of specified real estate or the transfer of securities. More commonly, a POA is designed to be used more generally, so that the client has someone who can act on his behalf in the event that he becomes ill or meets with an accident and cannot handle his own financial affairs. With a general POA, the attorney can do virtually anything the principal could have done, with the exception of making or changing the principal's will, or giving a new POA on the principal's behalf.

The POA is effective while the client is alive, and the attorney's power ceases when the client dies. At this point, the executor of the client's estate takes over responsibility for acting on behalf of the client.

Although the terminology differs in various jurisdictions, the provinces and territories make a distinction between a general POA for property and an enduring or continuing POA.

In all provinces except Quebec (where a POA is known as a mandate), a general POA terminates when the person granting the power becomes mentally incompetent. However, enduring POAs survive incompetency, remaining in effect until revoked. An enduring power of attorney can be extremely useful for older clients who want to ensure that their finances will be taken care of even in the event they develop dementia in their later years.

As the laws that govern the creation and use of POAs are not uniform across Canada, advisors need to involve competent legal counsel when advising a client to appoint an attorney.

The individual who is appointed attorney should of course be competent and trustworthy, and should be someone who has a clear understanding of the client's estate and financial plan. This person will be relied on to see that the client's desires are carried out.

Sometimes clients are concerned about the possible misuse of a POA. The best protection against misuse is to name a trustworthy attorney in the first place. However, there are some strategies that can minimize the risk. For example, two or three individuals can be named as attorneys, with the requirement that they act jointly. In that case, all attorneys must agree on the action to be taken. This is different from acting jointly and severally, which means that the attorneys can either make decisions together or separately. However, if joint action is required, and one of the attorneys cannot be contacted when a decision is needed, the remaining attorney cannot act independently.

A POA can also be designed as a springing POA, meaning that it becomes effective only in the event of the principal's incapacity, rather than immediately. However, this introduces the problem of how to determine and prove that the client is actually incapable of managing his or her own affairs. The document itself should describe how this is to be done; for example, it could state that two doctors must agree that the principal cannot manage his or her affairs. Third parties, including family members, with adverse financial interests ideally should not be given the authority to determine the client's capability. Clients must also recognize that the need to prove incapacity will likely result in delays and inconvenience.

Another alternative is to execute a general POA and place it with a trusted third party (possibly a relative or the client's lawyer) with an instruction letter containing the criteria for determining disability and specifying when the instrument is to be released to the attorney.

A client can generally revoke a POA at any time as long as he or she is legally competent. If this happens, the principal should ensure that all relevant parties are notified of the revocation.

Some financial institutions incorrectly insist that their own forms be used to convey POAs. Clients should think carefully before they sign these forms. Doing so could cause a previously drafted POA to be revoked, leaving the client with no one able to handle other affairs if necessary. If a financial institution refuses a client's POA, the issue should be raised with senior staff at the institution's head office. A lawyer may need to be consulted.

Some clients may feel that a POA is unnecessary if all assets are held jointly between spouses. In the event one spouse becomes incapacitated, the other can simply take over the paying of bills and handling of finances. However, clients and advisors should be aware that, in some jurisdictions, a spouse is unable to sell or mortgage a matrimonial home without a POA, even if his or her name is on title.

See Chapter 7, Where to Live, for additional comments relating to POAs for snowbirds.

The Power of Attorney (POA) for Personal Care

A power of attorney for personal care names an individual to act on the client's behalf with regard to health and medical care decisions. Some jurisdictions incorporate this type of POA into a living will or health care directive. Again, the formalities are handled differently in different jurisdictions, but the main distinction is that the POA or proxy names the individual responsible, while the living will or health care directive gives specific directions to treatment providers as to the treatments that the principal consents to or refuses. It is a good idea for clients to discuss the content with their doctors to ensure that their instructions are clear and that healthcare providers will be able to understand their wishes.

A copy of the directive should be given to the client's attorney or proxy, close family members, and the family doctor.

Trusts

A trust is a relationship among three parties:

- the settlor, who transfers property to the trust

- the trustee, who legally owns the property for the benefit of another

- the beneficiary, who is entitled to the income earned in the trust and/or the property of the trust itself.

Trusts can be created during the lifetime of the settlor (*inter vivos* trusts), or they can become effective on the settlor's death (testamentary trusts). Depending on the type of trust, they can be used to provide for disabled or spend-thrift family members, reduce taxes paid by the family, minimize probate fees, and protect a client's privacy.

Note that the federal budget released in February 2014 proposed a number of changes to testamentary trusts that would limit their usefulness as a tax minimization technique. This will be discussed in greater detail under the section *Testamentary Trusts*.

In order to be properly constituted, a trust must meet a number of tests, referred to as the "three certainties". If the trust is not properly constituted it will not be effective, and may cause the entire estate plan to fail.

The three certainties are:

- Certainty of intention. In the realm of estate planning, this will be evidenced by a written document, such as a will or trust deed, that establishes the trust.

- Certainty of subject matter. The property that is to be held in the trust must be described in the trust document.

- Certainty of objects. A trust can be established to serve a purpose or to benefit certain individuals. In either case, the purpose or person(s) must be clearly identified. In the case of a group of individuals, Frostiak points out that they must consist of an ascertainable class – for example, "my brothers" would qualify, where "my friends" would not. [1]

Trusts may be either revocable or irrevocable. A revocable trust is one in which the settlor retains the right to revoke or amend the terms of the trust to take back some or all of the transferred property. From an income tax perspective, all income and losses and any capital gains or capital losses on the disposition of the property transferred to the trust will be attributed back to the settlor while he or she is a resident of Canada[2]. Because of the attribution rules, there is often no income tax advantage to a revocable trust. However, revocable trusts can be used for a number of other purposes, such as avoidance of probate and creditor proofing.

The more common irrevocable trust is one in which the settlor does not retain the right to revoke or amend the terms of the trust to take back some or all of the transferred property. These trusts can be discretionary or non-discretionary in nature. Discretionary trusts usually confer on the trustee the broad power to pay or to accumulate income of the trust. Discretionary trusts also often confer on the trustees the power to encroach on the capital of the trust in favour of one or more eligible capital beneficiaries. Irrevocable trusts can be used in an estate freeze to hold the common shares of a private company, or to hold property or other investments.

Inter Vivos Trusts

An *inter vivos* trust or living trust is one created by a settlor during his or her lifetime. With an *inter vivos* trust, property transferred into the trust is subject to a deemed

---

[1] Frostiak, Larry. Practitioner's Guide to Trusts, p. 11-12.

[2] CRA Interpretation Bulletin IT-369R, Attribution of Trust Income to Settlor.

disposition, thereby triggering any capital gains or losses on the property. However, in the case of small business assets, it is possible that any gains could be sheltered by the $800,000 capital gains exemption at that time. If the trust is considered revocable, ongoing income of the trust property will be attributed back to the settlor, as described above.

Inter vivos trusts can be a useful estate planning tool for small business owners as part of an estate freeze. For example, if the client is concerned about maintaining influence over his or her private company following an estate freeze, the client can either continue to hold the controlling shares of the company or be appointed as one of the trustees of the trust holding the common shares of the company. Depending on the terms of the trust, this may give the client significant influence over the future income stream of the trust. This would also allow the client to decide in each year who should benefit from the trust, and by extension, from the company. By naming himself or herself and/or the spouse as a beneficiary of the trust, the client may also be in a position to ensure that he or she has an income stream into the future. Naming himself or herself as beneficiary of the trust would be only one of a number of ways in which the client could access money from the company. If the client is a director of the company, he or she may direct that the company pay him or her a salary or bonus. Also, so long as the client owns his or her own "freeze" shares, that is, converted preferred shares, the client should be in a position to access money from the company by way of dividends or redemptions.

A trust can also be useful for clients who have several children, but are currently unsure of which of the children should ultimately take over the business. Rather than give a child shares outright, the client can have the future growth of the company held by a trust and then, if the client makes a decision before his or her death, the trust can distribute one or more of the shares to that child or those children at that time, usually on a tax-deferred rollover basis.

Advisors should note that any income retained by an *inter vivos* trust is taxed at the top marginal rate. In order to avoid this, it is important to ensure that the income of the trust is paid or payable to the beneficiary in the year, so that it will be taxed in the beneficiary's hands and not in the hands of the trust. The flow-through nature of a trust may enable the trustees to sprinkle income among the lower income beneficiaries, thereby reducing the total tax payable on the income passed through the trust. However, advisors should be aware that the "kiddie tax", introduced in the 1999 federal budget, limits the effectiveness of this technique. Since January 1, 2000, income from a private company or business attracts the highest marginal rate of tax when paid to minor beneficiaries, even when the income flows through a trust.

Income retained in an *inter vivos* trust is taxed at the top marginal rate in the jurisdiction where the trust is deemed to reside. Historically, the residence of the trustees was the deciding factor in determining where the trust was resident. So, for example, if an Ontario couple (the settlors) set up a trust in a low tax jurisdiction like Alberta, income retained in that trust would be taxed at Alberta rates by virtue of having an Alberta-based trustee. The same logic applied to trusts set up offshore in tax-favourable jurisdictions. However, in April 2012, the Supreme Court ruled in the Garron case[3] that the residency of a trust should be based on where the central management and control resides, parallel to the laws governing the residency of a corporation. Planners will need to take this decision into consideration when planning for a trust.

Inter vivos trusts are also used to hold assets such as cottages for the benefit of family members, while capping

---

[3] Fundy Settlement v. Canada, 2012 SCC14 (Garron Family Trust).

the capital gains tax exposure of the original owner. If the cottage has gone up in value over the years, a tax liability will be triggered on transfer into the trust. But it's possible to reduce the tax impact through a number of mechanisms, such as the principal residence exemption, and increasing the adjusted cost base for the value of repairs, renovations and additions to the property over the years. Transfer of cottage properties will be explored in more detail later in this chapter.

Inter vivos trusts are subject to the 21-year deemed disposition rule. Essentially, there must be a deemed sale of the trust assets every 21 years, resulting in capital gains tax. The impact of the deemed disposition can be reduced or avoided entirely by distributing the trust assets to the beneficiaries prior to the deemed disposition date, thereby deferring the tax until the beneficiaries sell the assets.

Alter Ego / Joint Partner Trusts

An *alter ego* trust is an *inter vivos* trust that can be set up by an individual who is at least 65 years old for his or her exclusive benefit. No one else can access the income or capital of the trust during the settlor's lifetime. Similarly, a joint partner trust is set up by partners who are both over the age of 65. The partners can be married or common law, same or opposite sex. No one but the partners can access the trust income or capital until both partners have died.

Unlike other types of *inter vivos* trusts, capital gains are not triggered when assets are transferred into the trust. With an *alter ego* / joint partner trust, capital gains are deferred until the assets are sold, or the settlor dies or gives up Canadian residency. Similarly, the 21-year deemed disposition rule does not apply to *alter ego* / joint partner trusts.

The client setting up the trust can act as settlor, trustee, and beneficiary. This allows the client to manage the trust without directly owning the assets inside it. The trust document can allow for trustees other than the settlor to administer the trust if the settlor becomes incapacitated. In this way, the trust can be used as an alternative to an enduring power of attorney for property to ensure continuity of asset management, at least for the assets held within the trust. The legal obligations imposed on a trustee are more onerous than the fiduciary duties expected of an attorney; therefore, the *alter ego* / joint partner trust can provide greater protection for the client.

Because the assets held in the trust no longer legally belong to the settlor, they don't form part of the estate at death, and are not subject to probate. The assets remain in the trust and their distribution is determined by the terms of the trust. There will, however, be a deemed disposition on death, which could trigger capital gains tax.

Unlike wills, which become public documents when submitted for probate, trust documents are private. Disgruntled beneficiaries who might have been inclined to challenge a will don't have the same opportunity with a trust. For clients who plan an unequal distribution of assets among their children, for example, this could be an important consideration.

Assets held in an *alter ego* / joint partner trust are protected from creditors, and, in some jurisdictions, are exempt from dependants' relief legislation.[4]

While there are significant benefits to be gained by using an *alter ego* / joint partner trust, there are drawbacks as well. When the settlor dies, there will be a deemed disposition of the assets held in the trust. Any capital gains will be declared at this time and will be taxed at the top marginal rate currently in effect for capital gains. If these assets had been held personally, the gains would be taxed on the terminal return at the graduated rates that normally apply to individuals. Note that this same deemed disposition will apply if the settlor gives up Canadian residency.

---

[4] Frostiak, Larry. Practitioner's Guide to Trusts, p. 80.

Another drawback is that the use of an *alter ego* / joint partner trust can interfere with certain estate planning opportunities. For example, many clients choose to transfer their assets into a testamentary trust on death. This can provide protection for spendthrift beneficiaries and unsophisticated investors, as well as provide tax relief for beneficiaries with substantial personal income of their own. However, assets in an *alter ego* / joint partner trust do not pass through the estate at the settlor's death, and cannot be used to fund a testamentary trust.

Alter ego / joint partner trusts are designed primarily for people who want to avoid the impact of probate fees, without losing control over their assets. However, setting one up may not be worth the expense unless the assets to be transferred into the trust are substantial, generally over $1,000,000. The cost to set up and maintain the trust, including an extra annual tax filing, could outweigh the probate savings. Advisors should bear in mind that real property such as homes and cottages can be transferred into the trust, and that the principal residence exemption continues to apply to such property.

Testamentary Trusts

Trusts established as a consequence of an individual's death are called testamentary trusts. Unlike *inter vivos* trusts, testamentary trusts are taxed at the same graduated rates that apply to individuals. However, a trust cannot claim any of the personal tax credits that are used by individual taxpayers. The fiscal year of a testamentary trust is established following the death of the settlor, and can be different from the calendar year. The first year begins on the day following the date of death, and extends for a maximum of 12 months following the date of death. Future fiscal years adhere to that same 12-month period.

The federal budget of February 2014 proposed a number of amendments that would substantially change the tax treatment of testamentary trusts for taxation years ending after 2014. Under the new rules, graduated rate taxation would apply only for the first 36 months after the individual's death, except in the case of beneficiaries who are eligible to claim the federal disability tax credit. The proposals would also require testamentary trusts to have a calendar year end. At the time of writing, these proposals had not yet been passed into law.

Testamentary trusts can be used for a variety of purposes. A testamentary family trust could be used to hold the estate until the children are of a certain age and capable of managing the funds, to protect the trust assets from spendthrift children, or to assist a physically or mentally challenged child. Even where there is no personal reason to avoid placing large sums of money directly into the hands of a beneficiary, there can be good tax planning reasons for doing so, although these may disappear when proposed new legislation is passed. Bear in mind that income from a testamentary trust can be taxed in the hands of the trust, even when it is actually paid out to the beneficiary. In effect, creating a trust creates another taxpayer. Where the beneficiary's income is already fairly substantial, tax savings can be realized by having investment income taxed in the testamentary trust, rather than on the beneficiary's personal tax return. As noted above, the government has proposed to limit the advantage of graduated rates to the first 36 months after the individual's death, except in the case of beneficiaries who are eligible to claim the federal disability tax credit.

A spousal trust is another common form of testamentary trust. A qualifying spousal trust stipulates that the surviving spouse or partner is entitled to receive all of the income from the trust during his or her lifetime, and no other person is entitled to receive any of the income or the capital of the trust during the lifetime of the surviving spouse. Property can be transferred into a spousal trust at the contributor's adjusted cost base, unless the settlor's representative elects otherwise, for example, to absorb unutilized capital losses.

As with the family trust, a spousal trust can be used for situations where the beneficiary may not be able to handle the investment and management of large sums of money, or for tax minimization. However, spousal trusts are also used to ensure that there will be a gift-over to the children of the marriage at the surviving spouse's death. Here, the income of the trust is available to the surviving spouse, but on his or her death, the capital is available to the children. A spousal trust is often used where the testator wishes to ensure that his or her assets will not pass on to someone the surviving spouse may marry after the testator's death.

Planning Strategies

Reducing Probate

The probate process is the judicial verification of the deceased's will and the distribution of the property according to that will. Many clients are interested in avoiding probate, sometimes for legitimate reasons, but often because probate avoidance has been promoted so much by the media in recent years.

Probate fees range from non-existent in British Columbia and Yukon for estates under $25,000 to 1.553 percent of the estate value over $100,000 in Nova Scotia. Some jurisdictions cap fees at amounts ranging from $140 to $400. Therefore, the amount of the fee does not always warrant elaborate avoidance techniques. See Table 3 at the end of this chapter for a listing of provincial and territorial probate rates.

However, there are other reasons why a client might prefer to avoid probate. In some jurisdictions, the will is a matter of public record, and the information it contains is available to anyone for the asking. Many clients do not want the potential public disclosure that goes with the probate process.

Other clients are concerned that the availability of funds may be delayed and that creditors may receive a priority interest against the probatable assets.

Probate fees can be reduced simply by reducing the value of the assets that flow through the estate. One way for clients to accomplish this is to gift assets while they are still living. Many retirees choose to help family members in this way, so that they have the pleasure of seeing their gift put to good use and benefiting others. However, clients must be absolutely certain that there is no chance they will need to rely on the asset to be gifted for income in future years.

Advisors and clients should also be aware that gifts of property, particularly to non-arm's length individuals, can have tax consequences. Generally speaking, the transferor is deemed to have disposed of the property for its fair market value and the transferee is deemed to have acquired it for the same amount. In addition, if the transferee is a spouse or a child, grandchild or niece or nephew under the age of 18, any income from the property will be attributed back to the transferor. In order to avoid any surprises, gifts of property in these circumstances should be carefully reviewed.

In general, a gift involves the gratuitous and voluntary transfer of property from one person to another. Therefore, there are a number of legal details that are required to complete a gift. For example, the donor must be legally competent to make the gift and must attend to and in fact transfer the title and control of the property. In addition, the gift must be delivered and accepted. There may also be restrictions on the transfer of the property, either by contract, such as in a shareholder's agreement, or at law, such as restrictions on defrauding creditors. If a gift is to be contemplated as part of a formal estate plan, it is prudent to review the gift with a lawyer.

Gifting of money or assets has to be considered carefully in the context of the overall estate plan. Consider a situation where a client has three daughters, two of whom are married and doing well financially, and one who is single and struggling to make ends meet. The client's will leaves his assets divided equally among the three daughters. However, before the client retires, he decides to give his single daughter $100,000 so that she can pay off her mortgage and improve her financial situation. When the client dies, there may be some disagreement among the daughters as to whether the $100,000 was intended as an outright gift over and above the estate distribution, or whether it was in fact an advance on her inheritance. Proper legal documentation at the time of the gift serves to establish the client's intention.

If the individual wishes to maintain somewhat more control over the property, he or she may wish to loan it to a family member, with or without interest or security on the loan.

From a tax perspective, if a client simply loans money, there is no immediate income tax impact although, as discussed earlier, if the loan is made to a spouse or a minor child, grandchild, nephew, niece, or to a non-arm's length adult in some cases, the income from the money loaned (or from property substituted for that money) may be attributed back to the lender, unless a fair market value rate of interest is charged and paid every year within the prescribed time limits set out in the *Income Tax Act*.

Unless the lender never expects to see the money back, he or she should have the loan evidenced by a promissory note and, if only to give him or her a preference over ordinary creditors, should seek security in the borrower's assets. Again, it would be prudent to use a lawyer in these circumstances.

Another technique for reducing the impact of probate is to name a designated beneficiary for registered retirement plans, pension plans, and life insurance policies. This results in the plan proceeds or death benefits being paid directly to the beneficiary, rather than flowing through the estate; therefore, probate fees will not apply. If the plan proceeds or death benefits are paid to the estate, these amounts will be included as part of the probatable assets.

In some jurisdictions, the use of multiple wills has been effective in reducing probate fees. The strategy here is to use one will to deal with assets that would be subject to probate (bank accounts, investment portfolios) and a second will to deal with assets such as private company shares, where probate would not be required. Clients must seek legal advice in setting up this strategy in order to avoid a situation where the second will revokes the first.

Finally, holding property in joint ownership is a much-touted means of passing assets outside of the estate, and thus avoiding probate. Property that is held as joint tenants with right of survivorship (JTWROS) automatically passes to a surviving joint owner upon an individual's death.

Issues with Joint Ownership

While holding assets in joint ownership may be effective in avoiding probate on those assets, it can lead to other problems that clients and advisors need to be aware of. First of all, let's clarify how the joint registration of assets works.

When assets are registered in the names of more than one person, the parties can be shown either as joint tenants or as tenants in common. When individuals hold assets as tenants in common, they are each entitled to the same rights over the property and an equal share of any income from the property. A tenant in common may transfer his or her interest in the property to someone else without the consent of the other tenant in common. When a tenant in common dies, his or her interest passes to his or her heirs, not to the other tenant in common.

Different rules apply to the registration of property in the names of multiple owners as joint tenants. When a joint tenant dies, his or her share of the property passes automatically to the surviving joint tenant(s). This form of ownership is sometimes referred to as Joint Tenancy with Right of Survivorship or JTWROS. Joint tenancy is seen as an advantage from an estate planning point of view, since jointly-held assets do not form part of the deceased's estate, and are therefore not subject to probate fees. Also, jointly held assets typically pass to the surviving owner with very little delay as compared to assets that flow through the estate.

While couples typically hold assets such as bank accounts, real estate, and non-registered investments in joint ownership for the reasons stated above, it has also become common for elderly parents to transfer assets into joint name with one or more of their adult children for estate planning purposes. However, this practice has resulted in many legal disputes after the original owner has passed away. These disputes revolve around the distinction between legal and beneficial ownership: is the surviving child entitled to full ownership of the asset, or is he or she simply holding it in trust for the estate?

Under the concept of legal ownership, the child is presumed to be holding the asset in trust for the parent's estate. As such, there are no capital gains tax implications on the transfer of assets, and the parent continues to declare all of the income from the assets on an annual basis. On the death of the parent, the entire asset will be subject to probate fees.

Under the concept of beneficial ownership, there is a deemed disposition of the asset that is being transferred. For example, if the parent transfers a $100,000 stock portfolio into joint ownership with one child, 50 percent of the portfolio is deemed to have been sold, and capital gains tax may be payable. Any future income from the portfolio will be split equally between the parent and the child for tax purposes. On the death of the parent, probate fees will not apply.

Two presumptions of law have developed over the years that have a bearing on these situations. The presumption of advancement applies to transfers of property by parents into joint ownership with minor children or between spouses. Here, it is assumed that the original owner intended to make a gift to the other party, and beneficial ownership has been transferred. The presumption of resulting trust applies to transfers of property by parents into joint ownership with adult children. Here, the assumption is that a gift was not intended, and legal, but not beneficial ownership has been transferred. The onus is on the transferee to demonstrate otherwise.

Planners should also be aware that where the presumption of resulting trust stands, the asset in question flows through the estate and is subject to probate fees.

Two cases heard by the Supreme Court of Canada in 2007 (*Pecore v. Pecore* and *Madsen Estate v. Saylor*) addressed this issue and emphasized the importance of having clients document their intentions at the time of making a transfer of ownership. A separate written document outlining the client's intentions should be created and signed as close in time as possible to the date when the joint asset is established. Where bank accounts are concerned, it is not enough to rely on the form used by the bank in opening up a joint account.

Another issue to bear in mind with joint ownership is that it precludes the transfer of assets to a testamentary trust on death. As outlined above, it may be preferable from a tax planning point of view to transfer assets into a testamentary trust rather than leave them directly to a beneficiary. Setting up a trust creates another taxpayer, thereby allowing for income splitting. The income from the investments held in the trust is taxed in the trust at the usual graduated rates. Under new proposals discussed earlier, this graduated rate tax treatment may be limited to the first three years after the settlor's death, unless the beneficiary is entitled to the federal disability tax credit. Where investments are left directly to a beneficiary, the investment income will be taxed on top of the beneficiary's other sources of income, resulting in a higher overall tax bill.

Yet another potential problem with joint ownership has to do with the division of assets following the breakdown of a marriage. Where a child receives an inheritance through an estate, the inheritance is normally exempt from the pool of family assets that must be divided in the event that the child's marriage founders. However, where the inheritance comes by virtue of survivorship, the law is less clear.

Supporting Charitable Causes

As people move into retirement, they begin to consider ways of giving back to the communities, institutions or causes that have been important to them over the years. Sometimes this is done through active involvement with a charitable organization, sometimes through the donation of money, insurance policies or tangible property. Donations may be made during the client's lifetime, or at death by a bequest in the will. Advisors have an important role to play in discussing their clients' charitable intentions, and making clients aware of tax-effective ways of supporting charitable causes.

During a client's lifetime, donations to registered charities are eligible for a federal donation tax credit of 15 percent of the first $200 donated, and 29 percent of any excess amount. The provinces and territories have their own donation tax credits, usually worth about 50 percent of the federal amount. Donations of up to 75 percent of net income may be made annually. If a larger amount is donated, the excess can be carried forward and taken as a credit during the next five years.

Donations made in the client's will are eligible for a donation tax credit of up to 100 percent of net income in the year of death. Excess amounts can be carried back to the year before death, and are eligible for a credit of up to 100 percent of net income in that year as well.

The 2014 federal budget proposed increasing flexibility for claiming charitable donations for deaths occurring after 2015. Under the proposed new rules, the charitable donation credit for gifts made in a will may be claimed by the estate or in the individual's final two tax years.

Where publicly traded securities are donated directly to a charity, special tax treatment applies. For donations made after May 1, 2006, there is no capital gains tax on the disposition of the securities. The planner must ensure that the assets are not sold prior to transfer to the charity, but that the actual securities are transferred directly.

Using life insurance to make a charitable gift often provides for a larger gift than would otherwise be possible. Where the client retains ownership of the policy, but designates the charity as beneficiary, the gift is made on death and qualifies for a donation tax credit on the deceased's final tax return. If clients wish to take advantage of the tax credits during their lifetime, they could transfer ownership of the policy to the charity. Any cash surrender value at the time of the transfer, as well any premiums paid by the client after the transfer, would qualify for the donation tax credit. However, because there is a deemed disposition on the transfer of the policy, there may be a tax liability if the cash surrender value exceeds the adjusted cost basis of the policy.

As the baby boom generation moves into retirement, there will be an increased interest in taking an active role in charitable giving. We expect to see more personal involvement in the charities they support, partly to ensure that their money is well spent, and partly for the personal growth opportunities that such involvement provides. One outcome of this trend is the increasing interest in charitable foundations and donor-advised funds.

Private foundations must be registered with CRA before any donation tax credits will be available for contributions. As of March 19, 2007, gifts of appreciated property to private foundations are subject to the same tax treatment as gifts to any other registered charity. Philanthropic Foundations Canada (www.pfc.ca) has extensive information on setting up a charitable foundation.

See Table 4 at the end of this chapter for a summary of the features and benefits of various charitable giving strategies.

Passing the Cottage on to the Next Generation

When it comes to estate planning, the family cottage is one of the most challenging assets to deal with. Most clients want to make sure that their children will continue to enjoy it after the clients have passed away, but if the property has increased in value, there can be a substantial tax bill to pay on the death of the original owners.

There are many ways of reducing the taxes owing on death with proper planning. First, it's important for clients to keep track of the valuation of the cottage at significant points in time. Prior to 1981, each spouse was entitled to claim a separate principal residence exemption. Therefore, if a couple owned both a cottage and a home at that time, both properties could qualify for the principal residence exemption, which would shelter any gains in value related to those years[5]. Similarly, when the $100,000 lifetime capital

---

[5] Note that, if both the cottage and the primary home were held in joint

gains exemption disappeared in 1994, taxpayers had the opportunity to increase the adjusted cost base of assets held at that time in order to use whatever remained of their exemption. If that was done, clients and advisors need to be aware of the cost base that was established at that time. The cost of any renovations done to the cottage over the years must be tracked and documented, since those expenses add to the cost base of the property for tax purposes.

If a client leaves the cottage to his or her children in the will, either directly or via a testamentary trust, capital gains tax and probate fees will be triggered at the time of the client's death. Capital gains tax will be calculated based on the difference between the adjusted cost base and the fair market value when the client dies. In Ontario, probate fees of 1.5 percent of the value of the cottage would result in an additional bill of $7,500 on a $500,000 property. In other jurisdictions where probate fees are lower, this will be a much less important consideration. The cash value of other assets in the estate can be used to pay the taxes owing, or life insurance can be used in order to keep the full value of the estate intact.

However, there are a number of ways of transferring ownership during the client's lifetime that can reduce the cost of the transfer.

Gifting the cottage to the children during the client's lifetime will eliminate probate fees, but capital gains tax will still be payable, even though no money changes hands. The tax will be calculated based on the difference between the adjusted cost base and the fair market value when the property is transferred. If the property is still going up in value, making a gift today will result in a lower tax bill than

ownership prior to 1981, title on both properties should be changed to reflect individual ownership prior to making any principal residence designations. In this way, both properties will be eligible for the principal residence designation for years prior to 1981.

passing it through the client's will many years in the future. However, it also means that the tax bill has to be paid today, which is a significant disincentive for a number of clients.

Transferring property to a married son or daughter can also put the value of the property at risk in the event of marriage breakdown. If married couples divorce or separate, the value of most of the property that they acquired during the marriage is subject to equalization. Often, the original values of gifts or inheritances received during the marriage are protected from equalization. However, in most jurisdictions, this protection does not extend to a property that could be considered a matrimonial home. Although under tax law, a couple can have only one principal residence, under family law, it is possible to have more than one matrimonial home. If the married child and his or her spouse use the cottage regularly, it could be considered a matrimonial home, and as such, would be subject to equalization. In this case, a marriage contract excluding the cottage from property division may be appropriate.

Clients who are concerned about losing control of the property by gifting it could consider placing the cottage into an *inter vivos* family trust. Capital gains tax will be payable when the cottage is transferred into the trust, but the future growth in value of the property is transferred to the children. Of course, the cost of setting up and maintaining the trust also has to be considered.

Putting the cottage into joint ownership with one or more children reduces the current capital gains tax, as only the gain on the portion being given away is taxable, with the gains on the client's share taxable when the client dies. But this technique can expose the property to claims of creditors and ex-spouses of any of the joint owners, as described above.

Selling the cottage to the children has the same advantages as gifting, but with the apparent disadvantage that the children have to come up with a sizable amount of money. However, the client could grant the children a demand loan that can be forgiven in the client's will. There is no requirement for the children to make payments against this loan while the client is alive. Because the client is not receiving all the proceeds of the sale right away, the payment of capital gains tax can be spread out over a five-year period.

Regardless of how and when ownership is transferred, clients need to realize that cottage ownership does not come without its costs. Consideration needs to be given as to how the children will pay for the cottage upkeep. In some families, all the children may want to use the cottage, but only some may be able to afford to pay their share of the maintenance costs. If this is a concern, clients could consider transferring the cottage into a testamentary trust, along with sufficient funds to pay for the maintenance.

In helping clients decide on the most appropriate strategy, consider the following factors:

- The amount of control the client is willing to give up and/or the level of involvement the client wishes to have

- The responsibility for paying the cost of upkeep and maintenance for the cottage, including property taxes, electricity, and insurance

- The level of interest the children have in the cottage, i.e. do they live close enough to make use of it, will career plans take them to other parts of the country or the world, do they have their own vacation properties

- The cost of making the arrangements to sell, give, or transfer the cottage, including legal and accounting fees, income tax payable, land transfer tax, and ongoing filing costs

- The implications of family law legislation for both the client and the children

- The possibility that an interest in the cottage will be seized by creditors to pay outstanding debts

The Question of Equal Distribution

Clients who have several children often want to ensure that they each inherit an equal amount from the estate. This can get complicated when clients plan to leave particular assets to particular children. For example, a client might plan to leave a bond portfolio with a current value of $200,000 to one child, a RRIF with a current value of $200,000 to another child, and a condo with a current value of $200,000 to a third child. Apart from the fact that these assets are unlikely to have similar values at the time the client dies, there is also the issue of taxation. If the second child is the direct beneficiary of the RRIF, that child will receive the full value of the plan, while the estate will be responsible for the income taxes on death, potentially reducing the value of the bond portfolio slated for the first child. The condo may or may not be subject to capital gains tax, depending on its status as the client's principal residence.

Advisors need to alert their clients to these complications when planning the distribution of their assets.

TABLE 1

GENERAL DUTIES OF AN EXECUTOR

1. Arrange for the funeral if it has not already been done.

2. Arrange for the funeral expenses to be paid from the estate.

3. Attend to personal matters. such as discontinuing utilities, re-routing mail, and cancelling provincial health cards.

4. Return or destroy charge cards.

5. Cancel subscriptions or charge accounts.

6. Notify Social Development Canada if the deceased was in receipt of CPP and OAS benefits.

7. Gather information regarding the beneficiaries, including full names and birth dates.

8. Gather information regarding other family members, including full names and birth dates.

9. Review contents of all safe deposit boxes and other personal papers.

10. Gather information regarding the estate inventory.

11. Locate all bank accounts and notify the respective account managers of the death.

12. Obtain all unpaid wages and other benefits from former employer.

13. Locate and analyze any life insurance policies and file claims.

14. Analyze inventory to determine which assets form part of the estate.

15. Arrange for the storage of any assets if required.

16. Value the estate assets.

17. Review the possibility of special valuation on farm and business real estate.

18. Protect assets before probate.

19. Advertise for creditors.

20. Probate will.

21. File claims for pension and profit sharing, and social security and military benefits, if applicable.

22. Open bank accounts for the estate.

23. Pay all debts of the estate.

24. Obtain prior years' income tax returns to verify assets, e.g., interest income declared, etc.

25. Obtain comparative financial statements for any closely-held businesses.

26. Decide whether any assets should be sold.

27. Schedule cash needs of the estate.

28. Obtain appraisals on real and personal property.

29. Obtain a list of the deceased's debts.

30. Allow for safeguarding of any assets distributed to minors.

31. Prepare an accounting statement regarding distribution of assets.

32. File a personal tax return for the deceased for the year of his or her death by the later of six (6) months following the date of death or April 30th of the following year.

33. Consult an accountant regarding the filing of other returns for the deceased where the deceased had "rights or things", partnership or business income, or income from a testamentary trust.

34. Consider post-mortem tax planning.

35. If the deceased died without filing income tax returns for any previous taxation years, these should also be filed.

36. Select a "taxation year" for the estate and file all income tax returns as and when required.

37. Keep proper accounts of estate assets.

38. Obtain a Clearance Certificate from the CRA.

TABLE 2

WILL REVIEW CHECKLIST

		Yes	No	N/A
INSTRUCTIONS This checklist serves as a reminder of key points to consider as the planner reviews the wills of the client and spouse.				
1.	Does the will reflect the client's current situation and not contain sections that may be obsolete? For example, is the will current for: (a) province of residence? (b) tax law changes? (c) executor suitability? (d) guardian suitability? (e) birth or death of an heir?			
2.	Does the will identify the sources from which debts of the deceased, funeral expenses, and estate administrative costs will be paid?			
3.	Does the will identify the sources from which taxes will be paid?			
4.	Are there bequests to charity either outright or in trust?			
5.	Does the will call for the disposition of a closely-held business according to the client's wishes?			
6.	If a non-corporate executor is named, is there a provision for a co-executor? (If not, are there reasons why naming a co-executor might be appropriate?)			
7.	Do any potential conflicts of interest exist between the named executor and the beneficiaries under the will?			
8.	Is the individual or institution named as executor competent to carry out the duties of administering the estate?			

	Yes	No	N/A
9. Does the will name an alternate or successor executor?			
10. Has the executor's bond requirement, if applicable, been waived in the will?			
11. Are specific powers granted to the executor? Some of these powers may be to: (a) retain or sell property; (b) invest trust and estate assets; (c) exercise stock options; (d) manage real estate; (e) allocate receipts and disbursements to income and principal; (f) make loans and borrow funds; (g) settle claims; (h) make decisions relating to the deceased's business interests; (i) distribute property in specie; (j) perform other appropriate duties.			
12. Does the will provide for disposition of property if an heir predeceases the client?			
13. Does the will state who will receive property if the beneficiary disclaims it?			
14. Is the ownership of the assets complementary to the provisions of the will, i.e., some assets may pass outside of the will by contract or by type of ownership?			
15. Is the custody of minors satisfactorily addressed?			
16. Does the will specify that any minor beneficiary's share of the estate will be held until he or she reaches a more mature age?			

	Yes	No	N/A
17. Does the will provide for a guardianship or trust to protect the inheritance of disabled or incompetent beneficiaries?			
18. Does the will give the executor the authority to make income tax elections at his or her discretion?			
19. If there is a spousal trust, does it comply with the spousal trust rules?			
20. Have clauses been included to take maximum advantage of family law protections for the beneficiaries?			
21. Has a foreign or international will been considered in addition to the Canadian one?			
22. Has the possibility of the will being defeated by the spouse through an election under the family laws of the province been considered?			
23. Where the client's investment portfolio is composed largely of mutual funds, have the executors and trustees been given the power to continue to use them?			

NOTES: _____

_____

_____

_____

_____

_____

_____

TABLE 3

PROVINCIAL/TERRITORIAL PROBATE RATES

Province	Estate Size	Fee
Alberta	First $10,000 $10,001 - $250,000 Over $250,000	$25 Progressive to $300 Maximum $400
British Columbia	First $25,000 $25,001 - $50,000 Over $50,000	No fee $208 + 0.6% $508 + 1.4%
Manitoba	First $10,000 Over $10,000	$70 $70 + 0.7%
New Brunswick	First $5,000 $5,001 - $20,000 Over $20,000	$25 $50 to $100 $100 + 0.5%
Newfoundland and Labrador	First $1,000 Over $1,000	$60 $60 + 0.5%
Northwest Territories	First $10,000 $10,001 - $250,000 Over $250,000	$25 $100 to $300 Maximum $400
Nova Scotia	First $10,000 $10,001 - $100,000 Over $100,000	$78.54 $197.48 - $920.07 $920.07 + 1.553%
Nunavut	First $10,000 $10,001 - $250,000 Over $250,000	$25 $100 to $300 $400
Ontario	$1,000 or less First $50,000 Over $50,000	No fee 0.5% $250 + 1.5%
Prince Edward Island	First $10,000 $10,001 - $100,000 Over $100,000	$50 $100 to $400 $400 + 0.4%
Quebec	Requested by natural person Requested by corporation	$99 $111
Saskatchewan	All estates	0.7%
Yukon	First $25,000 Over $25,000	No fee $140

TABLE 4

CHARITABLE DONATION STRATEGIES – FEATURES AND BENEFITS

Type of Gift	Features and Benefits
Outright Gift of Cash	• Reduces value of estate for probate purposes. • Provides immediate tax credit for gifts of up to 75 percent of net income – excess may be carried forward up to five years • Provides immediate support to charity
Outright Gift of Appreciated Property	• Reduces value of estate for probate purposes • Provides immediate tax credit for gifts of up to 75 percent of net income – excess may be carried forward up to five years • Provides immediate support to charity • No capital gains tax on disposition
Charitable Remainder Trust or Residual Trust	• Donor receives income from assets or use and enjoyment of property during lifetime • Immediate tax credit for present value of remainder or residual interest in trust • Reduces value of estate for probate purposes • Gift is irrevocable • Capital gains tax will apply on transfer of assets to trust • Provides future support to charity on death of donor
Charitable Gift Annuity	• Donor contributes cash to charity for purchase of life or fixed-term annuity • Immediate tax credit for a portion of the funds contributed • Donor receives tax-preferred income, possibly increased cash flow • Reduces value of estate for probate purposes • Gift is irrevocable • Provides future support to charity on death of donor
Bequest in Will	• Probate fees will apply on full value of estate • Tax credit for gifts of up to 100 percent of net income in year of death and preceding year* • Provides future support to charity on death of donor

Type of Gift	Features and Benefits
Naming Charity as Beneficiary of RRSP/RRIF	• Probate fees will not apply to value of RRSP/RRIF • Tax credit for gifts of up to 100 percent of net income in year of death and preceding year* • Provides future support to charity on death of donor
Gift of Life Insurance where Donor Transfers Ownership of Policy to Charity	• Gift is irrevocable • Probate fees will not apply on death of donor • Immediate and annual tax credit based on cash surrender value of policy and annual premiums • May be capital gains tax if adjusted cost basis is lower than cash surrender value
Gift of Life Insurance where Donor Maintains Ownership of Policy	• Donor can revoke gift during lifetime • Probate fees will not apply on death of donor if charity is named as direct beneficiary • Probate fees will apply if gift flows through estate and the donor's will provides for bequest to charity • Tax credit for gifts of up to 100 percent of net income in year of death and preceding year* • Provides future support to charity on death of donor

---

* Under proposed legislation, the tax credit may be claimed either by the estate in the year of donation or an earlier year, or may be claimed on the donor's tax return for the year of death or the preceding year.

Chapter 10: Working Effectively With the Retired Client

Much has been written about the communication and interpersonal skills required for a financial advisor to be able to develop and maintain a successful practice. And, of course, these basic skills are essential, no matter what the age of the client group.

But that's only part of what's needed to work successfully with an older clientele. Despite the TV and magazine ads that show retirees on the golf course and playing tennis, it's a fact of life that physical abilities decline with age. The Toronto Seniors Council has reported that 65 percent of people between the ages of 60 and 79 experience some degree of hearing loss. And anyone over 40 can tell you about the changes in eyesight that take place as we get older.

What this means is that financial planners who work with an older clientele need to make sure that their practices are operated in a way that accommodates people with a variety of physical abilities. Making a business senior-friendly means attending to space planning, furniture selection, and written and verbal communications systems to ensure that older clients feel comfortable working with the advisor and the planning team. And, of course, since physical disabilities aren't synonymous with aging, adapting the work environment means meeting the needs of a wide range of clients of all ages. This chapter discusses some of the changes that can be made to the physical environment of the office, as well as changes to written and verbal communications, that will enhance the financial planning experience for the older client.

The Physical Environment

The location of an office is sometimes a major consideration for older clients or those with physical disabilities. While not all advisors are in a position to make a decision about office location, those who are opening a new practice or looking to relocate should certainly think about accessibility. Here are some features to keep in mind about the location of the building and its overall features:

- Proximity to public transit
- Ease of parking, with drop-off facilities at the entrance
- Well-lighted parking lot
- Ramped entrance at the front of the building with automatic doors for wheelchair access
- Automatic entrance doors
- Elevators in addition to stairs within the building
- Accessible washrooms throughout the building, with features such as levered handles or automatic faucets, toilets and hand dryers or paper towel dispensers for ease of use.

Within the office itself, there are many design features that can be implemented in order to create a comfortable, welcoming environment. Above all, advisors should avoid crowding the office and reception area with furniture. Clients who may be in wheelchairs or walkers need spaces large enough to move through easily, as well as enough space to sit and wait without obstructing traffic. A good test of space is to walk through the area with your hands pointing out from your thighs. If you bump into furniture while doing this, a client in a wheelchair will be doing the same thing.

From an aesthetic as well as a safety point of view, office areas should be kept clear of loose carpets and items such as files and boxes stacked on the floor. Thick, plush carpets can be challenging for people with impaired mobility.

When selecting furniture, keep in mind that older people often have difficulty getting in and out of deep, softly cushioned couches and chairs. Seats should be comfortable, but with firm support, and not too low to the ground. At least some of the chairs should have arms to make it easier for clients with arthritic hips or weak knees to sit down and get back up again. In the reception area, make sure that there are occasional side tables nearby where clients can set down a cup of coffee within easy reach. This is often a more accessible arrangement than having a coffee table directly in front of the seating area.

Lighting is also an important consideration. Make sure that rooms where client meetings are held have bright lighting, but avoid having clients sit facing the glare of the sun. Make it as easy as possible for clients to read the forms and reports that will be put in front of them.

Consider the acoustic environment as well. Background music may be appealing to some, but for those with hearing difficulties, it can create a real distraction. Design features such as broadloom and soft draperies help to absorb background noise. Hard surfaces such as tile reflect noise and can cause reverberation of sound.

If there is a washroom within the office premises, it should be accessible and easy to use by those with limited mobility and dexterity. Full wheelchair accessibility is ideal, and, to the extent possible, toilets, sinks and hand dryers or paper towel dispensers should function automatically.

While making an office premises accessible is essential, consideration should also be given to providing home visits for clients whose mobility is limited. Although this practice takes more of the advisor's time, it helps to cement the relationship and provides a much-needed service for those who would be unable to travel easily to the advisor's office. It can also save time, in that it allows for easy access to documents that the client may have neglected to bring to the office.

Written Communications

Written communications, in this electronic age, take place both on paper and on-line. Anyone over the age of 50 can attest to difficulty in reading material in both media. A common problem with websites and electronic newsletters is that the font is too small. While some users may be able to adjust font size, this is an extra step that recipients should not be expected to take. The baby boomers are an impatient generation – when they reach retirement age, they won't take the time to adjust the font, they'll simply move on to another, easier to read website. Verdana is a highly legible font that is often recommended for websites and electronic communications. Dark print on a light background is easiest to read for most people.

Make sure that the design of the website is simple, and that the backgrounds do not interfere with the legibility of the type (for example, screened images behind the text). Avoid colour combinations that are difficult to read, such as light blue text on a dark blue background.

Beware of constructing websites that take too long to load, or contain too many Flash features. It's interesting to see what music and video features can be incorporated, but the interest wears off quickly. If you want visitors to return to your website, keep these features to a minimum. Your goal is to attract repeat visits, not to impress the clients with technological innovation.

Keep the needs of older clients in mind when designing any type of printed material for your advisory practice, including marketing letters, newsletters, brochures, and routine correspondence. Use dark print on a light background and choose matte paper to avoid glare. Use a plain, clear font of at least 12-point size (Arial is a good choice) and avoid using several different fonts in one document. Use upper and lower case letters in normal style, avoiding the use of capital letters and boldface for large blocks of text. Capitals and boldface should only be used for headings or occasional emphasis. Make sure that there is plenty of white space in documents, and that forms have adequate space for clients to write in the required fields or add a signature.

Special consideration should be given when preparing financial plans, illustrations, and reports for older clients. These usually contain complex graphs and tables with a wealth of information, but too much fine detail to be easily seen by many people. A simplified illustration may be more effective in getting the point across, with more specific detail provided on request.

Including people of all ages and varying physical abilities in pictures used on a website or in promotional materials is a nice touch that conveys a welcoming impression to older clients and prospects.

How do older clients prefer to receive their information? While those over 65 are among the fastest-growing group of internet users, it's always best to ask clients whether they prefer to receive printed or electronic information, and be prepared to provide it both ways to meet client needs.

Verbal Communications

Some older clients may be more comfortable with a slightly more formal approach than is the norm with the younger generation. For example, rather than automatically addressing a new prospect by his or her first name, let the client be the guide. Use "Mr. Brown" or "Ms. Jones" unless the client expresses a preference for the use of his or her first name. Advisors should also try to limit their use of slang expressions ("brain freeze", "snail mail", "hey" instead of "hello"), corporate-speak ("repurposing", "tasking") and acronyms in order to make themselves more clearly understood and avoid annoying their listeners.

Remember that older adults don't necessarily think of themselves as "old". Age is a very relative concept. The 20-something advisor may think of anyone over 40 as old, whereas the 60-something client may think of herself as middle-aged. Be very wary of using words that imply that someone is old.

Above all, remember that your older clients are, in one sense, like everybody else – they have their own unique style and preferences. Use the suggestions above as guidelines, but take the time to get to know them as individuals, and respect their unique differences.

Bibliography

Bengen, William P. "Baking a Withdrawal Plan 'Layer Cake' for your Retirement Clients." *Journal of Financial Planning*. August 2006.

Bengen, William P. *Conserving Client Portfolios During Retirement*. Denver. FPA Press. 2006.

Canada Mortgage and Housing Corporation. *Condominium Buyers' Guide*. 2002.

Carter, Barbara H. *Where Will They Live?* Toronto. Stoddart Publishing Co. 2001.

Cohen, Bruce, and Brian Fitzgerald. *The Pension Puzzle: Your Complete Guide to Government Benefits, RRSPs, and Employer Plans*. Toronto. Wiley. 2007.

Cooper, Sherry. *Take Control in the Acceleration Age*. Toronto. Prentice Hall Canada. 2001.

Cooper, Sherry. *The Cooper Files*. Toronto. Key Porter Books Ltd. Canada. 2000.

Cooper, Sherry. *The New Retirement*. Toronto. Penguin Group (Canada). 2008.

Diamond, Daryl. *Buying Time: Trading your Retirement Savings for Income and Lifestyle in your Prime Retirement Years*. Toronto. Wiley. 2008.

Diamond, Daryl. *Your Retirement Income Blueprint: A Six-step Plan to Design and Build a Secure Retirement*. Mississauga. Wiley. 2011.

Foot, David K. *Boom, Bust & Echo: Profiting from the Demographic Shift in the 21st Century*. Toronto. Stoddart. 2001.

Frostiak, Larry H., and John E. S. Poyser. *Practitioner's Guide to Trusts, Estates and Trust Returns 2006-2007 (Canada)*. Toronto. Thomson Carswell. 2006.

Gray, Douglas. *The Canadian Snowbird Guide: Everything You Need to Know about Living Part-Time in the USA and Mexico*. New York, NY. Wiley. 2007.

Hubbard, Carl. "Retirement Savings: Choosing a Withdrawal Rate That is Sustainable." *AAII Journal*. February 1998.

Klinger, William J. "Using Decision Rules to Create Retirement Withdrawal Profiles." *Journal of Financial Planning*. August 2007.

Lovett-Reid, Patricia. *Live Well, Retire Well: Strategies for a Rich Life and a Richer Retirement*. Toronto. Key Porter Books. 2006.

MacKenzie, Warren. *New Rules of Retirement*. Toronto. Harper Collins. 2008.

Milevsky, Moshe. *Wealth Logic: Wisdom for Improving your Personal Finances*. Captus Press Inc. 2002.

Milevsky, Moshe. *The Calculus of Retirement Income: Financial Models for Pension Annuities and Life Insurance*. Cambridge University Press. 2006.

Milevsky, Moshe. *Pensionize your Nest Egg: How to use Product Allocation to Create a Guaranteed Income for Life*. Toronto. Wiley. 2010.

Milevsky, Moshe. *Are you a Stock or a Bond? Create your own Pension Plan for a Secure Financial Future*. Upper Saddle River, New Jersey. FT Press. 2009.

Otar, Jim C. *High Expectations & False Dreams: One Hundred Years of Stock Market History Applied to Retirement Planning*. Toronto. Otar & Associates. 2001.

Otar, Jim C. *Unveiling the Retirement Myth: Advanced Retirement Planning Based on Market History*. Thornhill, Ontario. Otar & Associates. 2009.

Ritchie, Terry F. *The Canadian Snowbird in America*. Toronto. ECW Press. 2007.

Stone, Leroy O. (Editor in Chief). *New Frontiers of Research on Retirement*. Statistics Canada. 2006.

Tezel, Ahmet. "Sustainable Retirement Withdrawals." *Journal of Financial Planning*. July 2004.

Bibliography

Van Cauwenberghe, Christine. *Wealth Planning Strategies for Canadians.* Toronto. Carswell, a Thomson Reuters Company. 2009.

Wruk, Brian. *The Canadian in America.* Toronto. ECW Press. 2007.

Index

Index